What Only a Mother Can Tell You about Child Sexual Abuse

by **Karen Schaefer**

CHILD WELFARE LEAGUE OF AMERICA
WASHINGTON, DC

M000084416

© **1993 by Karen Schaefer**

All rights reserved. Neither this book nor any part may be reproduced or transmitted in any form or by any means, electronic or mechanical, including photocopying, microfilming, and recording, or by any information storage and retrieval system, without permission in writing from the publisher. For information on this or other CWLA publications, contact the CWLA Publications Department at the address below.

Child Welfare League of America, Inc.
440 First Street, NW, Suite 310, Washington, DC 20001-2085

Current Printing (last digit)
10 9 8 7 6 5 4 3 2 1

Cover and text design by Jennifer Riggs

Printed in the United States of America

ISBN #0-87868-508-1

DEDICATION

To "Angela"

I love you a googol, a gaggle, and a giggle . . .
and even more than that.

CONTENTS

PREFACE

Six years ago my family was like any other two-career, middle class American family. There were three of us then, not counting our tabby cat, Un. My husband, to whom I had been married 18 years, was a research scientist/professor who studied the effects certain drugs have on the central nervous system. I was a lending officer for the same bank I had joined ten years earlier after earning my MBA in finance from Emory University. And our daughter, whom I will call Angie throughout this book, was an only child with wispy blond hair and laughing brown eyes. It was the summer of 1986, and Angie was about to begin kindergarten at one of the better preschools in Atlanta—a preschool she had already attended for four of her five years.

All of that seems like a lifetime away. Angie and I are now a family of two; her father moved out 15 months ago. Un died three years ago at the ripe old age of 19. Angie and I live in a 60-year-old money pit that is never quiet, thanks to the antics of Joey, a floppy-eared Beagle, and Sera, a sweet little Tonkinese cat. And in a few months Angie will begin middle school.

Angie is looking forward to this new step up the academic ladder, just as she eagerly anticipated kindergarten six years ago.

However, that earlier advancement brought with it changes we could not have anticipated—changes in her personality and behavior that were so severe we ultimately sought the help of a child psychologist, Nancy McGarrah. It was during one of her sessions with Dr. McGarrah that Angie disclosed that she had been sexually abused at the kindergarten. That disclosure of abuse came in August of 1987, almost a year after she had begun preschool, and it started my family on a journey for which we were totally unprepared.

During the next year, a period I now refer to as the crisis stage of Angie's recovery, I maintained my own sanity by resorting to a habit I had developed as a child—I kept a journal. Out of the anguish and frustration I experienced during that year arose a desire to help others who might struggle with the painful task of parenting a victim of child sexual abuse. And so, in August 1988, exactly one year from the date of Angie's disclosure, I began writing this book. At first, it seemed to flow out of the journal I had kept the previous year. But as I wrote, I began to realize that Angie's story was still unfolding—her recovery was not as complete as I had thought at first.

It took me well over a year to write this book, working for one or two hours early each morning while my family slept. During that time, as I witnessed my daughter's continuing struggle to heal, I slowly began to understand that long-term recovery from sexual abuse was a process whose end was nowhere in sight. I had read extensively about child abuse. I had attended seminars and conferences. None of that prepared me for the months and years yet to come. I began to feel that my family was sailing through uncharted waters.

Gradually my motivation for writing this book broadened. I still wanted to help other parents of molestation victims, but I also wanted to educate the public. Perhaps if others understood the devastating, far-reaching effects of child sexual abuse, more resources would be mobilized to combat this crime that affects hundreds of thousands of children each year. If more people understood, then perhaps other children's pain would not be compounded by the insensitivity that Angie often encountered.

So what you, the reader, are about to begin is really two books in one. One book, arranged chronologically, is designed to guide parents through the phases of recovery that victims of sexual abuse and their families experience. The second book, in topical format, is designed to show how the sexual abuse of children affects not only the victim, but families, communities, and society as well.

Moving back and forth between these two formats as I have done may risk confusing the reader. To reduce this risk, I have done two things. First, I have included a rather lengthy epilogue at the end of the book that updates the material and ties it together in a larger context. Second, I have written a brief chronology, which begins on page xiii, to provide a sense of the order of events and developments.

About Angie

After reading my manuscript, Nancy McGarrah commented that I should let readers know somehow that Angie has extraordinary communication skills for a child her age. Otherwise, she said, no one will ever believe that the poems and statements attributed to Angie really were her words and not mine. It is hard for parents to describe their child's intellectual level objectively, so I will say only that psychological testing has shown Angie to be a gifted child.

One example Dr. McGarrah cited as an indication of Angie's developmental level was her answer to the question, "What happy things do you have to look forward to today?" Most children Angie's age would have looked forward to something like watching cartoons next Saturday morning. As Dr. McGarrah reminded me, Angie's answer was an excited, "I get to see Baryshnikov dance in three weeks." She had just turned six at the time. Angie still spells many words phonetically and her punctuation can be confusing. I edited the spelling and punctuation of the material I included in the book for ease of reading, but the words and the meanings are Angie's. All other quotes, descriptions of nightmares, and so on, are Angie's own, as I recorded them at the time.

A Note on Names

For reasons discussed within this book, criminal indictments were never sought against the two women Angie named as her offenders. I have deliberately omitted any descriptive information that might identify the individuals or school involved in Angie's case. I refer to the two women simply as Angie's "offenders," "abusers," or "teachers." Technically, perhaps, I should call them the "alleged" offenders, but in the interest of smooth reading, I have not. It is not the purpose of this book to "try" these individuals, the preschool where the abuse took place, or the administration of that school.

The names of most individuals in the book, including that of my daughter, have been changed, with the following exceptions:

Nancy A. McGarrah, Ph.D.; Robert E. Wilson, former DeKalb County (Georgia) District Attorney; R. Stephen Roberts, former DeKalb County Chief Assistant District Attorney; J. Tom Morgan, DeKalb County Senior Assistant District Attorney, now District Attorney; Jennifer Berryman, former DeKalb County Victim Advocate; Thomas G. Sampson, Attorney; and Marianne Celano, Ph.D. I am grateful to these individuals for granting me permission to use their names in this book and for their cooperation in reviewing for accuracy the sections of the book in which they appear.

ACKNOWLEDGMENTS

I want to acknowledge the many people whose friendship, love, encouragement, and support have made this book a reality.

The professionals who work so hard to help child abuse victims and their families: especially J. Tom Morgan and Nancy McGarrah, both of whom "Angie" and I continue to count as valued friends; also Bob Wilson, Steve Roberts, and former state representative Eleanor Richardson.

Our friends and family: my soul sisters Betheda and Janet; Kathy and Bob Houman, Peggy Maier, Wanda Rachael, Mom and Buford, Grandma Bauman, Dad and Phyllis, Mike and Anna, Trisha and Boyd. Also my friends and colleagues from "049," Jim Adams and the rest of "030," and the lunch bunch—Patty, Jennifer, Pam, Candace, and Diane.

Special individuals in my daughter's life, many of whom never knew about her pain. Each of them, by treating her with the respect and sensitivity every child deserves, helped her in her struggle to regain a sense of self-worth: Kathy Born, Vivian Stephens, George Daniel, Judy Greene, Ann Dugan, Virginia Cox, Kathleen Everett, Leslie Gourley, Mary Ann McTier, Joe Mason, Cassie Beattie, Dr.

Omar Najjar, Laura J. and family, and Angie's beloved Heidi and Paul Santa Maria.

Finally, the book experts: Phyllis Mueller, whose early encouragement kept me going; Gail Ross and Elizabeth Outka; and my CWLA editors—Sue Brite, Carl Schoenberg, and Mary Liepold.

CHRONOLOGY

December 1980
Angela's birth

April 1982
Angie is enrolled in preschool.

Summer 1986
The preschool hires a new administrative director.

September 1986
Angie begins kindergarten at the same preschool.

October 1986
Angie begins to show signs that I later learn are the classic symptoms of abuse.

January 1987
We schedule the first of a series of conferences with Angie's teachers and the preschool's director.

May 1987
Angie begins therapy with Dr. Nancy McGarrah.

July 1987

Dr. McGarrah suggests that we remove Angie from the pre-school.

August 1987

I take a four-week leave of absence from work to stay home with Angie. Angie discloses that she has been sexually molested. We meet with "Ms. Williams," the Department of Human Resources investigator.
Angie is interviewed and videotaped at police headquarters.
Angie begins first grade at a new school.

September 1987

The DeKalb County (GA) district attorney's office begins its investigation.

October 1987

The victims' parents meet with the district attorney.
The prosecutor, J. Tom Morgan, interviews one of Angie's alleged offenders. The other offender has already resigned from the preschool and moved out of town.
The director and board members of the preschool learn about the criminal investigation.

December 1987

Mr. Morgan interviews the preschool's director.

January 1988

The district attorney decides against taking the case to the grand jury.
The state begins its regulatory investigation of the preschool.
We consult an attorney regarding a possible civil suit against the preschool.

March 1988

Representatives from the district attorney's office meet with the parents whose children attend the preschool.
Mr. Morgan talks with Angie about his investigation.
Angie is seriously injured at her after-school camp.
I take a second leave of absence from work.

June 1988

We consult with a second attorney about a civil suit.

Angie is sexually harassed at summer camp by a former preschool classmate.

Angie and Jessica attend Summer Safari at the Atlanta Zoo.

July 1988

The state concludes its investigation of the preschool.

August 1988

Angie enters the long-term phase of recovery.

I begin writing this book.

October 1988

I learn that the state has concluded its investigation of the preschool.

February 1989

I meet with DHR officials to discuss the state's investigation.

March 1989

We move into a new house, partly because Angie is still afraid her offenders will come back to hurt her at the old house.

Summer 1989

Angie continues to suffer flashback episodes.

Angie confides in her summer camp counselor.

September 1989

Angie begins third grade. Her academic performance has improved a lot.

January 1990

Angie's classmates learn of her "secret."

My husband and I begin marriage counseling.

Summer 1990

Angie and I participate in a support group led by Dr. Marianne Celano.

September 1990

Angie begins fourth grade at a new school.

September 1990 through June 1992

Angie shows tremendous improvement in academic performance and social skills.

April 1991

My husband and I separate.

April 1991 to the present

Angie remains in therapy with Dr. McGarrah, dealing with the lasting effects of having been abused, as well as learning to cope with her parents' pending divorce. Preadolescence raises new issues for her.

A MESSAGE TO PARENTS

August 1988

It has been one year since my daughter, then six, disclosed during a therapy session that she had been sexually molested by her kindergarten teachers.

Did I believe her? Sort of. I knew she wasn't lying, but I wanted to believe there was some kind of missing information that would eventually explain away the horrible reality of what she was saying.

Was I upset? Sort of. During the first few days I managed to push her revelation out of my mind by telling myself it couldn't be all that serious, and concentrated instead on the daily tasks at hand—my job, other family and community matters. That was during the day. During the night, I tossed and turned and cried. There were no cohesive thoughts at that time, only a deep foreboding of what was to come.

Was I prepared? Not at all. If you had asked me a year ago if I knew about child sexual abuse, I would have answered yes. I had read the popular literature to my daughter, telling her it was "okay to tell." What I didn't know was that there are very few people out there in our society who know it is okay to listen and believe. I didn't know then how this misinformation and lack of education regarding child molestation would hinder our progress in the months following my daughter's disclosure, as my family tried to move forward to heal the wounds of her experience.

Of course, there were professionals who were experts concerning child molestation—the investigating police detective, the prosecuting attorney and others in the district attorney's office, my daughter's therapist—who believed my daughter's story. They have been sympathetic and kind.

But no one was able to prepare my family for the hell into which we were suddenly thrust. For the most part, we have had to pick our way through this mine field ourselves, never knowing when something else was going to blow up in our faces. And there have been many explosions this past year.

My daughter, my husband, and I have come down a long, treacherous road. We've stumbled many times and crawled even more. But the progress we've made is obvious when I look back on where we were six months, three months, even one month ago. It is a road that will never end because our daughter's abuse will always be a part of our lives. But the rocky road is finally becoming smoother and navigating it has become less exhausting. The past's hold on the present has been loosened, and it no longer permeates every day's thought and every night's dream.

More and more I find myself turning outward and wondering how many other parents are stumbling down the same road, struggling with the agony of knowing their child has been sexually molested and trying to make sense of it all. And I wonder if there is anything one hurting mother can do to lessen the pain for those other parents.

A friend has suggested that writing about my own experience as the mother of a molestation victim might be a way to bring some good out of a tragic experience. I appreciate the thoughtfulness of a well-intentioned friend, but I find it hard to believe that anything good can come out of something as terrible as the sexual abuse of a child.

The only good thing I can imagine is turning back time and changing events so that my child would never have to suffer abuse at the hands of someone we both trusted. But that's the stuff imagination is made of. Life's reality makes it necessary to go forward. Reality tells me there are many other parents of abuse victims who need help. If you are one of those parents, I want to make your path a little smoother.

Sometimes I think that what I needed most during this past year was a hug. Just a hug from someone who understood exactly what I was feeling—the anguish, the confusion, the frustration, and the anger. A hug would have made it a little easier.

I hope that many people will benefit from reading this book, but my heart goes out particularly to the other parents of children who have been sexually molested. My intention is not so much to tell you my own story as it is to share with you my thoughts and experiences, so that you may be better prepared for your journey as the hurting parent of an abused child. This is my hug for you.

PART I

What to Expect from Your Child

Do ye hear the children weeping, O my brothers
Ere the sorrow comes with years?
They are leaning their young heads against their mothers,
And that cannot stop their tears.
The young lambs are bleating in the meadows,
The young birds are cheeping in the nest,
The young fawns are playing with the shadows,
The young flowers are blowing toward the west
—But the young, young children, O my brothers,
They are weeping bitterly!
They are weeping in the playtime of the others,
In the country of the free.

—Elizabeth Barrett Browning, from "The Cry of The Children"

INTRODUCTION

$\mathbb{M}$ ost of us have seen lists of symptoms that victims of child sexual abuse exhibit. They can be found in pamphlets to help parents detect suspected abuse, and they are sometimes recited by the media as an epilogue to reported news stories about molestation cases.

If someone had asked me two years ago if my family was educated about child sexual abuse, I would not have hesitated to say yes. I thought we were. I found out the hard way that we were not.

First of all, my daughter's symptoms did not occur in a vacuum. Like most families, my husband and I had other things going on in our lives—the daily ups and downs every family experiences, plus the pressures of a two-career family. Looking back, the warning signs should have been obvious. They were right there on the list of symptoms I thought I knew. At the time, however, it wasn't so clear. My husband and I knew something was wrong in our child's life, but it took us almost a year to learn exactly what it was.

Second, we suffered from a very common defense mechanism—denial. We humans don't accept tragedy readily. We protect ourselves from hurt by pushing the hardest of truths away from our minds. It is the same thing that keeps us from rushing to the doctor the minute we sense that our health may be threatened. We know that once we go to the doctor we'll have to face facts we'd rather not think about. And so we delay, some of us longer than others, looking for easy, less serious explanations for our symptoms and secretly hoping that if we pretend they aren't there, the symptoms will go away.

CHAPTER 1

EARLY SYMPTOMS

My child's story began when she started kindergarten at the preschool she had attended since she was a year old. During Angela's first four years there, the school had lived up to its reputation as one of the best in Atlanta. Angie had blossomed in the school's loving, nurturing environment.

Shortly before the beginning of the school year in September, the school board hired a new director. She immediately transferred the experienced kindergarten teacher to another class and hired two new teachers for that year's kindergarten.

By the end of October, Angie was crying and begging not to go to school. With the hiring of the two inexperienced teachers, the general condition of the kindergarten deteriorated quickly and dramatically from its former level of excellence. Many parents complained about the academic and disciplinary problems that soon became obvious. I assumed that Angie's new unhappiness with the school had to do with general problems with the program, the more structured kindergarten routine, and an unbalanced boy-girl ratio in the classroom.

My husband and I spoke with the director about Angie's unhappiness, and she promised she would work with the teachers directly, bring in a consultant, and make changes in the curriculum.

Nothing improved, however, and by January we asked for the first of a series of conferences with the director and teachers. We were concerned because Angie's unhappiness had escalated and she was showing signs of extreme stress: moodiness and occasional withdrawal, clinging behavior, exaggerated fears (loud noises and storms), sleep disturbances (nightmares and tooth-grinding), regressive behavior (finger-sucking and baby talk), low self-esteem, and somatic complaints.

Our conferences with the teachers and director over the next few months left us perplexed. They insisted that Angie was perfectly happy at school. They said she showed none of the signs of stress we were observing at home. In the meantime, repeated visits to Angie's pediatrician revealed no physical basis for her constant stomachaches, sore throats, and headaches.

I asked other parents if their children were having problems at school. Some were; some were not. Some parents were pleased with the teachers and program; some were not. I was baffled even more by some parents' comments that Angie appeared to be happy when they saw her at school. But then others told me they had noticed how unhappy she looked and how she often sat in the corner, huddled dejectedly by herself.

The inconsistency in Angie's behavior puzzled my husband and me for a long time and created a confusion that provided us with another form of denial. It was a denial based on what I now call the "all-or-nothing myth."

Even though abused children show definite signs of stress, they still have good days. They still laugh occasionally and find some joy in life. Observing this, we adults seize on the good times to help us deny the bad. We see them having fun and we assume the nightmares and the crying must have been just another "phase." We have a mental stereotype of children who are experiencing trauma in their lives as distraught all the time. When we see them acting "normal," we decide that whatever was bothering them must not have been that serious after all.

It's a ridiculous idea, on reflection. Think of the times we adults experience tragedy in our own lives. I remember the pain I felt when my grandfather died. He had been very special to me for many years, and the loss seemed unbearable. I grieved and I mourned. But I still went on with day-to-day living. I hurt inside, but I was still able to enjoy the happy things going on in my life at the time. Why should we expect anything else from a child?

During the time my husband and I were searching for clues to Angie's distress, I noticed that she was beginning to have social problems with children who had previously been her friends. The preschool was a neighborhood school; most of the parents either lived or worked close by. Many of Angie's classmates had been friends for most of their young lives. Families and children often socialized outside of school events. Yet Angie, a social child by nature, suddenly complained of being friendless.

She felt excluded from the group. She said she was "different" from the other kids, like "I'm from outer space or something." She became convinced that no one liked her.

A more subtle change took place—Angie's gradual loss of interest in activities that used to be very important to her. Like most children, Angie had been a creative preschooler who enjoyed music and arts and crafts activities. Her main passion in life, though, had long been her love of dance.

Angie and I often shared a mother-daughter joke that her passion for dancing originated when we danced together for so many months before she was born. (I went to ballet class until two weeks before her birth.) She had danced before she walked, it seemed. When Angie was three and a half years old, she begged for dance lessons, so we enrolled her in a creative movement class for preschoolers. She progressed to pre-ballet the next year.

She danced constantly. Her favorite playtime activity was to dress up in any of a variety of dance costumes, turn on music, and dance. She would dance for hours at a time, often with sweat rolling off her face. She practiced movements she learned in class and she choreographed her own. Her quiet moments were spent playing dance class with her dolls.

Angie started beginning ballet at the same time she entered kindergarten. And then her love of dancing began to die. She continued to go to class, but there were no more playtime performances. Her enthusiasm disappeared, just as it did for other creative pastimes. The vibrant, active child I had known for five years was turning into a rag doll.

By April, Angie's somatic symptoms had become more serious. Her headaches became so severe and prolonged that we suspected a brain tumor. She would suddenly burst out crying and say that she felt as though someone had hit her in the head with a rock. The headaches lasted for days and aspirin could not ease the pain. Alarmed, we rushed her to the doctor. Her pediatrician agreed that the symptoms were indeed serious. Neurological screening, however, revealed no physiological basis for the headaches.

The doctor's only explanation was that Angie's problems must be "situational," and he suggested we pull her out of that school. Unfortunately, it was now so late in the school year and Angie's emotional condition was so fragile that we were afraid the disruption of a change in schools would do more harm than good. It would have required three changes for her in four months (public school for the rest of the school year, new arrangements for summer, and her new school and after-school program in the fall). Everything I had ever seen written about the effects of day care on children said that consistency was critical. We thought it would be better to help her cope with the present situation than to make her adapt to a long series of new ones.

By this time, though, Angie was becoming more verbal about her unhappiness, and she often exploded in outbursts of anger and hostility toward her teachers. She would say she hated them, but her reasons were vague and diffuse. She would say only that they were "mean" and that they hated her. Yet there were times she said she loved them, and again, the inconsistency was confusing.

Even after all this time, it tears me apart when I remember how hard she tried to make her teachers love her. How she would ask to take them small gifts or how she would declare in the morning that "I'm going to be real good and not get in any trouble so that today will be a good day." Her child's mind believed that she must be doing something wrong, and if she could only be "good" her teachers would stop being "mean" to her.

And so I returned for yet another conference with the school's director. I told her of the pediatrician's suggestion that we remove Angie from the school. She replied, "He's only going on what *you've* told him." I told her of Angie's complaints about her teachers. She answered that unless I could be "more specific," there was nothing she could do.

I showed her pictures Angie had drawn about how she felt at school. One was a gut-wrenching drawing of a skeleton standing in a pool of tears. Angie's explanation had been, "That's all's I am is bones and tears—no heart, no skin, no muscles, no nothing—just bones and tears."

The director finally agreed that there was a problem, but she went on to suggest family counseling. She believed the problem had to be at home, because in her opinion, there was nothing wrong with my child at school.

Before I could sort out my own anger and frustration, the bottom fell out. Angie, my six-year-old who had always been so full of love and life, began to threaten suicide.

All of us have events in our lives of such emotional intensity that they burn themselves into our minds, and can be recalled years later with great clarity of detail. Some of these are collective events, such as when a nation witnesses the assassination of its president or the explosion of a space shuttle that sends seven national heroes plunging into the ocean. But some are our private events. Who can forget the shocked moment when we learn of the death of someone we feel we can't live without? Or the joyous intensity of the moment a baby is born?

One of those private etchings in my memory is the Wednesday in May when Angie hit rock bottom. She was hysterical from the moment I picked her up at school. I did not even have a chance to change my clothes or make dinner when we got home. Angie and I just lay together on her bed and I hugged and cuddled her and stroked her hair, trying to comfort and calm her. She cried and cried and cried. Through her tears, she said that she hated herself, that she hated "this life," and that she just wanted to die. She wished she could kill herself, she sobbed. I could not comfort her. I tried to convince her of what a wonderful, bright child she was and of how much I loved her. She could not believe me. She insisted I would have been better off if she had not been born.

Gently, I told her again that I loved her and how special she was to me. I also told her that there was no way I could prove it to her or make her believe me. It was something she would have to believe within herself and accept. And, I continued, it is hard to accept love from someone else unless you love yourself first.

That comment brought a new flood of tears. She could never love herself, she said, because there was nothing good there for her to love. The only answer was for her to just "go ahead and die." The intensity of her despair overwhelmed me. All I could do was cry with her. For a long time she lay in my arms and we cried together. I was terrified. Could a six-year-old commit suicide? I knew then that we had to get outside help for Angie.

My husband and I had occasionally considered consulting a child psychologist during the months when we were trying to figure out what was so wrong in Angie's life. At our last appointment with her pediatrician, I had asked him to recommend someone. Now I knew we could wait no longer.

In desperation, I told Angie that I knew of a doctor who might be able to help. I told her that her pediatrician was a doctor who helped her body feel better when it was sick or hurt. I knew another doctor, "Nancy," who could help her with her hurt feelings inside and who could help her learn to love herself again. Angie calmed down a little and seemed hopeful. She wanted "Nancy" to help her, she said. She wanted to love herself, but "I don't know how. Mommy, I need help."

It was a glimmer of hope. The next day I made an appointment with Dr. Nancy McGarrah, and Angie began therapy the following week. At that first appointment, my husband and I talked with Dr. McGarrah before she saw Angie. We were concerned about two things, we told her. First, we did not know how to deal with the immediate situation at the school. We outlined the frustrations of the past eight months. Second, we were very concerned about Angie's total lack of self-esteem. We were especially worried about how she would be able to begin first grade in a new school in September in her current state of mind.

Angie took an immediate liking to Nancy McGarrah. They related well to each other. Dr. McGarrah noted that Angie was very verbal and very motivated, and that was definitely a positive sign. It seemed as though we were finally on the way back up. We were all encouraged.

We noticed an immediate improvement in Angie, although she still had a lot of problems. She continued to suffer from severe nightmares and fears. She still hated herself. But the headaches and stomachaches became less frequent. Angie showed less despair and more hope. She still had very bad days at school and there were many more tears, but finally, we all felt we were moving in the right direction.

Several sessions were devoted to psychological testing. After the first few weeks of therapy, Dr. McGarrah told us that she felt she and Angie were simply "treading water" as long as Angie remained in that school. I arranged for a leave of absence from my job to get Angie out of the place and to give her a therapeutic break before starting first grade in her new school.

CHAPTER 2

TEMPORARY EUPHORIA

Angie's spirits soared when she learned she had only a few days left at school. She declared that she was "in heaven." Finally, it was her last day at the school she had come to dread so much.

She had looked forward to her last day there, not only because she knew she would never have to go back, but also because she somehow believed that the teachers would finally show her they liked her. One of her friends had left school a few weeks earlier and the teachers had treated the child royally. They had even given her a gift.

Angie thought that her day had finally arrived! She was sure her teachers would love her at last. She helped me bake a cake to put in the teachers' lounge and picked out special snacks for her classmates.

I picked her up early on that last day, expecting to see the same joy that had been on her face when I dropped her off earlier in the day. The moment I saw her, I knew something had gone terribly wrong.

She was devastated. She cried uncontrollably as soon as she got in the car. She said one teacher had been "mean" to her and the other had told her she was a "liar and a terrible child." Angie was inconsolable for hours. She cowered in the corner of her room and cried hysterically. She would let neither my husband nor me come near her.

Each time I tried to approach her to comfort her, she screamed for me to stay away. She cried that she didn't deserve my hugs and kisses. She said, "They're right. I am a terrible child. I hate myself. I don't deserve a vacation. I deserve to be at that school and I want you to take me back on Monday." I told her that Daddy and I didn't want her to go back to that school. We wanted her to stay home with me until her new school started. She was not a terrible child and we loved her very, very much.

It took almost an hour to talk her into coming out of the corner. When she finally crawled across the floor to me, she looked like a little animal who had been beaten into submission. I took her in my arms and rocked and soothed her. She continued to cry for a long time. Eventually, she calmed down, but none of us slept much that night. Weeks later we learned that Angie had indeed received a "going-away present" on that last day of school. She had been sexually abused one last time.

By Monday, only three days later, Angie's exuberance was back. Our first week at home was heaven for all of us. My husband and I began to relax for the first time since the frustrations and stress had begun almost a year earlier. As for Angie, she was like a new child. Or rather, she was like the old Angela—the happy, bubbly, energetic little girl was back.

She played contentedly at home for hours on end. She also became surprisingly social. Just a few days earlier, she had been desolate and "friendless." Now, she thrived on having friends over to visit. During this brief interlude, Angie's fears and nightmares punctuated her newfound joy, but I wasn't concerned. I thought they would fade with time now that the worst was over. What I didn't know was that the worst wasn't over. Our euphoria was to be short-lived.

The second week of my leave of absence was interrupted by a trip to south Georgia for a company conference I had to attend. My husband took vacation time to stay with Angie while I was out of town. On Tuesday of that week, Angie went for her regular weekly appointment with Dr. McGarrah. It was my husband's birthday, so I called home later that afternoon to wish him a happy birthday. In a quiet but tense voice, he told me Angie had disclosed to Dr. McGarrah that she had been sexually molested at school. Details were still sketchy, but Dr. McGarrah said she was taking Angie's disclosure "very seriously."

Under Georgia law, Dr. McGarrah was required to report her information to the authorities, which she did immediately. By the time we talked on the phone, my husband had already been contacted by an investigator from Georgia's Department of Human Resources (DHR) Child Care Licensing Division. The police had also been notified and would be calling us, he said.

It was an end of sorts to our months of searching for clues to Angie's unhappiness. But it didn't end her pain—or ours. We didn't know it at the time, but it was only the beginning of a new hell for all of us. We were facing new battles for which we were totally unprepared.

When Angie finally opened up and began talking about her abuse, all the turmoil she had held inside for so long was unleashed. She suddenly found herself on an emotional and behavioral roller coaster with no restraints to keep her safe. A new Pandora's box of anguish had opened for all of us.

CHAPTER 3

EMOTIONAL UPHEAVAL

During the first weeks that followed Angie's disclosure, we painstakingly protected her from the flurry of activity that marked the beginning of the investigations into her case. We didn't talk with Angie about her experience unless she started the conversation. We didn't question her. We only listened when she voluntarily disclosed information to us. Details cascaded out at first. Then she would stop talking about it for brief periods, after which more information would follow.

Apparently this is typical of molestation victims once they begin talking about the abuse. The first disclosure is just the tip of the iceberg. It can take months or longer for the details to emerge. It was very stressful for Angie to talk about what had happened to her. She would mention certain incidents and this would create emotional havoc for her. Then she seemed to need a period of time to work out her feelings. When she began to level out again, new information would emerge, followed by another period of upheaval. And so she went through phases of disclosure and turmoil, each followed by a brief plateau, and then she would begin again. This cycle continued for close to a year.

On the last Friday in August, just days before she was to begin first grade in her new school, we were asked to take Angie to the police station to be interviewed. I panicked.

Angie was still unaware of the storm that had been swirling around her since her disclosure two and a half weeks earlier. By this time, she was struggling with her newfound freedom to talk about what had happened to her and she was trying to cope with the whirlwind of emotions that was being released in her because of it. Now we were about to introduce her to a whole new terrifying dimension.

I asked the investigating detective what I should say to Angie to prepare her for her visit to the police station. He said simply to tell her the truth—that he wanted to talk with her about what she had told Dr. McGarrah. And so I sat down with Angie the evening before and tried to give her just enough information to keep her from panicking when she walked into the police station.

I talked with her in very general terms about rules and laws. We talked about some rules, like being polite to people, which are good to obey—but if you don't obey them, you probably won't get in serious trouble. Some rules, though, are more serious. If you don't obey those rules, called *laws*, the consequences can be very serious.

As an example, I talked about my job. I told her how it was part of my job to be courteous and helpful to my customers. If I broke that rule by being rude, I might get in no trouble, or in a little trouble, but I certainly would not go to jail for it. But if I were to steal money from my company, I would be breaking not only a rule of the company but also a law, so I could be arrested and go to jail for that.

From that illustration I moved on to teaching and some of the rules teachers have to follow. One rule that is so serious it is a law is that no teacher, or anyone else for that matter, is allowed to hurt children the way Angie had been hurt at school. For that reason, I told Angie, some people wanted to talk to her about what had happened. And one of those people was the detective she would meet at the police station the next day.

Angie was immediately intimidated by the thought of having to go to the police station. I answered her questions. No, she was not going to jail. No, the detective would not be wearing a uniform. I assured her that I had already talked with him and that he was a very nice man. It was his job to help children, he was used to talking to children, and I thought he would be nice.

She wanted to know what it would look like there, and I said that it would be much like any other office building except that there would probably be lots of police cars parked outside and she might see some uniformed officers walking around. She wanted to know what she was supposed to do there. I told her simply to answer the detective's questions and to tell the truth about what had happened to her.

Angie was pretty calm about it during most of the next day, but once she got in the car she began wringing her hands over and over. I had never seen her do that before, so I knew she was terrified. When we arrived at the police station, Angie clung to my skirt. She didn't want me to leave her when the detective asked to speak to my husband and me alone. After our discussion, he wanted to interview Angie alone, and she went with him reluctantly. After Angie's interview, she went to another building to be videotaped. The detective seemed to be very good with children and tried hard to put her at ease, but she was still terrified. I don't think she was afraid of him as much as she was intimidated by the environment and the whole situation.

As soon as we got in the car to go home, Angie became hysterical. She had been terrified of the videotaping. She said that some of the detective's questions had been hard to answer, and she had been afraid that if she didn't tell the truth she would have to go to jail. Before we went, I had emphasized that she must tell the truth, and apparently the detective had done the same. We had scared her without realizing it.

Angie was also in a panic because she didn't understand what the tape would be used for. Not one of us had bothered to tell her why the tape was made, so she assumed it was to be used on television, on the news. After all, isn't that what TV cameras are for? She started crying, "I'm dead. I'm history. I'm a goner. When [the teachers] see the TV, they're going to come to get me." Once I realized that she associated the videotaping with TV, I assured her that the tape would not be used in that way. I explained that the tape was made so she would not have to tell her story over and over again, because we knew it would upset her to keep repeating it. My explanation didn't help; the damage had already been done.

That was just the beginning of one of the emotions that would dominate Angie's life for months to come—fear. I didn't know it at the time, but Angie had been threatened into silence. In fact, details of the threats made against her did not come out until the following March, six and a half months after that night at the police station. At that time, she told of one occasion when her daddy took her to the preschool after a morning appointment with Dr. McGarrah. After my husband left, one teacher grabbed her by the arm, pulled her aside, and asked Angie if she had told her therapist "anything." When Angie assured her she had said nothing, the teacher replied, "You'd better not or you're dead meat."

Now that Angie was talking about the abuse, she was sure the teachers would find out and come to get her. The problem was that the offenders really did know where Angie lived. They really did know where her new school was located. In fact, one of them had made it a point to tell Angie that she would be coming to her new school sometime to visit. Knowing all of this made Angie feel very vulnerable and very threatened.

Angie's fears manifested themselves in nightmares so terrifying to her that *night-terrors* might be a better word to use. It was not unusual during the first months that followed Angie's disclosure for us to awaken to her screams in the middle of the night. They were screams so chilling that my heart would be pounding in my throat by the time I reached her bedside. She would claw at me as though she were trying to crawl inside me for protection and her eyes would be wide and wild looking. Rarely did I go back to sleep after one of her nightmares—the look on her face would haunt me for the rest of the night.

At this time, Angie's entire world consisted of life at her new school and at home, and she could not feel safe in either place. One of Angie's offenders was a certified teacher, and Angie was afraid that she might suddenly show up one day to be her teacher again. After school, Angie rode a van to her new after-school program at a local church. The bus resembled the one that had been used for field trips at her old school. Each time she got on the bus, she was afraid that she might somehow end up back at the preschool.

In one of the nightmares Angie described to me at that time, she dreamed that the dismissal bell at school had just rung. She walked slowly down the stairs and out to the parking lot where the after-school bus was waiting. Suddenly, she felt someone grab her shoulder. She looked up and it was one of the offenders.

"You're coming with me," the teacher said, and pulled her into the bus. And then Angie realized that it was really the bus from her old school and the other teacher was in the bus waiting for her. At that point, she woke up screaming.

Even at home, Angie was unable to feel safe. The nights were especially bad, since she often dreamed of being kidnapped by her former teachers. She asked if we could put "big spotlights" around the house so they couldn't break in at night to get her. She asked me hypothetical questions such as, "Mommy, what would you do if the doorbell rang and you opened the door and [offender] was standing there?" "What would you do if she had a gun or something and forced her way in?" "What would you do if she tried to take me away from you?"

I tried to deal with her fears by being calm and rational. I explained that child molesters often threaten children to keep them from telling, but they rarely carry out their threats. I explained that one of her teachers had already left the city and was teaching at a school in another part of the state. And I told her that the teachers and principal at her new school had very strict instructions from us that *no one* was allowed to pick her up at school except her parents and the after-school driver.

Some of my explanations helped; most did not. My constant assurance that I loved her and would do everything I could to protect her from being hurt again relieved some of her fears some of the time.

In the end, it was the passage of time that gradually lessened her fears. As the months went by, I noticed that her nightmares became less intense and more generalized. First she dreamed of being kidnapped by her former teachers, then by strangers who were "related to" her offenders. Finally, she dreamed of being kidnapped by strangers. By the time a year had passed since her disclosure, Angie's nightmares were few and far between.

When Angie was terrorized by her fears that "it" would happen again, she was experiencing a jumble of other emotions, each as intense as the next. At times, she seemed to be almost overwhelmed by guilt. Children who are abused don't understand that bad things can happen to good people, so they assume they must have done something to deserve what happened to them. This belief is often reinforced by the child's offender, who tells the victim that he or she is the one who will get in trouble if anyone finds out. For example, Angie was told that she would be kicked out of school if she told, and then everyone would know how terrible she was.

Molestation victims often suffer from conflicting emotions that fuel their feelings of guilt. Children are taught to respect and obey adults, especially those with authority over them, such as parents, teachers, baby-sitters, or clergymen. When one of those adults betrays the child's trust, he or she experiences conflicting feelings of

hate and love, trust and distrust. Children don't think they are supposed to have these negative feelings about the omnipotent adults
in their lives, so, believing there must be something wrong with
them, they are faced with a confusing sense of guilt. For a while,
Angie tried to resolve her own conflicting feelings by saying, "I don't
hate [the teachers], Mom. I just don't like what they did to me."

I can understand why Angie felt confused about her feelings for
her teachers. She had always loved her teachers at that preschool,
and that love had been reciprocal. It was normal for her to assume
it would be the same with the two new teachers. She really wanted
to love them and to have them love her back. I think she thought
that if she kept trying, eventually they would. It just wasn't in her
repertoire of feelings to have it any other way. They betrayed her
trust, and I think that is why their abuse caused so much emotional
damage.

Children may also feel guilty over the uproar that results when
they do disclose the abuse. After all, in many cases, they were warned
not to tell. In Angie's case, the investigation that followed her disclosure revealed that she had not been the only victim. It was a
sensitive issue, but I tried to use this information to help her. I was
careful not to reveal the identities or details of the other cases, but
I told her that her disclosure helped the prosecutor find other children who had been hurt like her. As a result, these other children
could now get help like the help Angie was getting from Dr. McGarrah.
This helped Angie realize that she was not the only child in the
world who had been molested, and it reinforced the idea that she
had done the right thing by telling about it.

In my opinion, the most tragic consequence of child molestation
is the way it tears down the victim's sense of self-esteem. Angie's
feeling of worthlessness was apparent long before we knew she had
been sexually molested, and it has persisted throughout her period
of recovery. It has expressed itself at varying levels of intensity,
ranging from a lack of confidence to self-hate. It has affected every
aspect of her life—school, friends, and family life. Angie is a bright
child with above-average reading, verbal, and math skills, yet she
was convinced that she was "the dumbest kid in the world."

The school Angie attended from first through third grades used
an ungraded performance system for the lower elementary grades:
W(orking to capacity), U(nsatisfactory), N(eeds improvement),
S(atisfactory), G(ood), and V(ery) G(ood). Throughout first grade, An-

gie's progress reports consisted of G's and VG's, but she was always devastated when she brought them home. She insisted that her grades were both higher than she deserved and not good enough.

The hardest adjustment Angie faced when she began first grade in her new school was making friends. Of course this is probably true of any child, but Angie brought with her the extra baggage of friendlessness she had acquired in kindergarten. Even though she was making new friends, she didn't really believe she was worthy of their friendship, and she often complained that no one liked her.

The inconsistencies were dramatic. I would see Angie invited over and over to parties where children invited only their few "best" friends. And when she arrived, I would see her new friends run eagerly to greet her, throw their arms around her, and squeal happily, "Oh boy, Angie's here." But deep down inside, Angie didn't believe them. She couldn't believe there was anything for them to like. And she often came home crying because she had been unable to enjoy herself at the parties. She felt alienated from the rest of the children, and eventually, her feelings of alienation became a self-fulfilling prophecy and the party invitations began to be fewer and further between.

Closely tied to Angie's lack of self-esteem was her sense of rejection. She rejected herself and she felt rejected by everyone around her—her friends, her family, and even God. Angie thought God had deserted her. One day she blurted out that she thought God must have a hole in his head. Angie went on to explain, "I pray and pray and pray for a good day, but one never comes. I think my prayers just go in one side of God's head and out the other." Tearfully she added, "He just doesn't love kids like me."

Neither did she believe that we, her parents, loved her anymore. There were times when all the reassurance and hugs and kisses in the world couldn't convince her that we loved her. She insisted that we would have been better off if she had never been born.

Angie also struggled with the fear that we might reject the information she disclosed about her sexual abuse by the teachers. She seemed to need constant assurance that she had done the right thing by telling and that she was believed. Sometimes she would ask me if I believed what she had said, and then she would stare at my face, searching for clues to assure her that I was telling the truth when I said I did. The fact that her former teachers had often accused her of being a liar contributed to her constant need for reassurance.

During the early months following her disclosure, Angie's moods were volatile. She would frequently withdraw into her room in depression. When she internalized her pain, her face mirrored the sadness and despair she felt. As she progressed through therapy, her feelings turned outward, and hostility and anger began to dominate her emotional repertoire. As Angie told more and more of her experiences, she turned into a bundle of pent-up hostility. She was like a ticking bomb—I never knew when she was going to blow up. Some of her wrath was directed at her abusers. Because her former teachers were no longer part of her life, however, much of her anger transferred to the authority figures who were accessible—her parents.

Angie didn't begin to verbalize her anger until one Sunday five months after her disclosure. We had decided to stop at a grocery store after church to buy some donuts. As my husband went inside to get them, Angie told me of a time when her former teachers had gotten donuts from the same store for the kindergarten class as a special treat. All of the children had gotten one except Angie. The teachers had not given her one because she had been "bad." It broke my heart to think of how mean that had been and how hurt Angie must have felt. I held Angie close to me and told her how very sorry I was that this had happened.

Angie pulled away from me a little and asked, "Mommy, do you like me?" "Yes, I do—very much," I answered.

"Then how could you have put me in that school?" she exploded.

I asked her if that was why she had been so angry at me for so long. "Yes," she screamed and she began to cry. I talked then about how worried we had been about her all that last year at the school. I told her about the conferences we had with the director and the teachers, about the times we had taken her to see her pediatrician, and about our decision to take her to see Dr. McGarrah. I said that all of that was because we knew she was unhappy at school and we were trying to find out what was wrong. If we had only known what was really going on there, we would have taken her out immediately.

I told her that what happened to her at school was not her fault. Neither was it our fault, nor anyone's fault except the people who had hurt her. "If it's their fault," Angie replied, "how come they aren't being punished for it?" (The criminal investigation had not yet been resolved.) I told her I didn't have a good answer for that, but the important thing was for us to all work together to get over it—and for Angie to let us love her and believe that we do love her very much. She cried a little more and then asked, "Why did it have to happen to me?"

Angie never did eat that donut. It stayed around the kitchen until I finally threw it out. Until then I had never known her to turn away a donut. She loves donuts more than any other junk food. I guess she just didn't have any appetite for a donut from that particular store.

"I hate you," we would hear day after day, as she lashed out in anger at us. After all, we were her parents. We were expected to protect her and take care of her. Isn't that what parents are for? And we had failed her. We had been unable to keep this awful thing from happening to her.

It is not hard to imagine how Angie's behavior changed during this period, with a kaleidoscope of emotions turning inside her. This child of mine with whom I had lived for six years became a stranger to me at times. My daughter who had always been so easy to raise turned almost overnight into a problem child of the third degree.

CHAPTER 4

BEHAVIORAL BEDLAM

Like all young children, Angie had led her parents through a maze of normal emotional and behavioral developmental phases. Somehow we were fortunate enough to slip uneventfully through the terrible twos; but just when we began to feel pleased with ourselves, we got slam-dunked during her horrific threes.

Baffled by three-year-old Angie's newly asserted independence and obstinacy, my husband and I had enrolled in a positive-parenting course. The child-rearing theories presented in the class emphasized using positive reinforcement to build a child's self-esteem and to encourage appropriate behavior. Negative reinforcement was to be used as a last resort, and the punishment should "fit the crime," so that the child could understand the cause and effect of his or her behavior. Physical punishment should be reserved for life-threatening situations when the seriousness of an action requires an instant but lasting impression (like the time three-year-old Angie broke away from me and darted across the busy street in front of our house).

The course helped immensely. Overall, Angie was an easy child to live with during those early years. She was high-strung and active, but she was also very sensitive, and disciplining her had been relatively easy. She responded well to positive reinforcement. Rarely did we need to resort to spanking, because exile to her room or deprivation of TV privileges usually were effective negative reinforcers.

Then came Angie's disclosure that she had been sexually molested, and the emotional maelstrom that followed brought behavioral chaos with it. There were times when I would simply stare at Angie and wonder who that stranger was. She became unpredictable, and at times totally unmanageable.

When fear dominated Angie's days and nights, I saw a lot of regressive behavior. She would cling to me and whine, afraid that I might leave her. She worried that I might die or that I would stop loving her and "run away." She demanded constant reassurance that I loved her, that I would love her forever, and that I would never leave her. She would often crawl into my lap, curl up as small as possible, and ask me to rock her and sing lullabies as I did when she was younger. And she would pull out her baby book so we could reminisce about the good old days.

Along with Angie's fear came incredible sleep problems. It is a rare child who doesn't like to do battle at bedtime, but the battles we engaged in often escalated to global proportions. She was so terrorized by nightmares that her bed became her own little house of horrors, and she didn't enter it willingly. Her repertoire of delay tactics was impressive indeed, and my patience rarely lasted through the evening. She refused to go to bed alone and wanted my husband or me to stay in her room with her. We would tiptoe out of her room as soon as she fell asleep, but the slightest night sound would send her flying from her room for the safety of ours. The normal creaks and groans of an old house sounded to her like her abusers walking on the roof, trying to find a way to get in to hurt her.

We tried everything—night-lights, lights left on in the hall, and background music, but only the protective arms of her parents offered her enough security.

Angie's fears controlled a great deal of her life. Cues that seemed innocuous on the surface often reminded her of her ordeal and sent her into emotional and behavioral retreat. The Christmas following Angie's disclosure had given all of us a much needed lift, but one evening after the holiday I noticed that Angie seemed very upset. She vacillated somewhere between depression and hostility.

I made spaghetti for dinner—her favorite—but she refused to eat with us. Instead, she took off her clothes, loaded up her bed with stuffed animals, and climbed into it with them. I asked her if she wanted me to stay with her in her room. She shook her head no. I promised to check back with her in 15 minutes. When I did, I found her lying in bed, staring at the ceiling. I asked her to come and eat dinner with us. Again she refused. I put a tape on for her so she could listen to something pretty and promised to come back again in a few minutes.

Before I could go back to check on her, she bolted from her room screaming, "It's not fair, it's not fair, it's not fair!" She ran back to her room, flung herself on her bed, and cried.

I followed her. After she calmed down, she began to talk about an incident earlier in the day when her father had taken her to a fast-food restaurant for lunch. She had seen someone there who looked like one of her former teachers. The resemblance wasn't just in her imagination, because my husband had mentioned it to me earlier. He had noticed that Angie was upset at the time, but she seemed to forget about it as the day wore on. Apparently she had not forgotten about it at all, and it had gnawed at her until she exploded that evening. She refused to return to that particular restaurant for months afterward.

Other cues were directly related to specific incidents when she had been molested. For many months Angie had been afraid of going into the bathroom by herself. She wanted me to go with her, and yet she was embarrassed to have me there. So I would go into the bathroom with her but I would be careful not to look at her. I thought this was peculiar, but the only explanation Angie offered was that she was afraid of the noise the toilet made when it flushed.

One day four months after her disclosure, Angie asked me, as she usually did, to accompany her to the bathroom. Again I asked her why she wanted me with her. She said, "I'm afraid of the noise when I flush it. I'm afraid a monster is going to come out and get me."

I asked, "Angie, does it have anything to do with school? Was the bathroom a bad place for you?"

She began to cry and said that the bathroom was one of the places where "it" had happened. She went on to describe an incident when she had been molested while she was going to the bathroom at school. One of the teachers had come in, closed the door behind her, and scolded Angie for taking too long. Just as Angie stood up and flushed the toilet, the teacher grabbed her, pushed her against the wall, and fondled her. The teacher was rough and Angie said it hurt her. She told the teacher to stop it, but the teacher "had bigger muscles than I did" and she told Angie, "I'm not doing anything." She ordered Angie not to tell anyone or she'd see to it that Angie got kicked out of school, and then she left.

Angie said that when she walked out of the bathroom, she felt "sick all over and had goose bumps." She sat down in a corner and "shivered all over." Someone asked her what was wrong and Angie replied that she was cold, only "I wasn't really cold. I felt creepy. But I had to make something up."

With a memory like that to haunt her, it isn't hard to understand why a simple act such as flushing a toilet could evoke feelings powerful enough to influence behavior that should be routine for a child. Shortly after she told me about that incident, Angie began to go into the bathroom by herself. She continued to be afraid to flush the toilet, however, for more than a year.

Angie's feelings of guilt and her low self-esteem had a profound effect on her behavior. She blamed herself for everything and anything that didn't go quite right. If we were late for church, it was because "It's my fault isn't it? You hate me, don't you?" If she accidentally spilled anything it was because "I'm stupid. I can't do anything right."

This lack of confidence affected Angie's performance at school. She never experienced serious academic problems, but neither did she perform up to her potential. It was interesting to see how her moods affected her schoolwork. In first grade, the children's classroom work was sent home to the parents once each week. How she was feeling about herself was clearly reflected in her schoolwork. The swings in quality were dramatic.

Angie also developed a victim syndrome. She began to expect bad things to happen to her, and when they did, she was convinced that she deserved them. She seemed to set herself up in situations where she couldn't possibly win, and she became very accident prone, both physically and emotionally. This quickly developed into a self-perpetuating vicious circle.

Children who are sexually molested often develop a distorted sense of sexuality. They are exposed to sex in ways that are beyond their level of comprehension, and they respond with sexual interest and behavior that is inappropriate for their age. Sexually abused children often engage in aggressive sexual behavior with other children, or in excessive masturbation.

I have not observed Angie displaying overt, aggressive sexual behavior, and it is hard for me to tell if her sexual curiosity is appropriate for her age. Nevertheless, it is clear that Angie did not escape from her ordeal unscathed. Her sexual self-concept was badly damaged by her experience. This was demonstrated by one therapeutic exercise Dr. McGarrah used with Angie several months after her initial disclosure.

First, Dr. McGarrah had Angie draw a picture of herself. Next, she had her select her favorite and least favorite colors. Then, she was to color the parts of her body she didn't like with the colors she liked the least. Angie colored herself with pink and purple except for her head and sexual organs, which were colored in black. She explained that she hated her sexual organs because that's where the teachers touched her and she hated her head because she couldn't stop thinking about it.

Angie has continued to be extremely self-conscious about her body throughout her period of recovery. For many months following her disclosure, Angie adamantly ordered me not to look at her when she didn't have clothes on. She eventually relaxed a little at home, but she is still reluctant to undress around other people. When we go swimming at the YMCA, she showers with her swim suit on and changes after she gets home. At the dance studio, she changes her clothes in the bathroom instead of in the dressing room. When she sleeps over at a friend's house, she won't even take clean underwear along, because she will not change her panties at someone else's house.

The summer following her disclosure, Angie came face-to-face with the sexual implications of the abuse when she attended day camp. Several children from her former school also attended, and one of the little boys began to display extremely aggressive and inappropriate sexual behavior toward Angie. I have no idea why this happened. At first I wondered if Angie was initiating it, but a camp counselor observed one of the incidents Angie described and confirmed Angie's story. So I hypothesized that something may also have happened to the other child in kindergarten. Or perhaps he had observed something there or overheard his parents discussing Angie after news of the criminal investigation became known.

At any rate, it began when Angie came home agitated and angry because this boy was telling the other children that Angie had "had sex." He seemed to be obsessed with vaginas, and he repeatedly asked Angie if she would show hers to him. He asked her if she had any books at home with pictures of naked women in them. If she did, he wanted her to bring them to camp so he could see their vaginas. Whenever he got a chance, he would grab Angie in the crotch or poke her in the buttocks.

The first thing we did was to discuss how to handle the situation. I wanted to talk to the camp counselor and/or to the child's mother, but Angie decided that she wanted to handle it herself. And she did. The next time the boy grabbed her, she told him he had no right to do that to her and if he tried it again, "my mother is going to talk to your mother." She told him that she had already told me about it, and that got him very upset. She said he looked down at the ground and muttered that he "hadn't done anything wrong."

The second thing we had to do was answer the questions about sex that this incident raised. When the boy told others that Angie had "had sex," Angie was upset because she didn't know what that meant. "How do I know if I'm doing it, Mom, when I don't even know what it is?" I asked her if she would like me to explain it to her and she said yes. We agreed to set aside the next evening for a talk about what it meant to have sex with someone.

Angie already knew basic anatomical terminology, and she knew generally where babies come from and how they are born. She didn't know about sperm and eggs and the details of intercourse. I wasn't thrilled about having to broach this subject with a seven-year-old, but the next day I visited several bookstores to see what I could find that would help with my explanation.

It was hard to find material with the detail I needed presented in a way that would be appropriate for a child Angie's age. Most books on sex education were geared toward telling parents how to discuss sex with their children. I didn't have time to read a book like that before evening. I found a few books that had been written for children but were too general. One book went into more detail, but I was afraid I would have a hard time keeping a straight face when it described orgasm as a big sneeze.

I finally found a book I liked at a religious bookstore. It was written for children eight to eleven years old and it presented the anatomy and physiology of sex simply and factually. Then it went one step further and put the facts in a moral context. It talked about feelings and about having respect for one's body. This was the book I chose for the springboard of our discussion that evening.

During our discussion, Angie was surprisingly nonchalant. She commented that intercourse seemed pretty "gross" and then focused her curiosity on the development of the fetus after conception. She was fascinated by the way cells divide and develop into a recognizable human being. That was "neat," she thought. Our conversation took a serious turn when we started talking about how special our bodies are because they were created by God. Angie got upset because she was convinced that her body wasn't special at all.

She said, "It used to be special but it isn't any more because I've been abused." Once again she declared that God didn't love her anymore because of what had happened to her. And then Angie started to ask questions about sex-related topics. I was surprised at how many bits and pieces of information she had picked up from overhearing news broadcasts and adult conversations and from reading headlines in the newspaper. She asked about AIDS, rape, teenage pregnancies, and homosexuality.

We talked about all these things, and then she wanted to know if what her teachers did to her meant that she had had sex. She had been sexually molested by women—did that mean she was gay? For the first time I realized how much of my child's innocence had been stripped away from her, and I wondered how irreparable that damage might be.

The problem Angie faced with the little boy from her former school was not the only social problem she encountered. Her self-concept was so poor that she often had trouble relating to other children. She couldn't accept herself and she assumed she was not really being accepted by her friends. Her feelings were easily hurt; the least little disagreement with another child would send her off to self-imposed solitary confinement.

Angie and Jessica

Her most complicated relationship was with a little girl who had been Angie's best friend since they were both about two years old. She and Jessica (not her real name) met in the baby room at preschool and they soon became inseparable friends. The girls' fathers knew each other professionally, and Jessica's mother and I hit it off and became friends as well. Like so many other aspects of Angie's life, this relationship began to unravel in kindergarten.

In personality and interests, Angie and Jessica were a lot alike. They were both very imaginative, intense little girls, and they were capable of some pretty strong disagreements. No matter how much they fought, however, they always managed to part as best friends—until they reached kindergarten. Over a period of months, they became more and more competitive with each other. The competition spawned vicious arguments over who was "better," and their relationship dissolved into one of mutual antagonism.

The tension between Jessica and Angie also worked its way into my relationship with Jessica's mother, whom I will call Diane. We continued to be friends, but the friendship had definitely cooled by the time the girls left the preschool. We knew Angie and Jessica were having problems, but we thought it might be just the natural demise of a long friendship the girls were outgrowing.

Looking back on those kindergarten days, Diane and I suspect now that all four of us were deliberately manipulated by the girls' teachers. It didn't become apparent until almost a year later, when Diane and I finally were able to start talking about what had happened to Angie in that classroom. Once we started putting the pieces together, we felt foolish that neither of us had figured out what was going on sooner than we did.

Child molestation is not a random, impulsive act. Child molesters pick their victims carefully, and they create opportunities for their crimes. They especially like victims who depend on them to fulfill their emotional and/or physical needs. I think Angie was deliberately isolated from her friends, including Jessica, so that the attention she received from her teachers would become even more essential to her. Angie's abusers frequently set the girls up against each other by showing blatant favoritism toward one or the other.

During most of the conferences I had with the teachers and director during that kindergarten year, the teachers insisted that Angie was perfectly happy at the school. On one occasion, however, one of them admitted that Angie and Jessica were having problems. She speculated that the unhappiness Angie was expressing to me was a result of her inability to adjust to the cooling of that friendship.

The other teacher, in an inconsistent way that was typical of her, denied that there were any problems between Angie and Jessica. Then she turned right around and said that Jessica and Angie were always fighting but it never had anything to do with school. It was always, she said, over something that happened outside of school, such as at ballet or when they were visiting each other's home. She went on to say that she thought there was a problem "with the parents."

The teachers did a good job of pitting Diane and me against each other. They would often pull me aside and tell me confidentially how awful Jessica had been to Angie that day. They would tell me how "jealous" Jessica had been of something Angie owned or something she had done that day. I remember one incident in particular when Angie had a very bad day at school. One teacher explained it by saying that Jessica had acted like a "little queen bee" all day and had bullied Angie mercilessly. Jessica had been pretty "full of herself," I was told. I learned later that this was one of the days Angie had been molested.

When Diane and I finally began talking to each other about these things, I learned that the teachers had done the same with her. They had often told her what a problem Angie was. She told of one day when she came into the room and Angie was sitting tearfully in the corner, looking miserable. One teacher nodded toward Angie and said in a nasty tone that she couldn't wait until "that child gets out of here" because she was "such a problem." Angie's abusers fueled the tensions between the girls and between their mothers.

The minute both girls got out of that school, we saw an immediate improvement in their relationship. They became best friends once again. Right after Angie's last day at school, Jessica spent the afternoon at our house. I was amazed to see none of the rivalry and hostility that had been so obvious in recent months. Even though the two girls eventually entered first grade at different schools, their relationship continued to be a good, steady friendship until the summer following first grade, when it hit another snag.

That summer, Jessica and Angie attended a two-week camp at the Atlanta Zoo. They were there only a few hours each day, so Angie spent the rest of the afternoons at Jessica's house. After a few days, the old antagonism began to reappear. Angie complained bitterly that Jessica was "putting me down and trying to make me feel bad about myself." It seemed as though they were falling back into their old kindergarten pattern.

One morning on the way to camp, the girls got into a fight almost as soon as they got in the car. Jessica began tugging on Angie's ponytail. Jessica had done that before, and each time she did, Angie objected. Jessica wasn't doing it to be mean, but Angie just didn't like to have someone fiddling around with her hair. And by now Angie knew she had a right to tell anyone to stop doing things like that to her.

So Angie ordered Jessica to stop pulling on her hair. Jessica responded by teasing Angie about how short her hair was compared to her own. Angie answered with a retort, tempers flared, and by the time they got to the zoo they were in a rip-roaring argument.

When I picked Angie up that afternoon, the girls were still screaming at each other, and Angie stormed out of the house, vowing never to go back again. From what Angie told me that evening, no major incident had precipitated the arguments, but rather a series of exchanges where Angie felt put down by Jessica and responded by lashing back at her. She was so angry that night that she insisted she would not go back to the zoo the next day.

We talked a long time, and I said that I understood her anger if Jessica was putting her down. We talked about the camp and Angie admitted that she was enjoying it. I said that it would be a shame for her not to go back to something she enjoyed because of her fights with Jessica. I told her I wasn't going to force her to go back, but I hoped by morning she would decide to go to camp. If she didn't want to go to Jessica's house after camp, I would make other arrangements.

The next morning, Angie decided to go to the zoo, but she said she didn't want to go to Jessica's house that afternoon. When Diane arrived to pick Angie up, I told her I wasn't sure Angie would be going home with them after camp. We decided to talk about the situation later that day. Fortunately, my relationship with Diane had mended enough by this time that we were able to discuss the situation constructively.

It could have been a messy conversation, reminiscent of the ones we had attempted the year before. It would have been easy for each of us to take our own child's side, and in so doing, implicitly blame the other child for the problems the girls were having. It turned out to be a very frank, cooperative discussion. We analyzed rather than accused.

I told Diane that it was too much of a coincidence that Angie was having this problem with Jessica immediately after her encounter with the boy from kindergarten who was in her day camp. I wondered if all the children in that class had not been victimized to some degree. I didn't mean that they had all been molested, necessarily. But the atmosphere in that classroom had not been healthy, and children are perceptive.

Who knows what they heard or saw? Maybe the other children picked up cues from the teachers that Angie was some sort of victim—that she was vulnerable; that she felt so bad about herself that she was an easy mark to bully. Only now the rules had changed because Angie was beginning to stick up for herself. Maybe the other children didn't know how to adapt to this new, assertive Angie.

Or, I hypothesized, maybe her former classmates simply reminded Angie of what happened to her at that school and it was generating feelings of hostility in her. Maybe that was why she was getting so angry with them. Maybe it was a combination of the two. Maybe they were provoking her and she was reacting with unusually intense anger because of those old feelings. Or maybe the sexual harassment at camp reminded Angie of what had happened to her in kindergarten and she was taking it out on Jessica.

Diane agreed that what I said made sense. Our problem was trying to figure out what to do about it. Should we keep the girls away from each other for a while? We didn't want to do that. The situation had not been totally awful that past week. Even in her anger, Angie admitted she and Jessica had a lot of fun together and she still considered Jessica her friend. We decided their friendship needed to run its natural course.

I had promised Angie I would be at the zoo to meet her when camp was over. She could decide then if she wanted to go home with Jessica or not. When I got there, Angie and Jessica talked things over and decided to give it one more try.

Later that afternoon, Diane called me to ask if Angie could stay for dinner. Angie and Jessica were both begging to have Angie stay longer. I asked if that meant they'd had a good day. They had, Diane said. In fact, they were two excited, giggling little girls most of the day.

On their own, Angie and Jessica had talked about how they were going to try very hard to work things out so that they wouldn't get so angry and start fighting with each other. They made some sort of pact that the first one to start a fight would have to fall down on the floor and lie there for two minutes.

When Angie came home after dinner she was very happy. She told me how well she and Jessica had gotten along. I told her I was proud of them both for working it out on their own. And I could tell that Angie was very proud of herself.

The next day there was a remarkable difference in the demeanor of both the girls. The day before they had been tense and high-strung; now they were relaxed and natural with each other. They had a lot of fun together. Somehow they had broken that old pattern and had learned to respect each other's feelings.

At the time of this writing, Angie and Jessica are eight years old. Their summer at the zoo is over and the girls continue to have a healthy, relaxed friendship. And the same is true of their mothers. At least in terms of our relationships, the four of us have put the agony of the girls' kindergarten year behind us.

The Banshee

The volatility of Angie's emotions during the months that followed her disclosure often resulted in behavior that was completely unpredictable. Most days were "bad days," but how Angie reacted depended on how much she was internalizing her pain. There were times when she acted despondent. She would cry buckets of tears over hurt feelings or feelings of inadequacy. She would dread each day, expecting the worst to happen to her at any time. I remember her crying hopelessly, "It's just not ever going to get any better." She felt life had been unfair to her and she didn't understand why.

As she progressed through therapy, she began to externalize her anger, and instead of beating on herself all the time, she began to beat more and more on her parents. She acted out the anger and hostility that was bubbling inside her in physical aggression and defiance.

Some of Angie's behavior was so outrageous that I began to suspect that the little girl in the movie *The Exorcist* was not possessed at all—she was probably a victim of child molestation! Remember the scene with the pea soup? It wasn't any worse than the day Angie spit a mouthful of sticky cough syrup in my face!

My husband and I were totally unprepared for the dramatic change in Angie's behavior. Suddenly we were face-to-face with an incorrigible, defiant little rogue. None of our past experiences helped. Nothing we tried worked.

In desperation, I consulted Dr. McGarrah. "Is this drastic change in behavior a result of her abuse," I asked, "or is this a normal phase for a six-year-old?" It was definitely not normal, I was assured. In fact, it was textbook behavior typical of sexual abuse victims. Angie had been abused by her teachers, people she had been taught to respect, obey, and love. This betrayal of her trust had turned her young world upside down. The rules had been broken, and as a result, she no longer knew what the rules were. She began testing the limits because she wasn't sure what the limits were anymore.

Her abominable behavior suddenly had no limits. She attacked my husband and me both verbally and physically. She became destructive. There were times when she fought us over anything, everything, and nothing.

I remember one nerve-racking incident in particular. Angie had been a screaming, hostile little banshee for some time, so I finally confined her to her room until she could calm down. She did, but her repressed anger was obvious from the way she sulked when she emerged ten minutes later. She soon began to scream abusive language at me once again, and I warned her that if she screamed at me again I would have to spank her. She stopped yelling, coldly looked me in the eye, took a handful of crackers, crumbled them up, and dropped them on the floor.

I took a big breath and calmly told her that I expected her to clean up the mess she had just made. She exploded, and screamed out a barrage of venom—"I hate you" and "I wish I didn't have any parents." I gave her a swat on the bottom and sent her to her room, where she cried hysterically for what seemed to be forever.

Sometimes Angie's hostility attacks lasted for days. However long they lasted, the end would finally come when she simply seemed to collapse from emotional fatigue. Then she would be a whimpering, clinging child again, begging for reassurance that we loved her. It was as though she was pushing us as far away from her as she possibly could just to test how much we really did love her.

During this chaotic time, Angie's relationship with her father became so damaged that I wondered if it could ever be repaired. Angie and I had angry times, but we had a special closeness that eventually prevailed. Her confrontations with her father had a bitter edge. I'm not sure I will ever understand why. Maybe it had something to do with the different dynamics of father-daughter and mother-daughter relationships.

Angie often did battle with both of us, but when she went one-on-one with her father, it was hard for me to keep out of the middle.

She demanded that I take sides, taking great pains to detail all the injustices her daddy had inflicted on her.

One time she came storming into the room in complete exasperation. "Why did you marry Daddy," she hissed. "How could you *ever* have married a man like that!"

When I tried to act as a mediator, Angie felt rejected and her anger turned to self-pity. She would become angry with me because I "didn't care" and she became angry with herself because she didn't "deserve anyone's love." She would wail plaintively that "All I ever wanted from the day I was born were two parents who cared about me . . . but my parents don't care about me at all . . . and that's all I ever wanted . . . ."

And so we found ourselves in a tug of war with a child who pushed us away with her hostility at the same time as she clung to us desperately for help. We were faced with behavior that demanded both sympathy and discipline.

CHAPTER 5

SO WHAT'S A PARENT TO DO?

Being a parent in today's changing and complex world is hard enough without the complications of child abuse. Add this tragedy to a family's life and parenting suddenly becomes an overwhelming task.

As I write this book, I remember how my husband and I reacted to Angie's behavioral problems, and in retrospect a lot of what we did was logical. What worked and what didn't work seems to make some sense now. At the time, however, nothing made sense at all.

There was no rhyme or reason to what we did to help Angie recover from her trauma. In fact, to be perfectly honest, a lot of what we did wasn't designed to help her regain control of her life as much as it was to salvage our own sanity. We simply reacted desperately on a gut level from day to day. Fortunately, some of what we did ended up being right.

The positive parenting course my husband and I had taken when Angie was three years old made a lot of sense. Positive parenting is certainly healthier for parents and children than negative approaches. Unfortunately, when you're out there on the front lines, fundamental survival sometimes results in emotions that override logic, and the theories learned in the classroom can go right up in smoke. This simple fact of parental life is magnified many times over when the child to whom you are trying to be a good parent has been sexually abused.

During normal development the child learns the rules of the household gradually, beginning with the day he or she comes home from the hospital. Parent-child relationships are established, roles are learned, and family members know pretty much what is expected of them in routine family life.

Parenting is like building a house. Under normal parenting conditions, the house is built gradually, beginning with a foundation and adding on over time. The parents of an abused child, however, are faced with building an emergency structure after the home has been flattened by an unexpected, vicious storm.

When a child has been sexually molested, rules once taken for granted are demolished. The child is stripped of innocence, self-esteem, and security. It's as though a basic lifeline is severed, and the child is suddenly an untethered kite drifting in space at the mercy of unstable air currents. She needs an anchor, and she needs it fast.

So the parents have to start almost from scratch to reestablish the rules and boundaries of acceptable behavior. It's a crisis situation for which no parent is ever prepared. Most positive parenting concepts are based on reinforcing positive behavior and building on the child's self-esteem. But it's hard to accentuate the positive when you're overwhelmed with the negative. It's hard to build on self-esteem that no longer exists. And it's hard to try to be a good parent in a bad situation, when you're struggling with your own fears, anger, and insecurities. It's an enormous job, but the child's survival depends on the job getting done.

So what works and what doesn't? Generally, what worked for us was anything that effectively channeled Angie's negative emotions into constructive outlets. What didn't work was anything purely punitive.

Punishment was the first gut response we had. Angie was probably sent to her room, deprived of privileges, and spanked more in those first few months of turmoil than she had been in the entire six years before. At times, it seemed to be effective. At times, we managed to extinguish an unacceptable behavior, but then it was immediately replaced by another.

Angie often vented her anger physically. The least provocation would send her flying at me in fury. She kicked me. She hit me. I had heard that punishment was supposed to fit the crime. So I hit her back. It was the worst thing I could have done. It only escalated the conflict. The problem was that Angie really didn't mind being spanked. It reinforced what she had recently learned—that she was a victim, that she deserved to be abused, and that adults couldn't be trusted to protect her. In fact there were times when I didn't spank her that she would dare me to do so, saying, "I deserve to be spanked."

Nonphysical punishments were much more effective with Angie. We had always restricted the amount of television she was allowed to watch. The TV programs we did allow were very important to her. She would rather be drawn and quartered than have to miss *The Cosby Show*. Depriving her of TV privileges usually worked, and we were able to extinguish certain behaviors.

Unfortunately, Angie had so much anger bottled up inside her that it just had to come out somewhere. It would leak out in one place and we would try to cap the leak by attacking the resultant behavior. If we were successful, her anger would only show up somewhere else. For example, I managed rather quickly to get Angie to stop hitting and kicking me. But then I began to notice how frequently she would "accidentally" slam into me with her body ("Sorry, Mom, I didn't mean to bump into you"). Or she would casually stick out her foot as I passed by and "accidentally" trip me. I had only managed to replace active hostility with passive hostility.

Too often, we dealt with particular acts of behavior without trying to understand the emotions behind the behavior. Eventually we learned to help her cope with her feelings and their sources. This was much more effective. We still had to rely on punishment when all else failed, but we were very careful to let her know that we weren't punishing her. She was not a bad person and we still loved her very much. It was a particular behavior that was not acceptable. We let her know that we didn't want to have to punish that behavior, and that what we really wanted was to help her get rid of the feelings that were making her act the way she was. We tried to get back to being her parents instead of her adversaries.

The first thing I did when things started to fall apart was to rummage through bookstores for books written for victims of child sexual abuse. I found books on the subject, but many of them were for older children. Many were about incestuous situations and the possibility of the child being placed in a foster home. I had to be careful not to introduce Angie to new fears and worries that were not germane to her situation. The best book I found was *Something Happened to Me* by Phyllis Sweet.* It is written simply and effectively in the first person and talks mostly about feelings. For example, "Something happened to me. I feel different. I'm afraid to talk about it."

Angie and I read it together at first, and she really identified with it. "Yeah," she would exclaim, "That's just how I feel!" Afterwards I would see her sitting quietly in her room poring over the book by herself. It helped her to recognize her feelings and be able to express them. More importantly, it helped her realize that what had happened to her happens to other children, too. Much of her intense anguish came from believing that no other child had ever felt as she did. Learning that her feelings were typical for children who have been molested made her realize she wasn't alone, and reinforced what I had been telling her—that there wasn't anything wrong with her, and that she hadn't done anything to deserve what happened to her.

One constructive way Angie expressed her feelings throughout her ordeal was by putting them on paper with words and pictures. Children's drawings are recognized by many therapists as powerful diagnostic and therapeutic tools. They can offer valuable insights into the experiences and feelings of children too young to express themselves in words. They are also an important emotional outlet for young victims of trauma.

Angie's verbal and writing skills were very advanced for her age. She drew some pictures for Dr. McGarrah, but most of the graphic expressions I saw at home were notes or combinations of notes and pictures. She kept some of her notes and pictures to herself. She would scribble them out furiously, crumple them up, and throw them away. Others would be addressed to me and left out where I could find them. I have one note where she wrote her name and surrounded it with bright colors. Then she covered all that up with heavy black scribbles and wrote at the top, "I hate my self." It was folded up and on the outside was written, "To mom."

I have another note written five weeks later that says, "It is fun at my new school. I like my teacher and friends too. I enjoy life now."

---

*   See the Resource List at the end of the book for information on this and other helpful readings.

During hostile moments, it was not unusual for her to write hate letters to me. She would stomp up to me, thrust a "I hate my parents" note into my hand, and storm away. It certainly helped Angie to vent a little venom, but I felt as though I had just been served a subpoena.

Angie generally expressed her feelings pretty openly. The problem was that the way she expressed them was often not acceptable. We had to let her vent her anger, but we couldn't let her pound it out on us. After about a month of struggling with this dilemma, I took Angie to the toy store and we bought a "bop bag." I hoped it would lessen the likelihood of her hitting and kicking us if she could take her anger out on the bop bag.

Angie was enthusiastic. She seemed just as eager as I was to get her angry feelings under control. She selected her bop bag as carefully as she would have selected a new doll. She couldn't wait to get home to try it out. On the way home, she fantasized about how she wished she could have a bop bag that looked like one of her former teachers and would say "Ouch!" when she hit it. And then, Angie said, "Wouldn't it be neat if it turned out to really be [the teacher] I'm hitting?"

Angie made good use of her bop bag over the months that followed. As a matter of fact, she pounded on it so hard the day we bought it that it broke and we had to go right back to the store for another one. The thud-thud-thud of Angie's pounding on her bop bag routinely sounded from her room, and her physical attacks on us became less frequent.

By the time two months had passed since the disclosure, my relationship with Angie was showing some improvement, although it was still pretty unpredictable. Her relationship with her father, however, was awful. My husband was struggling with how to discipline Angie, and her behavior toward him was downright atrocious. Most of her attacks were directed toward him at that time.

Pounding on the bop bag was helping, but her behavior was still unacceptable. In desperation I decided to try a behavior chart. I told Angie that we needed some rules in the house that would help us all get along a little better.

I was surprised at Angie's enthusiasm for the idea. Even though she was fighting the rules, she seemed to be groping for more structure in her life. So that she wouldn't feel as though my husband and I were picking on her, I suggested that we do a behavior chart for ourselves, too. Angie loved that idea—she could think of lots of ways for us to improve! We sat down together and decided on the behaviors we wanted to work on. We tried to keep them positive.

Angie's chart included 14 items. Some were easy to do, some were hard; some related directly to her problem behavior, and some did not. Her items ranged from "I picked up my own clothes and toys" to "I did not hit or kick my parents today." The items we decided on for Angie's father and me were similar—"I did not slam doors today" and "I was patient today." All of us had, "I said 'I love you' to someone in my family today."

Each evening we sat down to talk about our day, and we assigned a plus or a minus for each behavior on our charts. We totaled the pluses, subtracted the minuses, and recorded a total for the day as well as a cumulative total. When Angie's cumulative total reached 50 points (up to about twice a week), she could choose her reward— either an extra 25 cents in her Saturday allowance, an extra TV program that week, or a special treat such as a trip out for ice cream.

The behavior chart was an immediate success. Allowing Angie to choose her reward was especially useful. Some of Angie's negative behaviors, such as swearing, disappeared almost immediately. The ones that stemmed from her hurt and anger were much more difficult. I tried to help her distinguish between the feeling of anger and what to do with that feeling. I wanted her to be free to tell me she was angry about something I had said or done, but to know that it was not acceptable for her to be abusive by calling me names or striking out physically.

There were bad days when Angie was devastated over her minuses. I tried to emphasize the pluses, and urged her to look forward to the next day, which would surely be better. It also helped that the point system allowed for fairly frequent rewards. She needed some quick reinforcement.

On many days she woke up in the morning seething with anger and hurt and she wouldn't let me near her. Other times we could talk about her feelings and this would help for a while.

Sometimes, when Angie was having a bad time, all it took to turn things around was a little humor to break the tension. It was a temporary fix, but it gave all of us time to catch our breath. On one especially nasty morning, I asked her if she thought it would help if we tried to unscrew her big toes. Then I could shake her up and down to see if we could shake her anger out. That was an offer she couldn't resist. So we shook out as much anger as we could and then I tried to blow some love into her toes to replace the anger. Unfortunately, we misplaced her big toes and she almost had to go off to school without them. By that time she was giggling in spite of herself and the day started out a little better than it might have otherwise.

Humor wasn't always appropriate, though. I had to be careful not to be silly when she was seriously upset about something. She would be insulted and hurt and think that I didn't take her feelings seriously. Humor can be mean when it shows up in the wrong place at the wrong time. But for those times when she was in a generally bad mood, a little light humor, tenderly administered, sometimes did the trick.

As Angie began to work out her anger, I was able to deal more effectively with her despair. The simple passage of time was the best ally we had. When she felt despondent because life seemed so unfair, we could talk about how much progress she had already made. Angie could remember back to the time, just weeks before, when she was so dominated by fear and anger that good days were almost nonexistent. The good days were becoming more and more frequent, and this gave her hope that life wouldn't always be ugly for her.

As her moods began to level off, her acting-out behavior began to be replaced by more acceptable behavior, and I found myself relying more on my old pattern of positive reinforcement. Also, I was able to relax more and look consciously for ways to help Angie rebuild her still-fragile self-esteem.

For example, I encouraged her to run in a one-mile fun run for children that was sponsored by the YMCA the summer following first grade. Angie frequently ran with me at the Y, so I knew she could handle the mile course. I emphasized that it wasn't a race—she wasn't competing with anyone. There would be no winners or losers. All the children who finished the course, even if they walked the whole thing, would receive a T-shirt, a ribbon, and free snacks.

The fun run was a wonderful experience for Angie. She knew a number of the children there and she ran with one of her friends from summer camp. Both girls ran the entire course, and Angie was bursting with pride when she finished. It gave her a chance to feel good about herself.

The race was something that would not have worked a year earlier when Angie was in the depths of despair. She probably would have felt that she was destined to fail, or she would have been miserable because she didn't run fast enough or well enough. By the time she ran at the Y, she had enough of her self-confidence back to make something to build on. By this time Angie had been in therapy with Dr. McGarrah for over a year. She had come a long way on her road to recovery.

CHAPTER 6

THERAPY AND PROGNOSIS

This entire experience has been so painful for my family that it is hard to believe it could have been any worse. But it could have been much worse if we had not had a number of things working in our favor. The best thing my husband and I did was to put Angie in therapy as early as we did and leave her there as long as we have. All children are different, but I can't imagine any child recovering from the effects of abuse without professional help. Children may be able to bury their pain and confusion on their own, but they will never forget it, and sooner or later they will have to deal with it. I'd rather it be sooner than later, so that they won't have to lose any more of their childhood than necessary.

It helped that Angie was in therapy at the time of her disclosure. She already had established a good relationship with Dr. McGarrah before she was plunged into the emotional turmoil that followed. After being abused, some children have a hard time learning to trust other adults, especially those who are the same sex as the offender. Angie didn't have that problem.

We were also fortunate that Angie had a therapist with special expertise in working with sexually abused children. A professional without that expertise would not have been nearly as effective, and in fact, might have done more harm than good.

There are several ways to find a therapist who specializes in child sexual abuse cases. The local child abuse prevention organization should be able to provide a list of therapists from which to choose. Parents can look for a local affiliate of the National Committee for Prevention of Child Abuse. (In Georgia, it's the Georgia Council on Child Abuse, a nonprofit statewide organization headquartered in Atlanta.) The people in the local district attorney's office may also be able to help. A special prosecutor who handles molestation cases could steer parents to a qualified therapist.

How well a child responds to therapy depends a great deal on the child's personality. On the one hand, Angie is a very sensitive child, and I think this may have kept her from bouncing back as quickly as she might have if she were a little tougher. On the other hand, she is extremely verbal, and her ability to talk out her feelings in therapy is encouraging.

I remember one evening when she told me she felt like she was full of anger "up to here," and she pointed to her chest. Several weeks before that she had told me she was so full of anger that there wasn't any place left for love. I asked her if she realized how much progress she was making with Dr. McGarrah's help. Angie replied that she wanted to keep talking to Nancy until her anger went from "here to here to here." She pointed to her chest, her knees, and her toes to demonstrate the anger leaving her body.

How long abuse victims should stay in therapy will depend on their responsiveness to the therapist, the support they receive from the rest of their family, and the extent of the damage inflicted on them when they were molested.

Sexual abuse of children encompasses a range of crimes that vary according to the type of abuse, the frequency of incidents, and the relationship of the offender to the victim. At one end of the continuum is one-time sexual exposure (noncontact) by a stranger. The other extreme is repeated intercourse with a member of the victim's family (incest). Where the crime falls on this continuum will affect the victim's reactions and prognosis for therapy.

Angie has gotten both short-term and long-term benefits from her therapy with Dr. McGarrah. I feel odd talking about short-term therapy, because at the time we were trying to get through those first months it didn't seem short-term at all. In fact, every day and week seemed interminable. But as time flies by the calendar, it really was a relatively short time until we were able to see signs of Angie's recovery.

During the first six to nine months of therapy, Angie learned to deal with the obvious effects of her abuse—the fear, the guilt, the depression, the anger. As overwhelming as her behavioral problems seemed at the time, they decreased significantly after only a few months. After Angie had been in therapy for approximately 18 months, I noticed that her fears and hostility no longer dominated her life. The nightmares and behavioral problems eventually became a bad memory for us. Her bright, vibrant personality began to shine through again, and her smiles far outnumbered her tears. Her performance in school improved dramatically year after year, and her creativity began to bubble up once more.

So why is she still in therapy? Because she still has a long way to go. Sexual abuse rips away a child's self-esteem in no time at all. Repairing that damage takes a long, long time. For the most part, Angie feels pretty good about herself now, but her self-esteem is still very fragile. I have often wished I could have taken my daughter, wrapped her in a protective cocoon, and just let her heal, but life doesn't allow that. The average slings and arrows of childhood experiences wound abused children more deeply than less traumatized children, and threaten the self-confidence the abused children are struggling to regain.

One long-term effect of child sexual abuse that frightens me is the victim syndrome Angie continues to exhibit. This syndrome is seen in adult victims of rape as well as in sexually abused children. Once they have been victimized, children feel they were put in the world to be abused, and this poor self-concept can lead to revictimization. Angie will remain in therapy until I am confident that the cycle of victimization has been broken.

Finally, Angie's body-concept is still badly distorted. She hates her body in general and thinks she is just about the ugliest creature on earth. And she is extremely sensitive about the sexual parts of her body. If I accidentally pat her on the behind, she will wheel around and scream at me to let me know she doesn't ever want to be touched there again. When Angie has a physical exam, she worries more about having to undress than she does about getting her finger pricked for a blood test.

Victims of child sexual abuse often have problems forming healthy sexual relationships in adulthood. I see how uncomfortable Angie is with her body and I worry about whether she will ever overcome this lingering effect of the abuse and be able to have happy, healthy relationships as she grows older. I am bracing myself for her adolescent years, when I suspect her sexual development will bring special problems.

And so Angie continues to be in therapy with Dr. McGarrah. I am also trying to find a group therapy session for her. I believe that talking with other victims her age will help Angie overcome the social problems she continues to have. Group therapy may help her realize that she is not "from outer space or something." She still has trouble relating to friends because she feels different. She thinks nobody likes her because there is something wrong with her.

I don't know how long Angie will remain in therapy. My only plan is to keep her in therapy for however long it takes her to recover fully from the effects of the sexual abuse she experienced almost two years ago. I can't go back and change the fact that someone else almost destroyed my child, but I will do everything within my power to help her get over it so she can enjoy the rest of her childhood— as every child has a right to do.

PART II

What to Expect from Family, Friends, and Society

Facts do not cease to exist because they are ignored.

—Aldous Huxley, from *A Note on Dogma*

INTRODUCTION

I had known for months that something was turning my child's life upside down. Then one day the answer was there, staring me in the face. Angie had been sexually molested.

It was an answer that would spawn many more questions in the months that followed. My attention immediately focused on Angie and her welfare. It was obvious she had been severely traumatized by her experience. I was there with her day after day to watch her struggle, trying to cope with a life she no longer understood.

Angie was the victim. She was the one who suffered the most. It was her future that had been placed in jeopardy by just a few months of childhood that had gone wrong for her. It was her pain, her confusion, her anguish that were the most intense and the most pitiful to watch. But it wasn't long before I began to realize that Angie was only part of a much larger picture.

She was the primary player in a drama with a cast of many. She was the vortex around which many rings of victimization swirled. As time went on, the circles rippled outward farther and farther until every corner of our lives was affected. Angie was the victim, but she wasn't the only one touched by what happened to her.

I lived with Angie every day, and I could see how badly she had been hurt when she was molested by her teachers. I assumed others would automatically sympathize with her and understand at least a little of what she was going through. After all, she was a child who had been sexually assaulted by adults. How could anyone be unmoved?

But the sympathy and help I expected wasn't there. Instead, I discovered the hard way that sexual abuse of children is a crime few people want to acknowledge, let alone understand. People don't want to believe such things can happen in real life. They're uncomfortable talking about it and so they don't. As a result, the sexual molestation of children is among the least understood of all crimes.

And so, at the same time as we were trying to help Angie recover from her trauma, we had to face the world outside our home. We had to contend with the insensitive—sometimes cruel—attitudes of others. While we were struggling with our own feelings of sadness, anger, and confusion, we had to face the ignorance, denial, and hostility of others.

Not everyone was that way, of course. There were a few persons—mostly professionals such as Angie's therapist and the prosecuting attorney—who believed and understood the things Angie said. And they were, for the most part, sympathetic and gentle with us. Some other persons were supportive because they knew we were going through some kind of hell, even though they couldn't comprehend the full impact of what we were experiencing. The vast majority of people we encountered, however, were at best, indifferent, and at worst, hostile and accusatory. My family would be revictimized many times over.

CHAPTER 7

INSTITUTIONS

Within days after I learned of Angie's disclosure, Dr. McGarrah and I talked about the implications of what Angie had told her. One of the first things Dr. McGarrah did was to warn me that the situation could get very messy. The teachers and the school would undoubtedly deny that Angie had been sexually molested. They would try to prove we had made the whole thing up because we had some sort of vendetta against the school, she said. That was typical in child molestation cases.

If evidence of Angie's abuse ended up being undeniably strong, their next line of defense would be that the abuse happened somewhere else, for instance, at home. Nancy's warning would prove to be prophetic. I could understand the teachers' denial. They were, after all, the alleged offenders. It would have been naive to expect them to roll over and confess. I have a much harder time accepting the position the preschool's administration eventually took.

The institution itself was not the subject of the criminal investigation. The director and the board did not face the same consequences as the individuals who were under investigation by the district attorney's office, although I learned later that these officials did face civil suit and damages. I assumed it would be in their best interests to cooperate with the investigation. I naively thought that a school, especially an institution characterized by an active parent body, would place first priority on the children entrusted to its care. I was wrong.

The defensive position taken by the preschool's director during Angie's kindergarten year set the tone for the school's official position later on. Over and over again, during our parent-teacher conferences that year, the director had defended the teachers, and had supported them unequivocally when they insisted Angie was having no problems at school. When we kept coming back to them with examples of her stress and unhappiness, they looked for ways to place the blame on us and on Angie.

At our very first conference, the director suggested that my husband and I examine our own "attitudes." Perhaps it was we who were unhappy with the school, she said. Perhaps we were communicating our feelings to Angie, and she in turn was projecting them into her own attitudes toward her teachers and school. The director pointed out how important it was for Angie to understand that we (parents and teachers) were "on the same side" and that we were working together to deal with her unhappiness. She stressed that it would be detrimental if Angie should think she could get her parents to "take sides" with her against her teachers.

As the months went by, and my husband and I returned again and again to the school to search for clues to our daughter's unhappiness, the answers the director and teachers offered increasingly focused on Angie. They suggested that Angie was unable to cope with the structure and discipline at school because she was undisciplined at home.

We knew this was nonsense because in all four of Angie's previous years at the school she had been everyone's "angel." Every year we were told at our parent-teacher conferences that she was a joy to have in the classroom. She was bright and well-behaved. It was especially ironic that only months before, Angie's teachers from the previous year had given her a glowing year-end report. One of them had chuckled a little when she reported that Angie rarely needed to be disciplined, but when she did get in trouble, she was easy to work with. All the teachers had to do was ask Angie what had happened, and she would hang her head and confess.

Now, less than a year later, Angie was constantly being disciplined and she was portrayed as a lying, spoiled little brat. Angie's credibility was seriously challenged in the weeks before we pulled her out of the school. One afternoon when I arrived to pick her up, one of the teachers pulled me aside and reported that Angie had injured the inner, upper part of her arm during nap-time. She said Angie claimed to have hurt it on her cot, but the teacher was convinced Angie had bitten herself.

I asked the teacher if she had talked with Angie about it. She said, "No, I wanted her to come clean on her own without me forcing her." She said she had seen Angie biting her arm. I asked to look at Angie's canvas cot. There was a long screw sticking out on the underside and I wondered if it might have caused the mark. Later, when I asked Angie about her injury, she told me that her teddy bear had fallen under her cot during nap and when she reached under to pull him out, her arm started to burn "like a rug burn." I asked her if she had bitten herself and she said no, but she had tried to lick the wound to keep it from burning because the teachers had not put medication on it.

The next day the mark was still prominent and looked like a burn or scrape of some sort. I told the teacher what Angie had told me, and she agreed that the mark did not look like a bite and that it could have come from the cot. I was curious about the way she had overreacted the previous day, but I dropped the subject.

Several weeks later, another mark appeared in the same place on Angie's arm. When I asked the teachers if we could do something to fix Angie's cot to keep this from happening again, I was startled by their sudden hostility.

One teacher replied curtly that the mark had nothing to do with the cot. "Angie's doing it herself," she said. "We both saw her do it." I asked the other teacher, "What about the screw we saw on the cot?" She repeated the charge that the mark had nothing to do with the cot and that Angie was biting herself "to get attention." They made it a point to tell me that they had taken Angie to the office and the director, after seeing the injury, agreed with them that Angie obviously had bitten herself.

By the time I got home, I was so angry that I asked my husband to take a picture of Angie's arm. I didn't know what I would do with it, although I thought I might show it to Angie's pediatrician the next time I saw him. All I knew at the time was that I wanted a picture to prove it was not a bite mark. My husband did take several pictures that were eventually shown to the police, the prosecutor, and the Department of Human Resources investigator. No one ever came up with a solid explanation for the injury, but everyone agreed that it looked like some sort of burn or scrape. It definitely was not a bite mark.

I cried the day my husband took the pictures. Why were the teachers trying to make me believe that Angie was deliberately hurting herself? The next day, Angie had an appointment with Dr. McGarrah. The injury was still prominent, so I asked her if there was any way Angie could have bitten herself. Dr. McGarrah confirmed what I had thought—the mark looked like a burn or scrape. It was not a bite and it could not have been self-inflicted.

Dr. McGarrah explained that it is not unusual for children to exhibit certain physical signs of stress, such as nail-biting or thumb-sucking. Only children who are severely emotionally disturbed, however, will inflict pain on themselves to an extent that would leave a mark such as the one on Angie's arm. Angie obviously was not an emotionally disturbed child, and Dr. McGarrah was curious about why the teachers wanted me to think Angie was so disturbed that she would do something like that to herself. She asked permission to call the school and talk with the teachers and the director about it. I agreed and signed the necessary release papers.

It took a number of weeks for Dr. McGarrah to contact the people at the school, and by that time Angie was no longer a student there. Dr. McGarrah's approach was very low-key. She said that she was working with Angie and was interested in their input about Angie's experiences in kindergarten the past year. She first talked with the director. As expected, the director immediately pointed her finger at my husband and me. She said the teachers were unable to see any of the problems we thought Angie had been having at the school. In her opinion, the problem was that Angie was totally undisciplined at home and consequently could not cope with rules and structure at school.

She also mentioned that my husband and I had "withdrawn from the school long ago." I wasn't sure what that meant, but Dr. McGarrah's impression was that the director was saying we didn't like the school and our attitude had contributed to Angie's dislike of the place. When asked about the marks on Angie's arm, the director said they were self-inflicted bite marks. She and the teachers had seen Angie do it, she said.

"Did *you* actually see Angie bite herself?" Dr. McGarrah asked. The director backtracked a little and admitted that she had not. But she insisted the teachers had seen Angie bite herself and she believed them.

Dr. McGarrah talked with the teachers several days later. Those conversations were carbon copies of the one she had with the director. One teacher went a little farther and said they'd had a problem with Angie telling lies. A few sentences later, however, she noted that Angie was no problem at all at school, never got in trouble, and always told the truth. She said that it was "the parents" who were the most trouble. She thought that we "could not accept reality as far as Angie was concerned." It was clear that the defensive stage had already been set long before the charges of sexual molestation became public.

What made this so pitiful was that we started out with a normal, happy, loving child. Then she was sexually molested. And as a result of that abuse, her personality and behavior changed. She developed somatic symptoms. She began to have social problems. She whined and she cried. And then her abusers and the school for which they worked used those behaviors, which were the result of her abuse, to "prove" that Angie was the source of her own problems!

It took a long time for news of the child abuse charges to get back to the school. The district attorney's office conducted the first part of their investigation in complete secrecy. J. Tom Morgan, whose title at that time was Senior Assistant District Attorney, specialized in child abuse cases in our county. After Mr. Morgan reviewed Dr. McGarrah's report, the police report, and Angie's videotape, he told me that he believed Angie's story. He believed that her charges were legitimate. Unless there were other victims, however, he could not prosecute the case because it would be Angie's word against the word of adults. Children have little or no credibility in court unless their testimony can be corroborated by physical evidence (which is absent in most sexual abuse cases), adult witnesses, or the testimony of other victims.

Mr. Morgan began to interview the parents of other girls in the class. To prevent the "contamination of evidence," we were sworn to secrecy. We could not talk about the investigation to anyone.

As a result of the interviews, Mr. Morgan concluded that Angie had not been the only victim and he decided to proceed with the investigation. The next step was to question the two kindergarten teachers and the director of the school. One teacher had just resigned and moved to a new job in another part of the state, which complicated the investigation. Mr. Morgan first interviewed the teacher who was still in Atlanta.

The evening following that interview, I received a frantic telephone call from Jessica's mother, Diane. She was a member of the school board and she had just come from a special meeting, at which the director had informed the board that allegations of abuse at the school were being investigated. A few minutes later I met Diane at a restaurant. She was visibly shaken. She already knew of the investigation because she had been one of the parents interviewed by Mr. Morgan. She had also been ordered not to talk about the investigation with anyone who had not been interviewed by the district attorney's office.

The rest of the board now knew something was going on and they suspected that Diane had information they did not have. She was caught in the middle. She was the mother of a girl who could have been a victim. She was loyal to the school on whose board she served. She was my friend. In addition, she was still struggling with the first phases of denial. If she accepted the fact that Angie had been molested at the school, she also had to accept the fact that it could have happened to Jessica. She was in turmoil. And to add to her dilemma, she was suddenly in conflict with the rest of the board.

Diane questioned her own sense of loyalty. She kept saying that she didn't know if she had done the right thing by calling me, and she wondered if she had done the right thing by not telling the rest of the board everything she knew about the investigation. I told her that it was not a question of loyalty. This was a legal matter, and she had a responsibility, not to me and not to the school, but to the legal system, to cooperate with the district attorney's office. I suggested she call Mr. Morgan and ask him how she should handle conflicting situations like this in the future.

When the teacher had been questioned the day before, she was ordered not to talk with anyone else about the investigation. As soon as the authorities left, however, she called the teacher who had moved out of town. That teacher in turn called the director, and the information generated by those conversations was reported to the board the following night.

Interestingly, the report to the board included details that had not been revealed by the investigators when they questioned the teacher the night before. Someone on the board thought that if the charges involved female students, the parents of the other girls must know what was going on. The other board members had stared at Diane then as if to gauge her reaction. Diane ignored the comment and asked if it didn't seem peculiar, in light of the charges, that two of the original four girls in that classroom had been unexpectedly pulled out of school in midyear.

The director immediately pointed out that there had been other reasons for those children leaving school. She went on to explain that one of the girls had left because of "academic problems." The other had left because the parents "just wanted a new school." They were also having marital problems, the director added. Then the board targeted me as the one who was the most likely to have "filed the charges." Diane said they thought I was crazy, vindictive, and out to get the school. Dr. McGarrah had warned me to be prepared for that kind of attack, but it still hurt a lot when I heard it.

Apparently the members of the board, all of whom were parents themselves, and some of whom were friends of mine, never even considered the possibility that the charges might be true. Their first response was to attack me. What's more, they never expressed any concern for the children. They immediately began to take steps to protect themselves. They talked about hiring an attorney and they instructed the director of the school to "begin documenting everything."

Diane mentioned that a major part of their "defense" would be an incident from two years before when I had confronted the board about an unexpected school closing. Until Angie began having problems in the kindergarten room, I had never challenged or even questioned program- or classroom-related matters. I didn't need to—Angie was happy and there was nothing to complain about. I was fairly active at the school. I participated in parent workdays and fundraisers, and I always went to Angie's Christmas programs and school picnics. I volunteered for extras such as helping with field trips, and I had Angie's classes over to our house each spring to pick flowers in our huge patch of daffodils. I had worked with earlier boards on special projects such as long-term funding strategies.

Even though I questioned administrative policies from time to time, I never spoke up until Angie was four years old—her fourth year at the school. I was still delighted with the school overall. Angie had two wonderful teachers then and it was a good year for her. But when the next school year started, the school calendar included an extra holiday that had not been presented to the parents for approval.

It didn't have to be presented because the board had complete authority at the school, but a sense of partnership had always existed among the board members, teachers, and parents, and changes like that were normally discussed with the parents.

I was concerned about the way this was handled and about the holiday itself. School closings are murder on working parents. It was one more day to juggle around. I wrote a letter to the board expressing my concern and I went to the next board meeting to discuss the matter. A number of other parents who had the same concern also attended. The meeting was approached as a problem-solving session. The parents offered a number of alternative suggestions that would give the teachers time off and still provide adequate day care coverage for working parents. The parents were pleased when the board promised to reconsider.

After the meeting was officially dismissed and the parents left, the board members immediately reconvened and voted to uphold their original decision. That got me upset all over again, and I wrote a follow-up letter expressing my disappointment. This time the board's response was not friendly at all. I was accused of being ungrateful and unappreciative of how hard they worked for the school. I realized that my objections were being taken personally and that there was nothing to be gained by pursuing the matter. I backed off and never again challenged another issue at the school. That had been my one transgression and now it was coming back to haunt me.

When Diane told me that the board would surely use that incident as proof that I was a disgruntled parent with an ax to grind, I was flabbergasted. They were more concerned with protecting themselves and the school than they were with finding out the truth. And I kept asking myself, "What if I had been a troublemaker? What if I had been the most obnoxious parent in the history of the school? Would that justify what was done to my child? Don't they care about her at all?"

That meeting in October, two months after Angie's disclosure, laid the foundation for what was to become the school's official position of denial and cover-up. The director would defend the teachers and the board would back the director.

Mr. Morgan had intended to question the second teacher as soon as possible after her former coworker was interviewed. His efforts were complicated by the fact that she no longer lived in Atlanta and had been alerted by the first teacher. She managed to avoid him for over a month, but finally he arranged a meeting with her. The day before the scheduled interview, the teacher called Mr. Morgan and canceled their meeting because she wanted to talk with an attorney first.

Diane told me, and this was later confirmed by another board member, that the teacher had called someone on the school's board after her meeting with Mr. Morgan had been arranged. That board member advised her to cancel the appointment and to consult an attorney before talking with the authorities. She was also told that the board would hire an attorney to represent both the school and the teachers. So the teacher canceled her appointment with Mr. Morgan, and to this day she has never been questioned by the police or the prosecutor. The board later changed its mind about hiring an attorney to represent the teachers, but the damage had already been done.

Two months later, in December, Mr. Morgan visited the preschool and interviewed the director. He told her that a former student had disclosed sexual abuse while in therapy. This report had led to his investigation, during the course of which he learned that there was more than one victim. He explained how the investigation had been conducted and how parents and children had not been allowed to talk with each other so that there had been no contamination of evidence. He said that the victims closely fit the psychological profile of sexually abused children. There was no physical evidence to corroborate the charges, but in his opinion, the psychological evidence was "overwhelming."

In spite of this information from the prosecuting attorney, the board took the position that the abuse charges were "unfounded allegations" trumped up by an irate parent. Even if indictments should be forthcoming, they were convinced they would not reflect on the school in any way, because by this time both teachers had voluntarily resigned. The board decided to bury the entire affair. They vowed that no one, including the school's parents or the staff, would find out about the charges. They literally made a pact of silence among themselves, promising not to discuss the investigation with anyone.

At one point, someone on the board asked how they should handle the investigation that they knew would be conducted by the Department of Human Resources Child Care Licensing Division. The director assured the board that it would be "nothing to worry about" and that the only result would be "a bunch of extra paper-work." The entire situation was viewed as nothing more than a nasty inconvenience for the school.

Once the board knew the details of the investigation, they directed much of their anger at Diane, because they felt she should have told them about the investigation as soon as she was contacted by the district attorney's office. Only one other board member supported Diane's actions and agreed that she had done the right thing by honoring Mr. Morgan's request not to discuss the investigation. After all, she had been interviewed as a parent, not as a board member. Nevertheless, the rest of the board and the director accused her of "betraying their trust." When Diane told me that, I wondered bitterly if the board ever worried about how their school had betrayed the children's trust.

Five months after it began, the criminal investigation had gone as far as it could under the circumstances, and Mr. Morgan decided not to present Angie's case to the grand jury. He believed he could prove that the girls had been sexually molested and that the abuse had taken place in the kindergarten room at that preschool, but he would also have to prove "beyond a reasonable doubt" that he was prosecuting the right perpetrator(s), and the fact that the children had implicated two teachers complicated his case. The defense attorneys could have generated so much confusion over which teacher did what to which child that convictions were unlikely.

The decision not to prosecute was all the director and board needed to bolster their claim that the charges had been frivolous from the beginning. They insisted that Mr. Morgan's decision not to seek an indictment was the same as saying the crime had not occurred, although they were told the opposite was true.

Even though the case would not be prosecuted, Diane pressured the board to inform the school's parents of the investigation. For the sake of their children, parents had a right to know and a right to ask their own questions, especially since other children had been in classrooms with the alleged offenders before the teachers left the school. The board refused.

Diane's relationship with the board eventually became so strained that she resigned from the board and took her child out of the pre-school. Another couple who were peripherally involved in the investigation removed their child from the school shortly thereafter because they were unhappy with the board's cover-up of the investigation. The school typically had a huge waiting list, and once parents got their children enrolled in the school, they rarely pulled them out. The sudden departure of two longtime, active families started other parents asking questions, and before long, news of the sexual abuse charges leaked out.

Parents and teachers began to ask the director and the board about the investigation, and were told that the charges were nothing more than "unsubstantiated rumor." Finally, several parents called the district attorney's office for information and learned that the investigation and charges were more than just a nasty rumor. Those parents organized a group that asked the board to inform the school's parents and the staff about the sexual abuse charges and investigation. They wanted a meeting held at the school so that representatives from the district attorney's office could answer parents' questions.

The board refused the parents' request, so the parents arranged their own meeting and asked Mr. Morgan to attend. When the parents tried to distribute information at school about the meeting, the director and certain board members confiscated the notices and canceled the meeting. The school's attorney contacted Mr. Morgan to inform him that the meeting could not be held because it had not been "properly authorized by the board."

After much confusion and maneuvering by both sides, the meeting was finally held at the school and attended by a majority of the preschool's parents and staff members. Four representatives of the district attorney's office, including Robert Wilson, then DeKalb County's District Attorney, attended at the request of the parents. Mr. Morgan told the parents how the abuse had been reported and he described how the investigation had been conducted. He explained why, in spite of the evidence, he was not going to prosecute the case.

He and District Attorney Wilson explained that their decision not to seek indictments did not mean that the children had not been molested. In fact, they made it clear that there was no doubt in the minds of anyone who had been involved in the investigation that the girls had been sexually molested and that it had happened at that school.

Many parents became angry with the school's administration when they learned how the board had tried to keep them from finding out about the abuse charges. The school's officials in turn defended their actions by blaming the district attorney's office for failing to keep them "properly briefed" during the investigation. The district attorney responded that of all the cases his office had investigated that involved "ancillary institutions," this was the first case in which the institution had not cooperated.

Some parents knew about the many efforts we had made during Angie's kindergarten year to find out what was making her so unhappy at school. They criticized the director for not having been responsive to our concerns, especially since it was now known that we had not been the only parents to seek help from the director. Like us, other parents had tried to ferret out the cause of their daughters' sudden unwillingness to go to school. Like us, they had been told to seek family counseling, because, according to the director, the source of their daughters' problems had to be at home.

By the time the meeting was over, the school was badly divided. Many of the parents believed that the abuse had taken place and that the board and director had acted irresponsibly. Many parents supported the administration and believed that if there was no indictment, there had been no abuse. Still other parents felt that even if the abuse had occurred it didn't matter, since the teachers were no longer at the school. One parent, who didn't realize I was the mother of one of the victims, told me that he thought it was "a lot of commotion over nothing."

I have spent an inordinate amount of time talking about the preschool where my daughter was abused. My purpose has not been to vent my own frustrations or to condemn the school. The point I am trying to make is that while our school's response was extreme, it was not unusual. Parents of molestation victims need to be prepared for the indifference and hostility of friends and acquaintances who just don't want to believe that child sexual abuse can occur right under their own noses. People often feel threatened when it happens too close to home, so they will find ways to deny the reality that child molestation can, and does, happen anywhere.

I recently saw a news report about a minister who was indicted on multiple charges of child molestation. Similar charges had been investigated, but not prosecuted, at his previous parishes. Yet, when reporters interviewed members of the minister's parish, the parishioners were angry, and defended their minister, calling the charges "absurd." The obvious extension of this statement was that the victims must be lying. I couldn't help but ache for the victims and their families. After all, they were also members of that parish and they were being rejected by people who should have offered them support. It is all part of the process of revictimization, a process that adds agony to the family's anguish over and over again.

CHAPTER 8

TEACHERS AND OTHER CHILD CARE PROFESSIONALS

The negative responses of people associated with the school where Angie had been molested were hard to accept, but not impossible to understand, considering the strong sense of loyalty to the school that its parents tended to develop. The stronger their emotional investment in the school, the more extreme their reactions seemed to be. I imagine this is true in most situations where a child's offender is associated with an institution such as a school, church, camp, sports team, or social organization.

But what about other people who are not directly involved with the organization? Are they more supportive of the victim and his or her family?

The first question is, who knows the abuse has occurred? We had no control over people at Angie's former school finding out what had happened. Legally, the identities of the victims were protected. The school was so small, however, that it wasn't hard for people to figure out who the victims were. As we moved away from that school and into other situations, I had to decide who to tell and who not to tell about Angie's abuse.

I tried to look at each situation carefully and tell only those persons who had legitimate reasons to know that Angie had been sexually abused. My primary consideration in each instance was whether it would help Angie in some way if that person knew. A secondary reason to disclose Angie's abuse was if telling someone might help educate that person so other children could benefit. I also tried to anticipate the reactions of the people I considered telling. Would they be understanding or insensitive? Even in a situation where Angie might benefit, it would do more harm than good if the person reacted negatively.

The first big decision was how to deal with people at Angie's new school when she entered first grade. I believed there was a legitimate need to tell Angie's first grade teacher, and Dr. McGarrah agreed. Children who have been molested can be traumatized by any behavior that reminds them of their ordeal. Many of them don't want to be touched, for example. An uninformed teacher may pull a child close, hug the child, or put the child on his or her lap. The teacher may inadvertently upset the child and have no idea why the child reacts negatively. Also, most schools now include a module on child abuse to teach children how to protect themselves. Teachers should understand how these lessons might affect a child who already has been victimized.

So when Angie started first grade, I knew I should let her teacher know what my daughter was going through. The problem was that Mr. Morgan had said we could not talk with anyone, and that included her new teacher. (If news of the investigation leaked out at that point, it could have jeopardized the entire case.) Finally, though, after Angie had been in school over five weeks, Mr. Morgan gave me permission to talk with her teacher.

By this time I was already worried about what kind of impression Mrs. Davis, Angie's teacher, had formed of her. If you knew what Angie was going through, the clues she was dropping at school were obvious. For example, one of her early reading words happened to be the name of one of her offenders. As luck would have it, Mrs. Davis called on Angie to make up a sentence with that word. Angie's sentence, delivered with vehemence, was "I hate [teacher's name]." Mrs. Davis thought that was peculiar and asked Angie why she made up that sentence. Angie explained that the word had been her kindergarten teacher's name, and she had been a "mean" teacher and had "broken the rules."

During this period, Angie was terrified that her old teachers would show up at her new school. To alleviate some of her fears, Dr. McGarrah gave Angie a little container of "worry dolls." She was to tell one worry to each doll every night before she went to bed. Then she could put the dolls in their container and close the cap. The dolls could take care of her worries for her and she wouldn't have to stay awake worrying about them herself.

Angie was so pleased with her worry dolls that she decided to take them to school with her the next day for "share time." "Oh great," I thought to myself, "all the other children will bring fashion dolls and racing cars and my child will come in with her worry dolls." I wondered what Mrs. Davis would think. Angie promised she would say only that a friend had given her the dolls. She came home the next day and announced that her worry dolls had been a big hit with the other children. I could just imagine the rest of the first grade class running home and asking their parents for worry dolls of their own!

Six weeks after Angie entered first grade, my husband and I finally had a conference with Mrs. Davis. I had wanted to talk with her about Angie for all those weeks, but when the time finally came, I found that it was very hard to do. I could hardly choke back the tears while I explained to Mrs. Davis that Angie had been sexually molested at her previous school.

I was surprised by Mrs. Davis' reaction. She said that she had just about figured out what had happened from the few comments Angie had made and from some peculiarities in her behavior. For one thing, Angie was unusually aloof and serious for a child her age. Even more noticeable was Angie's reluctance to get physically close to Mrs. Davis. If she had to approach Mrs. Davis to turn in work, for example, she stood as far back as possible, getting no closer than arm's length. Mrs. Davis also said she noticed how exhausted Angie looked at times, and I told her about the nightmares and the sleep problems.

Angie was fortunate to have Mrs. Davis for a teacher during that first year following her abuse. Mrs. Davis was informed about child abuse, and she was unusually sensitive to Angie's special needs at the time. She asked what she could do to help. I couldn't think of anything she could actually do, other than being aware of what was going on with Angie and letting me know if she noticed behaviors that I should know about.

I didn't want Mrs. Davis to single Angie out for special treatment. She had to be sensitive to Angie's special needs, but Angie still had to be subject to the same academic and behavioral expectations as the other children in her class. As a matter of fact, Angie's need for consistency and structure in her life at that time may well have been greater than average.

Under the circumstances, I was relieved to see how quickly and easily Angie adapted to her new school. Her enthusiasm for going to school was in dramatic contrast to her reluctance the year before. Angie's new school was a private school with a well-defined code of conduct and a system of penalties that left little room for interpretation. It was interesting to see how easily Angie accepted all the rules and regulations—especially when the teachers and director of her previous school had so painstakingly painted her as an undisciplined child who couldn't cope with rules!

Telling Mrs. Davis about Angie's abuse was helpful because she was able to understand where some of Angie's unusual behavior was coming from. For example, one day when a brawl between the girls and the boys broke out on the playground, it was broken up by the whistle that signaled the end of recess. As the children began to line up to go back to class, one little boy decided to get the last word in by slapping Angie on the rear. Angie freaked out. That touch reminded her of what her offenders had done to her. She cried hysterically and had to be escorted inside by a teacher. It was an extreme reaction that surely would have left the teacher baffled if she had not understood how it was triggered by Angie's past.

That incident made me wonder how many young victims of sexual abuse become labeled as problems by teachers who don't understand the emotional and behavioral turmoil these children experience. It is an unfortunate fact that children's reputations in school become established very early in their academic careers. A child entering first grade with the problems Angie was experiencing at the time could easily be stuck with a self-perpetuating label and never be able to shake it.

A teacher dealing with an abused child faces much the same dilemma as the child's parents. On the one hand, the teacher has to be careful not to overreact and ignore or excuse unacceptable behavior because of what the child has been through. On the other hand, a sensitive, understanding teacher can be an invaluable ally in the child's struggle to regain some sort of equilibrium. Angie was blessed to have had the best possible teacher during that first critical year of her recovery.

Angie's first grade year wasn't all smooth sailing, however. In fact, her brush with an insensitive substitute teacher at the end of the school year set back the progress she had made by several months, and created a minor crisis for all of us.

Angie's regular teacher went on maternity leave shortly before the end of the school year. My husband and I debated whether or not to tell the substitute about Angie's abuse, and we decided it would not be necessary. First, Angie had made tremendous progress in the four to six weeks before that, and she was beginning to feel pretty good about herself. Second, Angie and I both knew the substitute teacher. She was a lovely person we both liked.

The problem was that she was substituting for a very popular teacher at the end of the school year. I think that she felt she had to take firm control of the class so the children wouldn't think school had ended three weeks early. Unfortunately, her idea of firm control was too harsh for a student who was trying to patch together a shattered childhood.

From the first day, the substitute relied on negative reinforcement, and frequently threatened the children with demerits and detention. Angie's fragile self-esteem began to crumble immediately. The teacher also had a bad habit of physically grabbing the children by the arms or shoulders. Instead of simply asking or telling them to "come with me," or "go over there," she would grab them by the arm and pull or push them in the direction she wanted them to go. After a few days, Angie began to panic. She felt threatened, and tried to become "invisible" in class, but the harder she tried, the more negative attention she got.

Several months earlier, Angie had a bad accident at her afterschool camp when another child threw a brick that accidentally hit her in the face. The injury left her with four gashes on her face that required 12 stitches to close. Her plastic surgeon told me to keep her out of the sun as much as possible to reduce the amount of scarring, and to have her wear a sun visor whenever she went outdoors.

Shortly before the school year ended, Angie went to recess without her sun visor. She asked for permission to go back for it, but the substitute teacher refused. Angie protested, and the teacher refused again. Angie got upset and told another child that she thought the substitute was "ugly" and she wished Mrs. Davis was back. The teacher overheard Angie and made her spend recess on the time-out line, in the direct sun.

The next day I sent a note to school explaining how important it was for Angie to wear the sun visor at all times. Keeping the sun off her facial scars would reduce the probability of reconstructive surgery later on, I explained. When Angie gave the teacher the note, the substitute pulled her aside and scolded her for "running home and telling your mother every little thing."

That was strike three. The verbal threats of demerits, the harsh touching, and now being told to keep secrets from her mother—it all began to feel too familiar to Angie. She cried all night long, and said she was afraid of the substitute. She said that she knew the teacher wasn't like her two kindergarten teachers, but "if she's doing these things to me, how do I know she isn't going to abuse me like they did?" Angie was terrified that she might be molested again.

It took a lot of special support, reassurance, and love to get Angie through those last few days of school. It was an unfortunate end to a school year that had been good for almost nine months. And it took much of the summer to repair the damage that was done in that short time.

I don't know if we could have avoided that situation if I had talked with the substitute teacher at the beginning. I do know that good, well-intentioned people can do a lot of harm if they are not sensitive to the behavioral consequences of child sexual abuse.

Angie's second grade teacher was a dedicated, wonderful woman. Unfortunately, her voiced support for Angie did not always work for Angie's benefit. Teachers, like parents, must be careful not to overreact by inadvertently putting an abused child under a microscope and searching for signs of unacceptable behavior. More than once I wondered whether Angie's second grade teacher watched her a little too closely for problems.

She reported one incident when she thought Angie had exhibited "inappropriate sexual behavior." It happened the day that a little boy in Angie's class got down on his hands and knees and crawled under the desks. He said he was looking for something he dropped, but Angie got upset because she thought he was trying to look up her skirt. The teacher defended the boy, saying that he was "a nice boy and certainly wouldn't do such a thing." And she disciplined Angie for making up a story "just to get the boy in trouble."

Interestingly, that was the same boy who had displayed aggressive sexual behavior toward Angie a few months before in summer camp. Within that context, I thought Angie's reaction was understandable. And I couldn't help but wonder how the teacher would have reacted if any other little girl in the class had been involved in this incident instead of Angie. Would the boy automatically have been absolved and the girl accused of inappropriate sexual behavior?

Another school issue I had to consider was the fact that each grade in Angie's school had a unit on personal safety sometime during the year. The first graders were shown a film about how to protect themselves from sexual abuse. Angie's first grade year was so fraught with fears and nightmares that the last thing she needed was another reminder of the horror she was trying so hard to forget. Mrs. Davis agreed that Angie should not be there when the film was shown, and we decided that the film would be shown on an afternoon when I picked Angie up early for a doctor's appointment.

Since I work full time, Angie spends several hours each day at an after-school camp, and I had to decide whether those people also should know that she had been sexually molested. It was, after all, an extension of the school day, and some of the same considerations were involved.

Angie started the school year in a large after-school program that had many children in a relatively small amount of space. The counselors were primarily baby-sitters, who watched the children, but rarely interacted with them one-on-one. Even in the few weeks we tried that program, we could tell that staff turnover was a problem. The constant sense of chaos there intimidated Angie, so we moved her to another program after three weeks.

Even if we had not moved Angie from that program, I would not have talked with the program director or counselors, because I don't think it would have done any good. It seemed as though they never really got to know the children individually, and I couldn't see that it would have helped Angie in any way to tell them. With the turnover in staff, the information soon would have been lost, anyway.

Angie's new after-school program was a world apart from the first. She loved it from the first day—so much so that she wanted to stop by there and visit on holidays and vacation days when I picked her up directly from school. The after-school camp was run by a local church. It had a small number of children and lots of space for them to run and play. The people who ran the program were warm and caring, and quickly became our friends. And the counselors, many of whom were young people from the church, played with the children as friends rather than as baby-sitters.

I decided to talk with the camp director and her boss, the activities minister, for several reasons. First of all, Angie would be spending a lot of time there. In addition to the daily after-school camp, she went there for part of the Christmas camp and during the summer. Second, I believed I could trust them. The camp was a ministry for them, not just a business, and they had an honest concern about each child under their care. Third, I did not have to worry about turnover, because the staff was quite stable.

Like the conference with Angie's first grade teacher, this one was packed with emotion. We talked about child sexual abuse in general and about Angie in particular. The activities minister said that child abuse was one of his greatest concerns in running the program. He said that he knew it could happen anywhere, so his staff members take as many precautions as they can in screening job applicants. They go far beyond the minimum regulatory requirements. The counselors attend conferences and training sessions on abuse. The camp director and the activities minister both knew a lot about child sexual abuse and they were very sympathetic and supportive.

The third situation I struggled with was Angie's dance school. That was a hard one to call, because it was a more peripheral part of her life. She would, however, be spending more and more time there. In addition to her weekly classes, she sometimes attended ballet camp in summer and performed in special productions. I waited a long time, but I finally decided it would be wise to talk with the school's director.

Angie's dancing has always been very important to her. She is a good dancer and she is proud of her talent. When her self-esteem crumbled, her dancing was the one area where she was able to hang onto a shred of self-confidence. Also, I hoped that pride in her dancing body would help restore her damaged body concept. It was a small foundation she could build on, and I didn't want a misplaced touch by a teacher to scare her away from something she enjoyed so much.

Moreover, the probability of her being touched was great in a discipline where body awareness is an integral part of training. Dance instructors have to touch their students to help them achieve proper alignment. They press on the spine to encourage a flat back and they rotate the thighs for a proper turnout. An unwanted touch was a genuine possibility.

Angie had taken classes at the same school for over three years, so I felt comfortable talking with the director about Angie's experience. The staff was small, Angie had the same teachers in more than one class, and all the staff members took a personal interest in their students. The director was glad I told her for the same reasons I had thought it necessary. She had encountered molested children before, and she understood the problem.

So, I ended up confiding in the people Angie spent the most time with—people at her school, her after-school camp, and her dance school. Every one of those people knew something about child molestation and acted in Angie's best interests. They understood at least a little of the trauma she had experienced, and they sincerely wanted to help her with her recovery. We were incredibly fortunate—at least during that first critical year following Angie's disclosure.

Not everyone is so lucky. The mother of another victim told me about her experience when she talked with the principal of her daughter's school. The first words out of his mouth were accusatory—"How in the world could you have allowed such a thing to happen!" Misinformation and a lack of understanding of child sexual abuse can have a devastating effect on victims and their families.

There were other people I chose not to tell. Angie sometimes took swimming classes during the summer. The only reason to consider talking about it there was because of possible physical contact on the part of the instructors, but classes were short group lessons and the instructors didn't spend much time with each student. Also, the instructors often changed from class to class. I didn't say anything to anyone there.

Neither did I tell any of Angie's baby-sitters, most of whom were high school girls. To avoid problems at bath time, however, I always made sure that Angie was bathed and dressed for bed before the sitter arrived. In fact, that was Angie's idea, and it worked well.

Another point to consider, when it comes to telling people about a child's having been abused, is whether or not to tell the child which people know about his or her experience. I did tell Angie that her teacher and the afterschool camp director knew. I wanted her to know she could go to someone there for help if she felt that need. It also helped her to know that someone else understood and cared about her.

There is a fine line between protecting children's right to privacy and making sure they have the support of the important people in their lives. Parents have to consider carefully the potential benefits and dangers of each situation.

CHAPTER 9

FRIENDS AND FAMILY

Friends and family—two of the most important groups in the world when tragedy strikes—are the people we turn to for support. But just how strong is this support system when a family is confronted with the tragedy of a molested child?

Obviously, the answer will vary from family to family, but the support most families receive in an abuse situation is much more tenuous than what they would expect in any other family crisis.

Why? Because most people just don't understand child sexual abuse, and they react out of their ignorance and lack of understanding. Because stereotypes and misconceptions abound when it comes to child molestation, even people who mean well can hurt more than they help.

Friends

My most likely source of support and understanding should have been my friendships with other parents. Those were relationships that had grown along with our children. Those were the friends most likely to help each other out in time of need, especially if it involved our children. Unfortunately, most of those friends were associated in one way or another with the school where Angie was molested.

These people reacted in different ways, but they all had strong feelings of their own to resolve. No matter which way their sympathies eventually fell, they all saw me as the mother of the victim "who started it all," because Angie was the one whose disclosure brought the abuse out into the open. Every friendship was affected in some way. Some survived; some did not.

Diane, Jessica's mother, was my closest friend. Our relationship had been sorely strained during the girls' kindergarten year, and by the time Angie and Jessica left the preschool there was a lot of tension between us. Diane knew about the problems Angie had in kindergarten. She knew of my frantic efforts to understand what had happened to change Angie so dramatically. She knew Angie began therapy with Dr. McGarrah shortly before the girls' kindergarten year ended. But sometimes she seemed to believe what the teachers wanted us all to believe—that Angie was just a "troubled child." And I resented it.

My relationship with Diane, like that of our daughters, began to improve as soon as the girls left the preschool. Diane could see the immediate change in Angie, and she began to acknowledge that something must have happened to her. We became more comfortable with each other, but just when I needed to communicate with her the most, I couldn't talk with anyone. The weeks following Angie's disclosure were hell. Diane could tell something awful was going on in my life, and she volunteered to listen if I needed to talk, but I knew I couldn't tell anyone about the investigation. I kept brushing her off by saying that I didn't know exactly what was bothering me.

Finally, six weeks after Angie's disclosure, Mr. Morgan said it was okay for me to talk with the parents who had been interviewed, as long as we did not discuss specifics about what the children had disclosed. I waited several days before calling Diane, because I didn't know how to broach the subject. Our conversation was strained and awkward at first. Then Diane's anger broke through.

She was angry at Mr. Morgan because "everything was going along just fine around here and then this damn lawyer comes into my house and turns my life upside down." I guess it was the proverbial desire to kill the messenger who bears bad news. Diane was also angry with me, and it rang in her voice when she asked me to confirm her suspicion that "this did all start with you, then."

Eventually she calmed down a little and her anger gave way to sympathy for me and for Angie. She wanted to know exactly what had happened, and asked me for details I could not give her. Mostly I told her generalities about how the investigation had started and how it had progressed so far. I told her that Dr. McGarrah had reported it to the authorities as required under Georgia law. I wanted her to know I had not "started" anything; we were simply responding to the system as she had done when she was contacted by the district attorney's office. I felt very defensive.

After our first conversation on the subject I felt relieved, because Diane accepted the fact that Angie had been molested at school. Her emotional investment in the school was so great that I had expected her to deny the possibility. Instead, her first response was one of horror, and she immediately thought about pulling Jessica's little brother out of the preschool.

Less than a week later, however, Diane's attitude changed dramatically. By then she had distanced herself completely from the entire issue. She would not even entertain the possibility that Jessica might also have been a victim, and she began to question whether anything really did happen to the others. Even if it had, she was convinced the school should not be held accountable in any way. She no longer considered moving her son to another school. It was business as usual for my friend, the member of the board of the school where my daughter had been sexually abused.

Once again our relationship was strained, although our children still played together and the four of us occasionally went on outings. But our friendship was a roller coaster. One minute Diane was sympathetic and the next minute she was staunchly defending the school. The night she called me after the board meeting represented a major turning point. As we sat in that restaurant talking about how events were unfolding, Diane still searched for reasons to convince herself that the charges might not be true.

Mr. Morgan had told me of his brief conversation with one of the alleged offenders the evening before. When Diane told me the details that had been discussed at that evening's board meeting, it was clear that there were major discrepancies. Someone involved in the chain of information that had led from the first teacher, to the other teacher, to the director, and then to the board, had revealed details that had not been disclosed by the investigators. The only people who could have known some of those details at that point were the victims, their parents, and the offenders. The discrepancies were incriminating, and I asked Diane where she thought some of that information could have come from.

The impact of what I said hit Diane slowly, but when it finally sank in, she looked as though I had doused her with a bucket of ice water. I remember looking her straight in the eye then, and struggling to keep my voice as steady as possible. I told her that there would be no easy answers for us. It was a very complicated situation. But the one thing I wanted with all my heart for her to believe, was that *it did happen*. Children had been molested at that school. There was no way to deny it—the evidence was too strong.

Diane began to cry, and said that if she let herself believe that, she didn't know how to deal with the fact that Jessica had not been a victim. And if Jessica wasn't a victim, how could it have been that "my child was so blessed that she escaped?" Diane seemed to be experiencing some sort of survivor syndrome, similar to that observed in survivors of plane crashes or other catastrophes in which some people survive and some do not.

That talk got us over a major hurdle in our relationship. Diane never again questioned whether Angie had been molested during her kindergarten year. She did continue to struggle with her loyalty to the school, however. Even after she resigned from the board and took her son out of the school, her goal was to "save" the school. She was shaken by the fact that such a horrendous crime could have been committed at the school where we had all been so comfortable for so long. What had gone wrong, and what could be done to make sure it didn't happen again?

Diane was the only member of the board who ever expressed any concern for the victims and the other children in the school. Eventually, both of Angie's offenders left the school, but before that happened, they had been assigned to other classrooms and had been in contact with other children. Only a handful of parents were interviewed during the investigation. There were many other parents who had a right to know. There were other children who might have been involved. With the exception of Diane and one other person, the board members cared only about their own liability and the reputation of the school.

Before Diane resigned from the board, she told me of one meeting at which the district attorney's ongoing investigation was the main topic of discussion. I asked Diane if anyone at any time during the entire discussion had even once expressed any concern for the children. I told her I could understand that they might question the validity of the charges—denial is common in these cases. I could also understand their being concerned about the school—that would be a natural response. But surely, at some point they would have to contemplate the possibility that it might be true. And if it was possible, what did that mean for the children? I asked, "Does anyone care about the children?"

Diane stammered a little, and then, hesitatingly, she answered, "No, I have to admit that no one has ever expressed any concern for the children." As Diane became more and more alienated from the rest of the board, our relationship grew stronger. She agonized over the course her fellow board members chose to take, and she was badly hurt by the hostility they directed toward her when she challenged them on it. She and I often disagreed during those chaotic months, but we comforted each other as much as we could when we weren't too busy licking our own wounds.

Occasionally I felt resentful, because it seemed I was trying to help her more than she was supporting me. After all, I was the mother of a confirmed victim and she was not. But I also pitied her, because she would have to learn to live with a question mark in the back of her mind. Jessica had been interviewed once by a psychologist during the criminal investigation and she had not said or done anything to indicate that she had been molested. Diane could relax. But Jessica was one of only two girls who had "probably" escaped victimization, and there are never any guarantees—not all children exhibit the obvious symptoms of abuse. Diane would have to live with the possibility for the rest of her life.

The circles of victimization ripple far beyond the victim and his or her immediate family. Diane and her family were one example of how others were pulled into the whirlpool. Through it all, however, my friendship with Diane not only survived but grew stronger.

I was not so fortunate when it came to my relationship with another friend, Carla. Like Jessica, Carla's son Sam had been Angie's friend since they were toddlers. As Angie says, "It's almost like Sam is my brother. After all, we've known each other since we were in diapers." We also knew Carla and her family through church, and Sam attended first grade at Angie's new school.

Like Diane, Carla served on the board of the preschool where Angie's sexual abuse occurred. Like Diane, Carla had known of our struggle to find out what was happening during Angie's kindergarten year. She knew of the teachers' conferences and of how frustrated I had been over our inability to get to the bottom of it all.

Carla found out about the molestation charges at the same time as the rest of the school's board. Carla never mentioned the investigation to me, and her silence became deafening when we met at school or church. We often had coffee and donuts with Carla's family after church on Sundays, so five months after the criminal investigation had begun, I decided it was time to break the ice. Our husbands were engaged in a conversation at the other end of the table and our children were off somewhere playing, so I was able to talk with Carla in semiprivacy.

I began by saying that I really didn't want to talk about the situation at the preschool, but I knew she knew what was going on and I would be more comfortable getting it out in the open than walking around playing "does she know that I know that she knows." Carla immediately lowered her voice, explaining that her husband knew nothing about the investigation.

I was shocked! She obviously had taken the board's pact of silence very seriously. I couldn't believe she had not told her husband about the investigation, especially since they had another child who was still attending the preschool. In a hushed voice, Carla began to ask me questions to which I knew she already had the answers. I immediately put up my guard and told her only what I knew Mr. Morgan had relayed to the preschool's director.

Carla's reaction took me totally by surprise. She kept asking me, "You don't really believe it happened, do you?" Or, "Really now, don't you find it impossible to believe that anything like that could happen at our school?" I felt like I might pass out. I remember thinking, "My God, she knows I'm the mother of a child who has been sexually molested. I've been through hell these past five months. And she can't believe that I believe it happened!"

I gathered a few wits about me and told Carla that I had learned a lot about sexual abuse during those past few months, and that she had to understand that molestation can happen anywhere—and it did happen at our school. She didn't seem to hear me.

"Angie certainly looks OK," said Carla blandly. I wondered if she expected Angie to run around with a big scarlet "A" on her chest, for "Abused." I told Carla that she should be around sometimes to witness Angie's fears and nightmares. Then she said something really bizarre. She told me that I would just have to remember that Angie was still "a child" and that I shouldn't think of her as being "different." I think that was a warning that I should be careful not to think of Angie as some sort of "damaged goods." That was the closest Carla would ever come to expressing any semblance of concern for Angie or for me.

Carla went on to defend the school, its director, and its board. She said she felt sorry for one of Angie's offenders, who was "so upset over this" that she had called Carla on the telephone and cried. That was as much as I could take, and I ended the conversation abruptly.

I was devastated. I had wanted to clear the air with Carla and defuse some of the tension I felt between us. Instead, I walked away wishing I never had to see the woman again. But as much as that conversation hurt me, Carla acted as though it had never taken place. For the next two months, she would smile and chat when we met like nothing had ever happened. All I could do was parrot back reflex responses.

The next, and last, time Carla and I discussed the abuse allegations came the day after the people from the district attorney's office spoke to the parents of the school about the investigation. Carla caught me completely by surprise. She called me at work and cried and talked at me for more than an hour. She was distraught over the previous week's events at the school. She was hurt, she said, because people who she thought were her friends didn't trust her anymore. She was stinging from the anger the school's parents had directed toward the board the day before. She talked on and on about how she had only been trying to do what was best for the school. And she was crying because she didn't want all of this to affect our friendship, because it was too important to her and her family. She had me there, because I didn't want to see the relationship damaged either, for the sake of our husbands and children. Between her sobs, Carla vehemently defended the school's director and board. She defended their actions by attacking the district attorney's office. She thought Mr. Morgan's investigation had been "shoddy." I told her I disagreed, and that I had nothing but the greatest respect for Mr. Morgan and the way he had handled Angie's case.

Carla also attacked Diane. It was clear that she and the rest of the board really hated Diane for her defection. They still blamed her for "betraying their trust" and not telling them about the investigation after she had been interviewed by Mr. Morgan.

There were a lot of inconsistencies in what Carla said. In fact, she said things that I knew were not true. The conversation left me in tears. I wanted to believe Carla had called on her own because she was concerned about our friendship, but I had a hard time convincing myself that was true. Sprinkled in among her tears and the "I just don't know what I'm going to do" were too many leading questions. Afterwards, I sat down and listed the points she made or asked about, and I wondered if she had been working off some sort of checklist of information she was trying to get from me, or things she was trying to get me to say. I wondered if the board had consulted an attorney and they were trying to put together some kind of defense.

I was suspicious for a number of reasons. First of all, I found out toward the end of the conversation that Carla had gone home from work just to call me. That meant the conversation was planned, and not the spontaneous call she had led me to believe it was in the beginning. Second, when she asked me questions that I ignored or dodged, she kept going back to those points as though she couldn't let go until she had the information she wanted. Finally, she really worked at putting words in my mouth. It seemed important to her that I admit certain things.

She quizzed me on the investigation itself. She wanted the who, what, when, and where details. She also tried to get me to name the victims. She said the board knew who the children were and she tried to nudge me into acknowledging that they had guessed right. The only confidential information remaining at that time was the identities of the victims, and I flatly refused to discuss any of the children with her. I suggested that the board members contact the district attorney's office if they wanted more information about the investigation.

Carla seemed to be looking for ammunition to support the board's "crazy, disgruntled mother and chronically unhappy child" theory. She asked me if I had been in therapy myself the past year or so. She asked about how happy I was at work and how I was handling the pressures there. She quizzed me on Angie's experiences at her new school and asked whether she was having any problems. Carla knew that I had switched after-school programs earlier in the year and she wanted to know why Angie had been unhappy with the first program and whether she liked her current one.

Carla also seemed to be feeling me out on how I might be disposed toward a civil suit. She tried to get at my feelings about the preschool, the director, and the board, and she wondered how I would feel about publicity, if details of the case should be picked up by the media.

What hurt me most about this discussion was Carla's insistence that she knew other reasons to account for each victim's unhappiness at the school. I asked her to explain that comment, and she began to point out that one of the girls' parents had been having marital problems. I cut her off and told her I did not want to discuss any other child. I warned her again that I would not say anything to identify the other victims, but I wanted to know what there was about Angie that she thought could have produced such extreme symptoms of stress.

Carla floored me with an absolute, out-and-out lie—one she then tried to nudge me into acknowledging as truth. She said she knew that Angie had been unhappy at school "for a long time." It just seemed that Angie had never been happy with any of her teachers, Carla said. Actually, Angie had adored all her teachers until she entered the kindergarten room, and I told Carla that. She insisted it wasn't true.

Angie had one teacher who was fired after only a few weeks at the preschool, when parents complained about an unauthorized field trip she impulsively took the children on. Without telling anyone she was leaving or where she was going, she single-handedly took Angie's class for a hike in the woods, where several children were stung by bees. Carla was now insisting that Angie had hated that teacher, and that I had been responsible for getting the teacher fired. Neither charge was true, but Carla was adamant. She had obviously bought the director's story that Angie and I were just chronically unhappy people who were out to make trouble for the school.

To this day I don't know if Carla believes that Angie was sexually molested. Since that telephone conversation the subject has never come up between us. In fact, I talked with her the very next day, and I was startled by the dramatic change in her voice and demeanor. The day before she had sounded exhausted. She had cried and said how the entire situation had made her physically ill. The next day she was energetic, perky, and buoyant. And that's how she's been ever since.

We still see each other around church, but we avoid each other as much as possible. When we do meet face to face, Carla is her usual bubbly, friendly self. As for me, I struggle to act cordial. I feel very defensive around her because I just don't trust her after the things she said about Angie. What hurts the most is that she has never once bothered to ask how Angie is doing, or expressed any remorse over what happened to her at that preschool. My daughter has never received an ounce of compassion from the mother of the friend she loves like a brother.

Family Members

So, with my friends, I won some and I lost some. As for family, the problem for my husband and me wasn't a question of whether or not our relatives would be understanding and supportive if we told them. Our problem was that our closest relative lived 900 miles away. Our immediate families—parents, brothers, and sisters—were scattered between London and California. It's hard to reach out and touch someone by telephone when what you really need is a warm shoulder to cry on.

My husband and I thought long and hard about whether we should tell our families of Angie's ordeal. Should we tell her grandparents, her aunts and uncles? We decided the answer to that question was no. We agonized over the tradeoff between protecting Angie's right to privacy and providing her with the support of the important people in her life. The problem was that those important people lived so far away that she only saw them a few days each year. Maybe she will want to confide in some of her relatives later in life, but at the moment we did not think they could be of much help to her.

We did have to acknowledge the possibility, however, that someone else in our families might end up raising Angie if anything ever happened to my husband and me. We decided to tell my husband's brother, who is named as Angie's legal guardian in our wills.

My husband eventually called his brother and told him briefly that Angie had been sexually molested in kindergarten and that we were sending a letter with information we thought he should have as Angie's legal guardian. And then I followed up with six typed pages of details. I outlined the investigation, basic facts about sexual molestation, the effects Angie's abuse has had on her, and the name and address of Angie's therapist. We received a brief note back from my brother-in-law's wife, saying how sorry they were to hear about Angie's ordeal. We have not had a chance to talk with them about it face-to-face yet. How supportive they, and the rest of our families, will be remains to be seen.

CHAPTER 10

*A*CQUAINTANCES AND *O*THERS

hild molestation is a crime that permeates every corner of a family's life. Angie's experience affected the ways we interacted with many people—not only friends and family, but acquaintances and others who touched our lives as well. I couldn't avoid unexpected encounters with people associated with Angie's old school. Those were people who knew what had happened and who sometimes made comments that cut me to the quick.

Two days after the parents' meeting with the district attorney, I picked Angie up from school. As I waited in the parking lot, someone tapped on my car window. It was the mother of a child who had attended Angie's old preschool the previous year, and was currently attending Angie's new school. As soon as I looked up and saw who was trying to get my attention, I knew what was coming.

I saw that person at school all the time and we never exchanged more than a polite hello in passing. If she was going out of her way to strike up a conversation with me, I knew what that conversation would be about. I tried to ward off the inevitable by launching into a monologue about the weather. She finally interrupted to ask, "So, how's Angie doing?"

I chattered on about how much Angie was enjoying first grade and how she loved Mrs. Davis, and I asked how her child was enjoying school. And then she plunged into a monologue of her own. She had been by the old school last week and had heard some rumors, she said. It was an unfortunate situation, she continued, but in her opinion we really had no one to blame but ourselves. After all, she explained, it is the parent's responsibility—not the school's—to figure out what is going on in a child's life.

Too many parents try to abdicate their responsibilities to the educational system, she told me. We should have been able to figure out what was going on with Angie in kindergarten. After all, she said, there are definite signs and symptoms related to abuse.

Ironically, it was this same woman who had criticized me only months before for pulling Angie out of her old school before the end of the session. I had run into her at the swimming pool the week after Angie left the school, and she had stunned me by announcing what a bad precedent I had set for Angie when I took her out of school early. According to her, "When Angie gets to her new school, has her first bad day, and then decides she doesn't like that school either, she'll expect Mom to pull her out of there and stay home with her again."

That interchange upset me at the time because it was clear that the preschool's director and/or Angie's kindergarten teachers had been talking about her to other staff members and/or to parents. And the picture they had painted of my child was an ugly one. As far as they were concerned, Angie was just a spoiled brat with an overly protective mother.

Months later, I was cornered by a mother whose child had attended Angie's preschool. Her child was currently a student at Angie's new school, and the mother actively participated in school activities. She pulled me aside one day to tell me that she had observed Angie at school, and in her opinion, the reason Angie had problems in kindergarten was that "the child obviously is unable to cope with stress." And that mother was one who had attended the parents' meeting with the district attorney!

Cruel comments like these were not everyday occurrences, but they were not isolated ones, either. Most of the parents we had known through Angie's old school acted very cool toward us when we met, speaking only when it seemed unavoidable. The biggest interpersonal problem I faced, however, was trying to make everything seem "business as usual," when in fact I felt that my world was collapsing around me.

This was especially true at work, and it was a test I failed miserably. I joined my company over 12 years ago, right after graduate school. I was in the first wave of women who were hired into the management training program en masse. Five years later, I became the first account representative to announce she was pregnant. My friends were as excited as I was. Others at the company were less enthusiastic. I remember some of the comments my colleagues made when they heard the news—comments like, "You didn't plan this, did you?" Or, "What? A hot-shot MBA like you?" Or, "Well, you just set the women's movement back 20 years." And then there were the first words of congratulations from a member of our top management: "Well, I heard the bad news!"

None of this bothered me much. In fact, it was rather amusing at the time. I was excited about the baby—I had wanted one so much for so long. And I was convinced I was one of the new breed of superwomen who could do it all.

I managed to be pretty successful at "doing it all" for the first five years of Angie's life. She was an incredibly healthy baby, and that made my job-juggling task relatively easy. Up until she began kindergarten, I had missed only four days of work because of her illnesses.

All of that changed when Angie began kindergarten. Suddenly I had a child who was constantly sick. Her unexpected headaches, stomachaches, sore throats, and chest pains kept me thinking she was coming down with a cold, the flu, or bronchitis. I began to miss whole days and part-days of work, not only because Angie wasn't feeling well, but also because of teachers' conferences and visits to the pediatrician.

Besides the anxiety I felt over Angie herself, I had to cope with the guilt I was feeling over having to miss so much work. I found it increasingly difficult to concentrate on my job.

To make matters worse, I was transferred to a new department at the same time Angie began experiencing severe headaches. Transfers are common at my company, but that one couldn't have come at a worse time. Just when I was in anguish over the possibility that my child had a brain tumor, I had to concentrate on learning the ropes of a new job. And I had no sooner moved into my new department than I had to ask my supervisor for a leave of absence to get Angie out of that preschool. Although my boss was cooperative and understanding about the leave, I was worried. I just wasn't used to that kind of conflict between my role as a mother and my role as a professional, and I wondered if it would all come back to haunt me.

With all of this, I already felt I was skating on thin ice before I was thrust into the turmoil that followed Angie's disclosure. Then came the agony of learning that my child had been molested and the pressures of trying to help her deal with her shattered life. Add to that the need to juggle my schedule around Angie's weekly therapy sessions. After four months of intense emotional and physical stress, a colleague walked into my office one day and said, "Look, I don't mean to pry, but I want you to know that we're all worried about you. You look as if you could drop over dead any minute."

It was not unusual at that time for me to go two or three days without sleep, and I realized that the stress was taking more of a toll on me than I had thought. I decided I had no choice but to tell my boss what was going on. He would have had to be blind not to notice that I was totally stressed out. So I walked into his office one day, closed the door, and reluctantly told him what I thought he had a right to know. I didn't go into a lot of detail.

Of course he already knew I had requested the leave of absence four months earlier because of problems with Angie's school. Now I told him I had learned since then that Angie had been sexually molested at school. I told him about the criminal investigation, which still was not resolved. I also told him I was taking Angie to see a therapist once a week, and that those appointments would continue indefinitely.

Working mothers have to contend with a lot of insensitive bosses in the corporate world. Fortunately, I was working for one of the nice guys. He didn't pump me for information, and he seemed personally shaken. He had small children of his own, so maybe that helped him understand a little of what I was living through. He said he had been concerned about me, because it was obvious I had been "preoccupied about something," and he thanked me for letting him know what was going on. Then he said he would pray for us. I left feeling very relieved.

Several weeks later, my boss called me into his office and said he had been thinking about our earlier conversation. He was grateful I had told him about what I was going through, he said, and he really "felt for me." He went on to say, however, that he was concerned that with all I had on my mind, I might "start letting things fall through the cracks" at work. As a result, he wanted to transfer me to a noncontact (i.e., no customer contact) job "until all of this blows over."

I went totally numb. It was a bombshell I wasn't expecting, and it left me speechless. I fought back my tears and asked him if my work had been unsatisfactory. He said no, but he was afraid I might start letting things fall through the cracks, and he didn't want "to see my strong reputation around the company get tarnished." All I could do was ask if we could continue the conversation after I had a day or two to think about what he had just said. I was in shock.

I fought desperately to keep myself calm and controlled at work. After several days, I returned to my boss's office to continue our conversation. I began by saying that I appreciated the concern he had expressed over Angie, but I was worried he might be overreacting to the situation. I thought the worst was over, because I was beginning to see the positive results of Angie's therapy, and by this time, I knew there would be no criminal trial to go through. I also said it would be hard to move me into a job until "everything blows over" because this was not something that would simply blow over. My family would have to learn to live with this tragedy for the rest of our lives.

I asked again if his desire to move me stemmed from any complaints about my performance. He reassured me that this was not the case. He was only concerned about what might happen. I went on to tell my boss that the thing I enjoyed most about my current job was the customer contact. Furthermore, I did not think I had the operational or technical expertise necessary for the noncontact job. I would do whatever he thought best, but I wanted him to know that a move into the other job would not, in my opinion, be in my best interests, either personally or professionally.

I asked him to consider leaving me in my current job, and volunteered to go on some sort of probation. If my work began to slip, then he could move me into a noncontact job. That left him at a loss for words, and he said he wanted to think all of this through again. We agreed to continue the discussion later.

Almost two weeks later, my boss and I met again. Again he amazed me, but this time it was a good surprise. He said that a lot of what I'd said earlier made sense to him. Rather than move me into the noncontact job, he could offer me another four-week leave of absence. By this time, I felt that I had regained much of my old emotional strength, but I knew I was still in bad shape physically. I was struggling to regain the weight I had lost over the past several months, and I still had trouble sleeping. My boss was right—I needed a break to get back on my feet.

I accepted the leave of absence gratefully. The four weeks off worked like a charm. I stayed close to home, devoting my time to writing and reading. I began a new self-imposed health regimen. I exercised, I ran, I worked out, and I ate right. I also spent a lot of time at Angie's school and enjoyed being with her those extra hours when she wasn't in school. Her spring break was especially fun for us.

Our ordeal wasn't over, by any means, but I went back to work physically strong and mentally refreshed. I did not step right back in where I had left off, however. When I got back, I stayed in my old job, but I didn't keep the same account responsibilities. In any sales job, there are good accounts, bad accounts, hard accounts, easy accounts, sensitive accounts, and accounts that almost run themselves. My boss reassigned territories and I took on the less attractive, less challenging, less sensitive accounts. It hurt my pride, but that was tempered by my gratitude over the leave of absence the company had given me. Also, I knew my boss was doing what he thought was best for the company and for me, so I swallowed my pride and dug in. Even now, I am tempted at times to feel resentful that I am having to prove myself all over again, but I try to push that out of my mind and concentrate on one day at a time. I know I am good at what I do and all I can do is hope I will be able to make up the ground I have lost at work eventually.

The circles of victimization kept rippling outward further and further. I can't think of a single part of my life that has not been affected in one way or another.

CHAPTER 11

SOCIETY

The people in my family's life were simply microcosms of the society in which we all live. We, the American public, don't want to believe that a crime as hideous as child sexual abuse can really be committed against someone we love. We protect ourselves from that reality by denying the crime itself, or we acknowledge its existence but downplay its significance. Few of us understand child molestation.

Even those who are sympathetic toward abuse victims are unable to grasp the impact the crime has on the victim, the victim's family, and society as a whole. I can't think of any other crime that is so engulfed in myths as child sexual abuse.

Many people don't even know what happens when a child is sexually molested. I remember another mother who was involved in our investigation asking me, "I don't want to offend you, but do you mind telling me exactly what happened? I mean, what exactly did they do to her?" She had no idea what it meant for a child to be molested. Her ignorance wasn't all that unusual, however. It took months of listening to my daughter's gradual disclosure of the details of her abuse before I fully understood the criminal acts that had been committed against her.

Sexual abuse of a child is any act that exploits a child for the sexual gratification of an adult or older person. It can range from exhibitionism, to fondling the child's genitalia (or having the child fondle or masturbate the adult), to sexual intercourse, to using the child for pornographic purposes. Child rape does occur, but it is the exception rather than the rule.

The absence of physical force allows many people to dismiss the significance of molestation. They don't think it really "hurts" the child. A business colleague of mine recently related an experience when she sat on the jury for a child molestation case. She ended her story by commenting that the jury had found the defendant guilty "even though he only molested the girls—I mean, he didn't rape them or anything."

What most people fail to realize is that physical force is rarely needed, because the difference in power and authority between a child victim and an offending adult provides overwhelming psychological force. And this is no less damaging to the child than physical force would be. I often wish we would stop referring to the crime as "molestation" and call it something more descriptive, such as child sexual assault. Sexual abuse violates a child physically and psychologically. It is an undeniable assault on innocence.

Most people also fail to realize how prevalent child sexual assault is in our society. Researchers stress how difficult it is to pinpoint the actual incidence of child molestation. Information typically comes from two sources—cases reported by various agencies and surveys of adults conducted by researchers. The lack of any centralized reporting facility or national standardization of reporting procedures is a large part of the problem. It is difficult to analyze and compare research results because of the inconsistencies in definitions, parameters, and methodology.

Nevertheless, the figure most frequently quoted by professionals is that at least one in four girls and one in six boys will be sexually molested before the age of 18.

Most professionals agree that these are conservative estimates. Like rape, child sexual abuse is a dramatically underreported crime. Although the exact numbers may be debated, it is clear that an alarming number of children become victims of sexual assault every year. As a result, not one of us can afford to be complacent about child sexual abuse.

One common misconception about child molestation is that it is a crime that happens to someone else's child in some other part of town. In fact, victims of child sexual abuse come from all socioeconomic strata. A comprehensive study by Diana Russell [*The Se-*

cret Trauma: Incest in the Lives of Girls and Women, New York: Basic Books, Inc., 1986] indicated that typical social indicators for victims, such as parents' occupation, level of education, or racial or ethnic background, were not significantly correlated with the incidence of incest. Russell also found that the social class background of perpetrators was not significant. Interestingly, social class distribution was evenly distributed, with 32% in occupations generally viewed as upper-middle-class, 34% in "middle-class" occupations, and 34% in those considered lower-class. Sexual assault can happen anywhere, anytime, to anyone's child.

Stereotypes also blind us to reality in regard to the types of people who commit crimes of sexual assault against children. It's easy for us to believe that the typical child molester is a dirty old man who hangs around public places looking for a lone child to victimize. That way we won't have to accept the fact that an offender could be the baby-sitter next door, the teacher in our child's class, or a counselor at camp.

In *The Silent Children: A Parent's Guide to the Prevention of Child Sexual Abuse* [New York: McGraw-Hill, 1980], Linda Tschirhart Sanford cites several studies that invalidate common stereotypes held by the general public. For example, studies show that 70% to 80% of child molesters know their victims. Eighty percent of one group of offenders studied had committed their first offense by the age of thirty. Child molesters rarely commit their crimes on impulse. They pick their victims carefully, often preferring certain ages, physical characteristics, or personality types. They plan ahead and create opportunities for the assault. Child molesters are also persistent. One study Sanford mentions indicates that the average molester of female children will molest 62.4 victims during his or her "career"; the average molester of males will assault 30.6 children.

One of the few common characteristics of child molesters is their inability to accept responsibility for their acts. Most offenders will categorically deny their crime. Those who admit the offense typically minimize its significance, or transfer blame to the victim or to external circumstances. If the crime cannot be denied, the offender may rationalize the act by insisting the child asked for it, enjoyed it, or "needed love."

But the child molester is not the only one who minimizes the effect his or her crime has on the child. One of the most amazing aspects of child sexual abuse is that so many people honestly believe it doesn't really hurt the child. I guess this goes back to the fact that so few people understand the crime. If one cannot comprehend the crime, how can one comprehend the significance of its effects?

Even a pediatrician for whom I have a tremendous amount of respect told me, "Don't worry about it. A year from now she won't even remember it happened." Children don't forget about it! They may bury the pain deep inside them. They may never talk about it. But it's there. It's part of them. And the adult who thinks the simple passage of time will erase the damage sexual abuse does to the child is suffering from a very serious delusion.

"Kids bounce back from anything" is another defense commonly used to deny the significance of child molestation. Adults should put themselves in the child's shoes long enough to imagine how they would feel if they were backed into a corner and sexually assaulted. Imagine how violated they would feel as an adult, and then think of how much worse it must be for a child still in his or her formative years. Imagine how it must feel to be assaulted by an adult you have been taught to respect, obey, and trust, such as a family member, a teacher, a neighbor, or a clergyman. Imagine how terrifying the child's life must become, knowing it will happen again but never knowing exactly when. Imagine how helpless adults would feel if they knew they couldn't tell about it because of threats made against them and/or their family. And finally, imagine how it must feel for children to know that, even if they do tell, the chances are they won't be believed, because adults are not likely to take the word of a child over the word of another adult. How can anyone possibly deny the impact child molestation has on its victims?

I have read magazine and newspaper articles about the emotional effects burglary has on its victims. Adults who have their homes broken into describe feelings of helplessness and rage. When a stranger invades the privacy of one's home and sorts through personal belongings, the victim often feels a sense of violation. Those feelings can stay with an adult for a long time—yet we adults expect children who have been physically violated to "just forget it."

Adults also minimize the effects of child molestation by thinking that all the parents or the authorities have to do is remove the child from the abusive environment. They don't understand that stopping the sexual abuse doesn't automatically undo the damage that has already been inflicted on the child. Someone recently told me of a teenage girl who broke down and cried one day in school.

Eventually, she revealed that she had been molested by her father. I asked if the abuse had been properly reported. It had. And I asked if the child was getting some kind of help. My question was dismissed with, "Oh, she's not living with her parents anymore." The person who told me that story seemed to think that getting the victim out of the home was all that was needed for a happy ending.

People also seem to think that all parents of abuse victims need to do is put the child in therapy for a while and everything will automatically be OK. Therapy is necessary if the child is to survive his or her trauma, but it is not a miracle cure. Therapy is a painful process as the child digs up and confronts horrors he or she wasn't meant to understand. A therapist works with the victim only an hour a week, at most. The child and his or her parents are ultimately responsible for the victim's recovery, and that recovery can take a lifetime. Therapy can help immeasurably, but it offers no guarantees. It isn't some kind of magic wand that bibbity-bobbity-boos away the child's pain.

As reluctant as society is to acknowledge the damage child sexual abuse inflicts on the victim, it is amazingly willing to defend and sympathize with the offender. Many people automatically jump to the defense of accused child molesters. Time and time again I watch news reports of indictments against "alleged" offenders. More often than not, the report will include interviews with the accused person's neighbors, friends, or employers, who inevitably vouch for the suspect's character. They are always described as model citizens—quiet, good, and God-fearing. People always find it "hard to believe." They just don't want to admit that the guy (or girl) next door could do such a thing. I call this the "nice guy myth."

People often use another version of the "all-or-nothing" myth to defend an accused offender. That is, if their child was not a victim, they can't believe anything could have happened to anyone else's child.

At Angie's preschool, parents refused to believe the molestation charges because their children "loved those teachers." What those parents failed to understand was that my child loved those teachers, too—until they assaulted her.

People will often conclude their declaration of the accused offender's innocence by pointing out that "these are, after all, only allegations." Someone will inevitably declare that the accused is "by the way, innocent until proven guilty." Innocent until proven guilty is certainly the cornerstone of our system of justice, and I don't mean to imply it should be any other way. I will, however, point out that child molestation is the only crime I can think of where a prosecutor's inability to get an indictment or a conviction against an alleged criminal is seized upon by the public as evidence that the crime never took place.

Perpetrators of murder, robbery, and rape remain at large either because the crime can't be solved, there isn't enough evidence against the individual to seek an indictment, the prosecutor fails to convince a jury beyond a reasonable doubt, or the accused is acquitted on a technicality. Do people automatically conclude the crime never occurred? Rarely. Rather, the public is likely to complain that our American legal system is designed to protect the criminal instead of the victim—unless the victim is a child who has been sexually abused. Then they will latch onto anything that will let them believe the crime wasn't committed in the first place.

We search for ways to convince ourselves that charges of child sexual abuse are unfounded, because if the charges are unfounded, that means someone lied. The victims and their families end up being the targets of suspicion and blame.

One of the cruelest myths surrounding child sexual abuse is the widespread belief that children can't be trusted to tell the truth. Common sense should tell us that a child would rarely, if ever, make up a story of sexual abuse simply to get attention. The type of attention that follows disclosure is hardly reinforcing. Neither is a child likely to make it up to get back at someone he or she doesn't like. A charge of sexual abuse is not the first weapon a child would think of for seeking revenge.

Most adults don't even understand what happens when a child is molested. How could a child make up details of sexual activity that would ordinarily be beyond their level of comprehension? How many children would be able to fake months and months of nightmares and terror? The typical answer is that children get these ideas from TV or from some avenging adult who has coached them. But how many children could be coached into consistent, believable stories that can stand the test of time and stand examination by experts on child molestation?

I am sure there are cases on record where charges of molestation have been fabricated. I am sure that somewhere, someone is serving time for a crime he or she didn't commit. But when it comes to the sexual abuse of children, we cling to the exceptions to keep ourselves from believing that the majority of reported cases are legitimate. Instead of making the truly unfounded cases an excuse to deny the existence and significance of child sexual assault, we should be demanding better education for ourselves and for the professionals, who should know more than most of them do. It is appalling that so many pediatricians, attorneys, prosecuting attorneys, social workers, psychologists, teachers, psychiatrists, and judges are as misinformed about child sexual abuse as the general public.

I have heard therapists complain about how frequently they report suspected cases of abuse to the Department of Family and Children's Services, only to hear the social worker's reflex response: "Are you sure he or she isn't just making this up?" And these are the people to whom, under Georgia law, therapists are required to report evidence of abuse.

Again, I am not implying that any charge of child sexual abuse should be blindly accepted, or that questions should not be asked to verify its validity. An investigation of any crime has to begin with confirmation that a crime was in fact committed. But child sexual abuse is the only crime I can think of where people reflexively start with the premise that it probably didn't happen, because we adults are programmed to believe kids are natural-born liars. Because children have great imaginations, we assume they can't tell the difference between truth and fiction.

Isn't it interesting that we credit children with being "imaginative," while adults are "creative?" We're impressed with creativity, but imagination is somehow synonymous with fantasy—and fantasy implies an inability to distinguish between reality and fiction. The assumption that children's stories of sexual abuse come from their imaginations is the cruelest fantasy of all.

We parents think we're doing a great job of protecting our children from potential abuse by reading them books and teaching them that "It's okay to tell." What good does it do to teach our children to tell, if we adults don't believe them when they do? Children have a right to be believed!

PART III

What to Expect from the System

*In the little world in which children have their existence,
whosoever brings them up, there is nothing so finely perceived
and so finely felt, as injustice.*

—Charles Dickens, in *Great Expectations*

INTRODUCTION

M ost of us manage to live a lifetime without getting directly involved with the judicial system. I spent a week on jury duty several years ago, but other than that brief encounter with justice, the closest I had ever gotten to the legal system was an occasional viewing of *Night Court* on TV.

When our daughter was criminally assaulted, we were abruptly thrown into the middle of judicial and regulatory systems that were completely foreign to us. There was no time to ease into the situation and no time to get ourselves educated. We were at the mercy of the authorities involved with Angie's case. I often felt helpless, confused, frustrated, and completely baffled by events that defied my own logic and sense of fairness.

Finding oneself unexpectedly enmeshed in the system is bound to be stressful. The degree of trauma experienced by the victim and his or her family, however, is largely determined by how responsive the judicial and regulatory jurisdictions in which the case is handled are to child abuse cases. Even more important are the responsiveness and sensitivity of the individuals who represent the system and with whom the family must work. In neither case does the family have a choice. Victims and their families have to work with the people assigned to their cases within whichever jurisdiction is applicable.

Having some idea of what to expect and knowing what questions to ask may lessen the feeling of helplessness and make the experience a little less traumatic. Generalizations are hard to come by; no one else's experience will be like ours. Nevertheless, there may be something to be gained from sharing experiences. If nothing else, our story shows how overpowering the system can seem and how dependent we are upon those people whose job it is to make the system work.

My family experienced both the best and the worst of situations. On the one hand, the sensitive professionalism of the people in the district attorney's office helped us tremendously as we struggled to cope with a frustrating criminal investigation. On the other hand, the way the regulatory investigation of the school was conducted added immeasurably to our pain. It proved to be a lesson in extremes.

CHAPTER 12

THE CRIMINAL INVESTIGATION

A criminal investigation is an inquiry into the guilt or innocence of the individual(s) accused of committing the crime. Institutions or organizations associated with the crime are not subjects of the criminal investigation. After all, you can't send a school to prison for molesting children. As elementary as that seems to me now, the distinction was not so obvious at first. In my mind, the teachers and the school were one and the same, and it took a while for it to sink in that the school's responsibility would have to be "tried" in the regulatory and/or civil arenas.

Federal efforts concerning child abuse are generally directed toward the funding of educational and treatment programs. The prosecution of child abuse cases is governed by the laws of the state in which the abuse occurs, and the effectiveness of child abuse laws varies dramatically from state to state. Even in a state with relatively progressive child abuse legislation, attitudes toward, and enforcement of, state statutes can vary widely from county to county.

The individuals within the system make it work or not work for our children. How progressive a state is in relation to child abuse depends on the people in legislative power. How effectively molestation cases are prosecuted depends on what priority the local district attorney places on child abuse. Some district attorneys may prosecute sexual abuse cases aggressively; others virtually ignore these cases. And if a case is prosecuted, how enlightened the judge is about sexual abuse can make or break a case.

Georgia is relatively progressive when it comes to child abuse legislation. The crime against my daughter was committed in DeKalb County, a jurisdiction where abuse cases are prosecuted aggressively. Former DeKalb County District Attorney Robert Wilson and Senior Assistant District Attorney J. Tom Morgan (now district attorney) have been instrumental forces behind legislative, educational, and social initiatives in the sexual abuse of children. We were fortunate that Angie's case was handled by someone with Mr. Morgan's expertise and sensitivity. He and others in the district attorney's office seemed to genuinely care about her welfare, and that was a great comfort to us.

Despite the positives we had going for us, however, the criminal investigation was incredibly stressful. If I had only known then what I know now, it might have been easier. If I could have had some idea of what to expect or what questions to ask, it might have been less frustrating.

The Investigative Process

The criminal investigation of Angie's case began two weeks after her disclosure, when a DeKalb County police detective called and said he wanted to talk with Angie. At first he planned to talk with her at Dr. McGarrah's office and to observe her therapy session. When the detective was unable to be there during Angie's appointment, he asked us to take her to his office at police headquarters. That slight change in plans was more significant than I realized at the time. Taking Angie to the police station turned out to be much more stressful for her than an interview at Dr. McGarrah's office would have been.

All of us were intimidated by our visit to police headquarters. Angie was terrified because she thought she was going to be arrested if she said something that wasn't true. I was still in a state of shock and disbelief, so I tried to play down the situation. I did not think Angie was lying, but I was still hoping there could be some other explanation for what she was saying. I tried hard to be objective so that the detective could draw his own conclusions without having to contend with the hysterics of a frantic mother.

The detective played the devil's advocate during our interview. He had small children of his own. He pointed out how imaginative children are, and he asked if we thought Angie might be making this story up so she could get out of school. I can hardly believe it now, but I tried so hard to be objective that I didn't even defend my daughter's credibility. I didn't even point out that Angie was no longer going to school when she began talking about her abuse, so the idea of a ploy to get out of school didn't make sense. I told him only the facts I knew at the time—Angie's stress symptoms, her disclosure to Dr. McGarrah, and the few details she had revealed to me.

After our discussion, the detective said he wanted to talk with Angie alone. When she emerged from his office, she brought along a piece of paper she had prepared at his request. On it she had written her name and the alphabet. At the time Angie was interviewed, Georgia still had an 1866 law on its books that required children to "qualify" as witnesses before being allowed to testify in court. (That law has since been amended.) Apparently, the detective had given Angie a primitive IQ test. He had also quizzed her on whether she knew the difference between telling the truth and telling a lie, and he had emphasized how important it was for her to tell the truth. Hearing this from a police officer made Angie assume she would be locked up forever if she did not tell the truth, and it scared her tremendously.

When the interview was over, the detective took Angie to a different building to be videotaped. The facility was an old one and the video camera was right there in plain sight. It sounds like a minor detail, but it added to Angie's stress. Sitting in front of a camera at a police station was a terrifying experience for my child.

Since then, DeKalb County has changed its procedures so that molestation victims are interviewed and taped in a playroom at a homelike children's center. The victims know they are being taped, but the camera is hidden from view. This arrangement is certainly more humane than what Angie endured.

When Angie and the police officer returned, the detective spoke with me alone. He said that Angie's story was very credible. She was obviously a bright little girl, he said, and I couldn't help but wonder what happened to molestation victims who didn't happen to be "bright" little girls. The detective believed what Angie told him and he said he was going to send the tape to the district attorney.

I had no idea what that meant, because I didn't understand how the police department and district attorney's office interacted. I was too overwhelmed and intimidated by the situation to ask questions, so I left police headquarters with no idea of what to expect next.

I didn't hear anything for over a week, so I finally called the detective to ask what was happening. He said he was going to send his report and Angie's videotape to J. Tom Morgan, the special prosecutor who handled child abuse cases. I was surprised to hear that there were enough molestation cases in the county to keep one prosecutor busy full time. I soon learned that Mr. Morgan was kept more than busy with such cases. In fact, he was carrying at least a two-person workload!

By the time I talked with Mr. Morgan the first time, he had reviewed Angie's videotape and reports from Dr. McGarrah and the police detective. He told me that Angie's tape was credible and he believed she had been sexually molested. He had two reservations, however, about whether the case could be successfully prosecuted. First, Angie had named two offenders, and second, both offenders were female. Most people have preconceived notions about child molesters, and the stereotype does not include someone who could be the girl next door. Further, the oddity of two females working together to molest children would be an even greater obstacle to overcome with a jury. Molesters typically work alone.

Technically, Angie's testimony was all that was needed. Realistically, it would not have been enough. Since there was no physical evidence, it would have been Angie's word against the word of adults. Mr. Morgan, Dr. McGarrah, and the DeKalb County police detective all believed Angie, but they were experts on the subject of child sexual abuse. The jury would have consisted of 12 people off the street—people whose knowledge of the crime would consist, for the most part, of stereotypes and misconceptions. Without corroboration, Angie's story would be impossible to prove beyond a reasonable doubt to a jury.

Shortly after Angie's disclosure, Dr. McGarrah and I talked about molestation trials. Dr. McGarrah had testified at many such trials. She told me the outcomes of child abuse cases were almost impossible to predict because they depend so much on the biases of the jury and the judge. She had seen cases with what she considered fairly weak evidence result in convictions. Conversely, she had seen strong cases end with acquittals. She told of one case that was tried in two counties. Those two trials, with the same victims, the same defendant, the same witnesses, and the same testimony, resulted in an acquittal in one county and a conviction in the other.

The problem is that the prosecution of child sexual abuse cases today is about where adult rape cases were 20 years ago. Rape victims were reluctant to report and prosecute their assailants because the victim's credibility was always suspect. Had it really been rape? Or had the victim somehow invited, deserved, or consented to the assault? To get a conviction, the rape victim had to be unquestionably blameless, and even then, her testimony often had to be corroborated by an eyewitness.

In child molestation cases, the accuser is a child, a creature whose credibility is immediately suspect simply because of his or her age. Physical evidence does not exist in most cases, and there is rarely an eyewitness. The prosecutor's case rests on evidence that is largely circumstantial—the testimony of expert witnesses such as social workers and therapists and the corroboration of other victims.

The first step in Mr. Morgan's investigation was to interview the parents of each of the other girls who had been in Angie's class to determine if there were other victims. It was critical that no one else know what was going on so that the evidence would not be "contaminated." I assured Mr. Morgan that none of the other parents knew about Angie's disclosure.

Mr. Morgan sent the other six parents a very general letter saying only that he wanted to schedule a meeting with them. All but one family agreed to see him.

When he met with the parents, Mr. Morgan reviewed a list of symptoms exhibited by abuse victims, without telling the parents what the list represented, and asked if they had observed any of those behaviors in their children. (This procedure has since been changed so that parents fill out a written questionnaire.) The object was to identify children who fit the profile of sexually abused children.

The parents were told not to talk about the investigation to anyone else, so that no one could later claim that new charges of abuse were the result of hysteria generated by information about Angie. Parents were also instructed not to quiz their children, but to listen if the children disclosed details of abuse. Next, the children would be screened by child psychologists who specialized in molestation cases, and those interviews would be videotaped.

One family did not want to have their daughter interviewed. The remaining four families agreed to proceed. From those four interviews, one other definite victim and one "possible" victim were identified.

By this time, I was beginning to realize that criminal investigations don't go as quickly or as smoothly as they do on TV. I guess we're all accustomed to seeing a crime committed, solved, and prosecuted in an hour. This real-life investigation would start, stop, burst open, and die again and again. Some of the delays were specific to our case and some occurred because Mr. Morgan was tied up with other cases.

At times the waiting seemed unbearable. We never knew if or when word of the investigation would leak out. We wondered how other parents from the school would react, and at times I was almost afraid to answer the phone. I never knew what to expect next.

Finally, over two months after Angie's disclosure, Mr. Morgan scheduled a meeting with the parents of the three girls, District Attorney Robert Wilson, and Steve Roberts, the chief assistant district attorney, in Mr. Wilson's office. The children were there also. It was the first time they had seen each other since all of this began, and the first time they learned each other's identities.

The children were introduced to DeKalb County's victim advocate Jennifer Berryman, the person who would help them if the case should go to trial. She showed them around the courthouse and entertained them while the parents met. She was wonderful with the girls; Angie later declared her to be "one of the nicest people I have ever met."

The purpose of the meeting, Mr. Wilson explained, was for us to let them know how we as parents felt about having the case prosecuted. Many parents ask not to have molestation cases prosecuted in order to keep their children from having to go through a trial. Mr. Wilson said he could understand parents' desires to protect their children and usually honored such requests.

I could understand a parent's reluctance to have a case prosecuted. In fact, my initial reaction had been to protect Angie from the trauma of a jury trial. It seemed cruel to expect a child victim to take the witness stand in front of the people who had hurt her so much and be cross-examined by a defense attorney who would do anything to get an acquittal for his or her client(s). He or she wouldn't give a damn about my child. The only reason the defense might not try to tear her testimony to shreds on the witness stand would be because it might evoke sympathy for her on the part of the jury. They would go as far as they could, though.

How could any parent subject a child to that? I knew now why so many incidents of child molestation are never reported or prosecuted.

By the time this meeting was held, however, I could already see the progress Angie was making in therapy. She was still very traumatized, frightened, and angry, but through all of her intense emotions I could see signs of remarkable strength. I was amazed by her sense of realism and by her fairly accurate perception of the judicial process. She seemed to understand the system, and that made me want very much to see the system work the way it should for her. Not proceeding with the prosecution might have been the easy way out in the short run, but in the long run I believed it would be healthier for Angie if we cooperated with the district attorney's efforts to prosecute the case.

Our decision would mean the difference between Angie looking back some day and knowing we did everything we could to bring her offenders to justice or knowing we turned our back on the system, thereby allowing the people who hurt her so badly to go free to hurt countless other children. I tried to relay all of that to District Attorney Wilson. It was a long way of saying, "Yes . . . do what you have to do."

Mr. Wilson said there was no doubt in his mind, after reviewing the tapes and the evidence so far, that the girls had been sexually abused. Being convinced a crime had been committed and being able to prove who did it beyond a reasonable doubt in court, however, were two different things. He echoed Mr. Morgan's earlier concern about the difficulty of prosecuting female offenders, especially when two persons were involved.

The biggest problem, however, was that the children, in their initial taped interviews, had not been consistent about the involvement of the two teachers. Angie named one teacher as the primary offender and mentioned the other secondarily. The other confirmed victim named the second teacher during her initial interview and did not implicate the first until later. People who are knowledgeable about sexual abuse know that children disclose details slowly over a period of time. Nevertheless, those taped inconsistencies would have provided ammunition for defense attorneys trying to destroy the children's credibility. Further, the other child who was definitely a victim was not in therapy at the time, so there was no psychological follow-up to her taped interview. Nevertheless, the prosecutors wanted to take the next step—Mr. Morgan would interview the teachers.

The remainder of the two-hour meeting was spent in a therapeutic free-for-all for the parents. We swapped stories about the school and some of the other questionable things that had gone on there. The most alarming news I heard was that, like us, other parents had requested conferences with the teachers and director that year. Two other girls had exhibited the same symptoms of stress Angie had shown. Like us, the other parents had been told to consider family counseling because there must be "problems at home." In fact, some of the comments made to them had been identical to those made to us during our conferences!

When we left the district attorney's office my mind was spinning, as I tried to sort out everything that had been said. That night I tossed and turned for four hours, until at 3 A.M. I finally decided to go ahead and get up. Not only was I unable to sleep any more, but I was afraid to sleep any more. I couldn't remember my dreams, but my anxiety was so intense when I awoke that I knew I had been having nightmares of my own.

So I got up in the middle of the night and made a pot of chili for dinner the next evening. While it simmered, I worked on an heirloom baby layette I was making for Angie's school's fund-raising auction. When I got tired of that, I went back to the kitchen to make cookies for Angie's lunch, and then I sat down to read a John Updike short story. I kept busy, trying to keep myself from thinking about the meeting with the district attorney. The thought of going to court scared me. The thought that the case might not go to trial scared me even more. I also knew that the secrecy surrounding the investigation was being lifted and I didn't know what would happen when people at the preschool found out about it.

What frightened me the most, though, was the fact that Angie would have to undergo an unpleasant gynecological exam if the case eventually went to trial. I had first learned of the colposcopic exam the evening before at the district attorney's meeting. The exam was a technical requirement that probably wouldn't add anything to the case, but the defense would make a major issue over the absence of such an exam. On the way to the parking lot, another mother had told me she would never allow her daughter to be subjected to the exam. She was familiar with the procedure and instrumentation, and she thought it would be too traumatic for children as young as ours.

Later that week, I talked with Dr. McGarrah about the colposcopic exam. She didn't have a lot to say except that it would be important to use a pediatric gynecologist with whom Angie could be comfortable. The exam wasn't necessarily a traumatic experience, she said, and she knew children younger than Angie who had undergone the procedure. She also mentioned that she knew of at least one case in which a child had been anesthetized for the procedure. I wondered if that might be a possibility for Angie. The conversation didn't resolve anything in my mind, but I decided to wait until the exam became more than a hypothetical possibility before getting upset over it.

Mr. Morgan interviewed one of Angie's teachers about a week after our meeting at the district attorney's office. There were inconsistencies in what she said, but they were not significant enough to affect the prosecutor's case. The interview with the other teacher never materialized, although Mr. Morgan tried for several months to arrange a meeting. She canceled their first appointment on the advice of one of the preschool's board members. Eventually, other appointments were arranged, but she either canceled them at the last minute or simply failed to show up. On one occasion, Mr. Morgan and a detective drove across the state in the middle of the week to a prearranged meeting at her new home, only to find that she had suddenly "left town." As of this writing, she has never been questioned by the prosecutor or the police.

The criminal investigation eventually stalled out. The other confirmed victim exhibited the classic symptoms of sexual abuse, and her parents believed the details she disclosed to them about that abuse. From the beginning, however, the parents were ambivalent about allowing the case to be prosecuted. One of the first things they did was to consult an attorney to defend their daughter's rights. They vowed to fight attempts by the prosecutor to put her on the witness stand. Then they reversed their position and agreed to cooperate with the district attorney's office—for a while. Next they seemed to go through a major phase of denial. The father told me he couldn't believe such a thing could happen to his daughter, especially "here in beautiful, warm, sunny Atlanta." He sounded very bitter, and in the end, the family wanted only to "get the hell out of this damn city" and try to forget this whole nightmare. My heart still aches when I think of that child and her family, and I hope they will find peace in their new home.

The third "possible" victim was never a factor in the investigation because she did not disclose significant information in her initial interview. She exhibited the classic symptoms of abuse, and she said things that indicated something had happened to her, but she "shut down" before she could disclose specifics. Her mother told me later that she had lowered her eyes, hung her head, and refused to speak. Her parents also went through a denial phase, and I don't think they ever came out of it. They assumed that since she was not a confirmed victim, she was no victim at all.

That left Mr. Morgan with Angie's disclosed information, backed up by strong psychological evidence. All he had for the other confirmed victim was her initial taped interview. The inconsistencies in the one teacher's statement were not incriminating enough to hold up in court. The second teacher had successfully avoided being questioned. In a last-ditch effort to shake something loose, Mr. Morgan visited the preschool and interviewed the director. He observed some problems with the school's bathroom policies, which could have provided an opportunity for abuse, but again there was nothing significant enough to help his case. The prosecutor just didn't have enough evidence to take before a jury of 12 people.

Five months after Angie first began talking about her abuse, Mr. Morgan acknowledged he had hit a dead end, and he told me officially that he was not going to take the case to the grand jury. He said there was strong psychological evidence for Angie, but that was not enough to go on, for the same reasons we had discussed earlier.

The inconsistency in the children's initial taped interviews continued to be his primary concern. He believed he could prove beyond a reasonable doubt that the girls had been sexually molested and that it had happened at that preschool. The defense, however, would have attacked those initial interview videos, generating so much confusion over which teacher had abused which child that convictions for either teacher were unlikely.

Mr. Morgan stressed over and over again that he believed what the children had said. The problem was that he felt constrained by the Prosecutors' Code of Professional Responsibility, which prohibits a district attorney from seeking an indictment before a grand jury if he or she does not believe there is a "reasonable likelihood of a conviction.'' Of course, the standard of reasonableness is a subjective one. Mr. Morgan was an experienced prosecutor, however, and headed up the Sexual Assault against Children Unit, so his opinion was to be respected.

In addition to the problems Mr. Morgan would have had in proving the identities of the abusers beyond a reasonable doubt, he was bothered by the probability that the defense would have subpoenaed the other kindergarten children and had them testify about how happy they had been in the kindergarten class. It would have been a cruel little circus, with the victims being set up against their friends. Was it worth putting the children through that for a case without a reasonable likelihood of convictions? Mr. Morgan sounded as frustrated as I felt over the way things had turned out.

One reason the criminal investigation was so hard on us is that it dragged on for so long. It was a five-month-long roller coaster ride. The other problem is that the investigation never really came to a conclusion. It just stalled out.

We had never been promised that Angie's case would be prosecuted, but there was always reason to hope something might develop that would strengthen Mr. Morgan's case to the point where he had a reasonable chance of convincing a jury beyond a reasonable doubt. I kept hoping the other parents would eventually put their children in therapy, providing evidence to back up the tapes. As time dragged by, that hope gradually faded, until one day it just wasn't there anymore. Nothing was ever resolved; there was no closure. We just waited until there was nowhere else to go.

What kept the criminal investigation from becoming intolerable was the kindness and dedication of the people we worked with. Then-District Attorney Robert Wilson made the fight against child sexual abuse a priority in DeKalb County. He was the first district attorney in the state to appoint a special prosecutor to specialize in abuse cases. That special commitment to the victims of child sexual abuse was evident in all the members of his staff with whom we came in contact. Not only were they concerned with the investigation and prosecution of the crime, but they were also concerned with the welfare of the children.

For several reasons, having Angie's case investigated by someone of Mr. Morgan's caliber helped us cope with the investigation. His reputation as an expert on the subject of child sexual abuse was well known. I quickly learned to trust and accept his judgment. A less credible, less competent prosecutor might have left us wondering if Angie's case could have gone to trial if it had been handled differently. At least we were spared that frustration.

Mr. Morgan communicated openly with us and that was also a great help. He made us feel that we were part of the process and not outsiders to the system. He didn't pick up the phone and call us with every detail, but he encouraged us to call him any time we had questions or information we thought might be important. He always returned our telephone calls, and he kept us informed of major developments.

Best of all, Mr. Morgan was able to relate to Angie and win her trust and affection. She wasn't just another victim. She was a child, and he genuinely cared about her welfare. More than once, I heard him express concern over the effect certain legal considerations might have on the children.

As the investigation dragged on and then faded away, Angie experienced problems of her own with finding closure. The investigation had begun with a bang for her—there had been the visit to the police station, videotaped interviews, and meetings with the state regulatory investigator and district attorney. For months we had reassured her that she did the right thing by telling about her abuse and that it was her offenders, not she, who had done something wrong. And then there was nothing—no arrests, no trial, no punishment, no anything.

We teach our children cause and effect at an early age. If they misbehave, they suffer consequences of some sort. So how was Angie to understand that adults who had misbehaved in a big way would suffer no consequences at all? When Mr. Morgan learned of the problem Angie was having understanding and accepting that there would be no trial, he offered to talk with her himself. He thought, and Dr. McGarrah and I agreed, that having it explained by the man who represented the system to Angie might help her put that phase behind her so she could move on with her healing.

And so Mr. Morgan sat down and talked with Angie about his investigation. He explained how it was his job to take people like Angie's offenders to court so they could be punished for hurting children. In this case, he said, he wasn't going to be able to do that. He explained how all the other children in the class probably would have been forced to go to court to testify. And he explained that it would have been easy to get a jury confused because there were two people, not one, who had hurt children at that school. Each one of them would have pointed her finger at the other and said that she had done it. If it had been only one of them, it would have been easier to prove the offense to a jury.

Mr. Morgan told Angie that he believed her. He believed she had been hurt by her teachers at that school. And he asked her whether she understood what he had just told her. Angie had not said a word while Mr. Morgan talked, but she nodded her head yes. He asked her if she had any questions and she blurted out, "They should go to court." Mr. Morgan said he agreed, but it just couldn't be that way.

I had a lump in my throat when we walked out of Mr. Morgan's office. He had been wonderful with Angie. It was not a simple situation to understand, but he had explained it to her gently and simply. It had taken a long time for me to comprehend the difference between being convinced a crime has been committed and being able to prove the critical details in court beyond a reasonable doubt, and I wondered if Angie really understood. Before we were halfway home, Angie began to cry.

"It's not fair," she sobbed. "Nothing in the whole world is fair." I agreed, but the important thing was for her to realize that everyone, including Mr. Morgan, believed her.

Later that evening, I heard Angie in her room, acting out a little courtroom scene of her own. She acted out one of her teachers, pointing her finger at the other teacher and yelling, "You did it." Then she switched roles and she was the second teacher, pointing her finger at the first and shouting, "No, you did it!" Angie put her hands on her hips, looked very stern and said, "Then I'd go to court and say, 'You're both lying. You both did it!'" She understood more than I had thought at first.

Mr. Morgan didn't have to take time out of his overloaded schedule to talk with Angie, but I am grateful that he did. I think it will be an important memory for Angie as she grows older. Someday I hope it will help her when she remembers that there was a little kindness in the legal system, even though the system didn't work as it should have for her.

If I Had Only Known . . .

There was no way I could have changed the frustrating outcome of the criminal investigation. I could have reduced the stress and anxiety we experienced, however, if I had asked questions—lots of them—at the beginning. I remembered that early conversation with Dr. McGarrah when she warned me that the school and the teachers would say I made everything up because I had some kind of vendetta against the school. She was right—that's exactly what they did, and their offense made me defensive and kept me from asking the questions I should have asked. I was afraid that if I was too assertive I would look vindictive, and that would reinforce the school's position. So I sat back and waited, trying to understand what was going on after the fact and feeling frustrated when things didn't make sense.

I recommend that parents of molestation victims immediately sit down face-to-face with the investigator assigned to their case and ask questions. Further, they should feel free to continue asking questions throughout the investigation and trial. There will be many questions to ask!

To start out with, parents should understand who all the players are and what their roles will be. In some cases, the police department will initiate and conduct the investigation. The police may initiate the investigation and then turn it over to investigators in the district attorney's office, or it may be a joint investigation. Other cases may be handled entirely by the prosecutor. Cases handled in jurisdictions with special prosecutors for child sexual abuse cases are more likely to be investigated by the district attorney's staff.

In any case, parents need not be shy about trying to get a sense of how much expertise investigators have with child sexual abuse cases and how well they work with child victims. Parents should ask if they investigate and/or prosecute only sexual abuse cases or if they handle other types of cases as well, how many molestation cases they have handled, and what their outcome has been.

Parents also should make sure they understand the typical sequence of events, including a realistic time frame. If there are complicating elements in their child's case, they should understand what effect those elements might have on the investigation and its outcome. If delays occur, they should not hesitate to ask why. Angie's case was complicated by the fact that two offenders were involved, so the investigation dragged on for an unusually long time while the prosecutor searched for ways to overcome that hurdle.

Before writing this chapter, I talked with Mr. Morgan and asked questions I wish I had asked over a year ago. I learned that the decision to prosecute a case is usually made within days of the initial interviews with a victim's parents. A prosecutor usually knows if he or she has a valid case almost immediately. A valid case for prosecution has to meet three tests. First, the prosecutor has to be able to prove that the sexual abuse took place. Second, the prosecutor has to prove where it happened, because the case has to be tried in the same jurisdiction as the crime. (I read of one case that was never prosecuted because the child was molested in a car and they couldn't prove which county the assault occurred in.) Finally, the prosecutor has to prove he or she has the right perpetrator. Angie's case met the first two of those three requirements.

As soon as the decision is made to proceed with the prosecution, a warrant is sworn out against the offender, an arrest is made, and a preliminary hearing is held. Bond is set at the preliminary hearing, so parents have to be prepared for the likelihood that the offender will be out on bail within 24 hours. It is possible, though, that the prosecutor will want to hold back on the arrest warrant and take the case directly to a grand jury, which will determine if there is enough evidence to warrant prosecution. In that situation, if the grand jury believes there is enough to go on, the arrest will be made after the indictment.

Once those preliminary events are out of the way, parents will turn their attention to the trial. The case may not come to trial, however, because many offenders plead guilty after they see the victim's taped interviews. According to Mr. Morgan, approximately 90% of indicted child molesters in DeKalb County, Georgia, plead guilty. Intrafamilial offenders are the most likely to plead guilty. If the offender enters a plea of not guilty, the trial date will be set. In DeKalb County, trials usually take place within four to six months. The length of time it takes for the case to go to trial will differ significantly from jurisdiction to jurisdiction.

Since we did not go through a criminal trial, I can't offer much insight on what to expect. I do, however, remember the questions that went through my mind when I considered the possibility of going to court. Foremost in my mind were fears and uncertainties over the effect a trial would have on Angie. I never raised the subject with Angie because we didn't know if her case was going to trial or not. It did come up on one occasion, however.

It was after one of her nightmares. As she clung to my neck for protection, she begged me to "keep them away from me." I promised her I would do everything I could to keep them away from her. She asked, "Will they ever get me again?" I promised her they would not. "Will I ever have to see them again?" I began to say that she would not, but then I thought of the possibility of a courtroom confrontation and I didn't want to make promises I couldn't keep. I told her that I hoped she would never see them again . . . unless it was in court.

Angie looked startled. "Would I have to see them in court?" she asked. I told her that if her case ever came to trial, she would have to see them in court.

Angie was very quiet for a long time. Finally she asked, "If they were in court, would they chase me? Would they be able to get me and hurt me?" I assured her they would not be able to come near her in court. Policemen would be there to make sure she wouldn't get hurt. But her offenders would be there in the same room, and she would see them, and they would probably look at her with mean looks to try to scare her. Angie thought about that for a while and then she said hesitatingly, "That would be OK . . . if it was in court. If that was where I saw them, I think that would be OK . . ."

The prosecuting attorney should brief the parents about court-room procedures, but parents shouldn't hesitate to ask questions of their own. Parents should ask if the child will have to testify in person if the case goes to trial. When Angie was videotaped, I assumed she would be spared having to testify in person. I was devastated when I later learned that was only partly correct. Her taped interview would have been used during the preliminary proceeding, but she would have been required to testify at the trial. (In some jurisdictions, the child has to testify in preliminary proceedings too.)

Even if a child's taped interview can be used as his or her primary testimony, prosecutors almost always need the child's personal testimony as well. In the unlikely case where a prosecutor decides not to call the victim to testify in person, the child would still not be spared a court appearance, because the defense attorney has the right to cross-examine the victim in person, and he or she will surely exercise that right.

Under the United States Constitution, an accused person has the right to confront his or her accuser. The interpretation of that constitutional right varies from state to state, so parents should understand how the child's testimony will be handled. Will the child testify in the judge's chambers? Behind a one-way mirror or screen? Who is allowed in the courtroom? What measures are taken to decrease the child's fear? Who will be with the child when he or she testifies? Will the parents be allowed in the courtroom during the testimony? (That will depend on whether the parents themselves are called as witnesses and on the discretion of the presiding judge.) Will there be a victim's advocate to help the child through the courtroom ordeal?

Parents should ask what will be required of their child before and during a trial. What kinds of physical and/or psychological examinations will be required? Can the defense attorney request that the child be examined by another therapist and/or physician of his or her choice? In Georgia, child victims are spared the trauma of multiple examinations, but some defense attorneys will file motions for additional examinations nonetheless. Unless the prosecutor is willing to fight for the child's rights, unenlightened judges may grant the request.

What about publicity? As soon as an arrest is made or an indictment is sought, the case enters the public domain. Parents should question the degree to which their child's privacy will be protected. Is there a possibility TV cameras will be allowed in court? Some abuse cases are of more interest to the media than others, because media coverage of sexual molestation cases is often more sensational than educational. Parents and victims should be prepared for attention they could do without.

Parents should ask the prosecuting attorney about statutes that specifically concern child sexual abuse cases. For example, Georgia waives the right of spousal immunity in molestation cases. That means that a person can be subpoenaed and forced to testify against a spouse. Another example involves the admissibility of hearsay evidence in child abuse cases. If the victim of a crime tells someone about a crime, that second person normally cannot repeat the details during testimony—that would be hearsay. In child abuse cases, however, details about the abuse that a child victim under the age of 14 reveals to another person can be used as testimony in court.

Until recently, Georgia's 1866 competency statute affected the prosecution of child sexual abuse cases. Children under the age of 14 were presumed to be incompetent witnesses, along with "idiots and lunatics during lunacy." The burden was on the prosecutor to prove that a child understood the meaning of an oath, the difference between telling the truth and telling a lie, and the consequences of telling a lie.

Although this Georgia statute has since been amended to exclude children, it is important for parents to understand how the laws of their jurisdiction can affect their child and the outcome of the case against their child's assailant. They should understand how the rights of the victim stack up against the rights of the accused, and understand their right to obtain information about their child's case. The answers will depend on the laws governing the case and on the personal beliefs of the prosecuting attorney. Some states have victims' rights statutes on their books. Georgia does not. Mr. Morgan believes in the parents' right to know the status of their child's case. Other prosecutors may not be that sensitive.

With all the questions and concerns that parents have to face, it is easy to understand why some parents ask to have their child's case dropped to protect the victim from the ordeal of going to court. I would never condemn a family for making that decision, because no one can walk in someone else's shoes and feel their struggle to decide what will be best for their child. Parents should understand, however, that although their first and most natural impulse will be to protect the child from going to court, that is not necessarily the best choice for the child in the long run. Parents should listen to what the prosecutor and the victim's therapist have to say about the effects the courtroom experience will have on the child.

Parents also have to understand that we are all part of the system. It is easy for us as individuals to feel victimized by the system, because we can be, and often are. But that doesn't mean we should turn our backs on it and stop trying to make it better. We have an obligation to try to help the system work for all our children. Each time a child molester is convicted, countless other children will be spared the agony our child has had to endure. I hope all parents of sexual abuse victims will bear that in mind as they stumble through their own legal labyrinth.

CHAPTER 13

REGULATORY AUTHORITIES

After Angie disclosed that she had been abused, we were told that three separate investigations would be conducted. The first would be the criminal investigation of the individuals involved in the abuse. Second, the Department of Family and Children's Services (DFCS) would investigate the school. DFCS is the agency to which abuse cases are reported under Georgia law. We were given the name of the DFCS worker who was assigned to Angie's case, but she never contacted us.

Months later, I learned that DFCS had decided not to conduct an investigation because the agency thought it was unnecessary to duplicate the criminal investigation. I was also told DFCS never investigates third-party abuse reports, because the agency is so understaffed that it concentrates its limited resources on incest cases where the child is in danger of continuing abuse.

The third investigation we were told to expect would involve the school. The Child Care Licensing Department of the Georgia Department of Human Resources (DHR) would investigate the school because it was a licensed child care facility. DHR's investigation ended up being an example of bureaucracy at its worst. The individual investigator was a very sweet woman I couldn't help liking, but she was completely ineffective. I don't know if it was the fault of the individual or of the bureaucratic system in which she had to operate. I suspect it was the latter. All I know for sure is that DHR's investigation added immeasurably to our stress and pain.

Waiting for DHR

The DHR investigator, whom I will call Ms. Williams, telephoned my husband and introduced herself within hours after Angie's disclosure. Two days later we received a one-page form letter from Ms. Williams that confirmed her telephone conversation with my husband and asked us to provide a parental statement of "the care received by your child while in [the school] as well as a description of the injury/condition." The form also requested that we submit medical and psychological reports.

Three weeks later Ms. Williams came to our house to talk with us and to meet Angie. We did most of the talking because Ms. Williams couldn't tell us much. All she said was that she wasn't sure what role DHR would play in Angie's case because it would take a back seat to the criminal investigation. At some point, though, it would have to confront the school, because the criminal investigation focused only on the individuals. The state would deal with the preschool, she said, "if they thought it was necessary," but it was too early to tell what would happen at that point.

The following week, Ms. Williams went to Dr. McGarrah's office to observe Angie's session through a one-way mirror. I talked with her briefly before she left. She was visibly shaken, and said Angie's story was "certainly believable." At that time, I gave her the parents' statement she had requested. My husband and I had taken a long time to write it. We were still trying to be logical and objective, so we had edited out anything that might sound emotional. We ended up with six relatively factual pages that summarized the previous year's events at the school.

Several months passed before I telephoned Ms. Williams again. She asked how Angie was doing and seemed surprised when I told her of the effect Angie's abuse was having on her. I told her about Angie's nightmares, her emotional turmoil, and her social and behavioral problems. The questions Ms. Williams asked gave me the impression that she didn't know a great deal about child sexual abuse. She suggested that we file a follow-up report to our parental statement detailing the information I had just given her about Angie.

In terms of the investigation, Ms. Williams didn't have anything new to tell me, because DHR was still waiting to see if Mr. Morgan was going to prosecute the individuals.

I wrote the report Ms. Williams had requested, only this time I didn't trip over myself trying to be objective. By this time, my husband and I had talked with the other parents, and we knew that two other couples had sought help from the school's director that year because their daughters had exhibited the same stress symptoms in kindergarten that Angie had shown. Like us, they were told the children were perfectly happy at school and that the problem was that the girls were undisciplined at home. Family counseling was recommended, as it had been for us. Those two girls turned out to be the other confirmed victim and the "possible" victim. We believed the director's defensiveness constituted negligence and I told DHR so. I ended that seven-page report with, "Could she really have believed that it was simply a case of three spoiled little girls? Especially when there were only five girls in that class at the time?"

Two weeks later, I called Ms. Williams again. The week before, Mr. Morgan had told me that Angie's case would not be prosecuted and that he had suggested DHR proceed with their investigation of the school. I called Ms. Williams to find out what we could expect to happen next. She didn't have anything to tell me. She was very vague and commented that Angie's was the first case of this type she had ever been involved in. She said she just didn't know what DHR could do since the teachers, by this time, had left the school.

Two weeks later, I called Ms. Williams again and asked what was happening. The answer was "nothing." Once more she told me, "We just don't know what we can do." Once more she said that Angie's was the first case like this she had ever dealt with. She went on to say that DHR still planned on doing an investigation "of some kind," but she was not sure when they would get around to it. She mentioned that she had so much "stuff" piled on her desk that she had to clear some of those items off first, before moving on to Angie's case.

My frustration got the best of me. For the first time, I began to press Ms. Williams for answers. I didn't get very far. The only new information I dug out was that there was something called a "civil penalty" that could be assessed by DHR in cases of "incorrectable offenses." DHR's investigations ordinarily involve seeing to it that infractions of licensing requirements are corrected. DHR gives the offending institution time to take corrective action and assesses penalties if the corrections are not made. If, however, the condition no longer exists, DHR classifies it as an "incorrectable" offense because there are no steps the institution can take after the fact to correct the situation. The civil penalty, however, was a way of acknowledging that an offense had taken place.

I asked her if a civil penalty for such an offense might apply in Angie's case, since Ms. Williams had repeatedly told me that she didn't know what DHR could do when the teachers had already left the school. Ms. Williams acknowledged that a civil penalty might be applicable, and she asked me what I would like to see happen.

I replied that I was not simply some avenging mother who wanted to see the school shut down. The school had been a good one for many years and Angie had four good years there. But children had been sexually molested at the school, and the school's administration had not acted responsibly, either while the crimes were being committed or after the charges were made known. "Shouldn't someone give them a message that their behavior cannot be condoned?" I asked. I thought there should be some kind of penalty—perhaps a fine—that would let people at that school and at other institutions know that they can't ignore or shrug off something as serious as the sexual abuse of children. They had to be reminded that their primary mission was the care and welfare of the children entrusted to them.

After my impassioned plea, all Ms. Williams managed for an answer was that she just didn't know what they could do, but she promised she would let me know when they decided to move ahead with the investigation. I hung up the telephone and cried. Two weeks after that conversation and over five weeks after Mr. Morgan ended his investigation, DHR officially launched theirs. Ms. Williams did not notify me as she had promised. Instead, I found out about DHR's investigation accidentally.

Maggie (not her real name) was a long-time veteran of Angie's old preschool. She had been Angie's teacher in the baby room and again in the three-year-old room. She was a popular teacher, a favorite with parents and children alike. Angie had always adored her. Maggie was still working at the preschool part-time. In the afternoons, she worked at Angie's new school in the after-school program.

I ran into Maggie one afternoon when I picked Angie up from her Girl Scout meeting after school. I asked Maggie a generalized, "How's life treating you?" and she blurted out that she thought everything at the old preschool was "about to blow sky-high." She explained that the teachers had just learned that the state was conducting some sort of investigation of the school. The teachers were upset because they couldn't find out what was going on. Someone from "State Licensing" had paid a surprise visit to the school, but the lady spoke in "generalities."

The teachers asked the director about the investigation, but she would say only that it was nothing to worry about. She told them, "Some parent has made allegations which have not been substantiated." "It's nothing more than a rumor," she continued. "And anyway, it doesn't involve the school because neither the child nor the adults involved are here anymore."

Maggie said the teachers didn't talk about it among themselves because they were afraid the director would overhear. The worker from the state had interviewed each teacher individually, but they had been afraid to say anything because the director had been sitting in the next room, right outside the door. The lady from DHR gave each teacher a questionnaire to fill out and told the teacher to either send it directly to DHR or give it to the school's director to send in. After the investigator from DHR left, the director told the teachers they had to turn their questionnaires in to her so she could send them all in together. Several teachers held their questionnaires back because they wanted to send them to DHR themselves, but the director came to their classrooms and insisted they turn them over to her.

Maggie was one teacher who had wanted to send her questionnaire directly to DHR, because she felt she had information that needed to be reported. When the director came to her room to pick up the questionnaire, Maggie told her she had left it at home and would send it in herself. The director gave her a blank form and made her fill it out while she watched. Maggie had wanted to fill it out confidentially because she knew of an incident when a parent had come in to pick up her child and found the child in the bathroom with a teacher, with the door closed. The parent was upset and confronted the teacher, who was unable to offer a reasonable explanation for being in the bathroom with the child or for the door being closed a long time. The parent had talked with Maggie about it rather than with the director because the director had been "unresponsive" to previous concerns the parent had taken to her. Then she had withdrawn her child from the school.

Maggie told me she had not even considered the possibility that something wrong might have been going on in the bathroom, but she mentioned the incident to the other teacher in her room because that person was relatively new at the school and had no experience in teaching or day care. She counseled the other teacher, saying that "you have to be careful when you're working with little children. There are some things you just don't do because they might be misinterpreted."

Apparently the director overheard, or heard of, Maggie's conversation with her colleague. She called Maggie in and disciplined her for "spreading malicious rumors about your coworkers." Maggie told her it was not a rumor, but the director insisted the incident had "never happened" and ordered Maggie to never mention it to anyone again. She accused Maggie of "just being negative."

At this point, Maggie didn't know that Angie was a victim, so I said as little as I could about the investigation and about the school. I did suggest that Maggie call the woman from DHR (who turned out to be Ms. Williams) and talk with her on the phone about that incident and anything else she had been afraid to include on her questionnaire.

Maggie hesitated. She was afraid the director might find out. She was even afraid the director would somehow find out that she had talked with me about the investigation.

Apparently Maggie's fears of retaliation from the school's administration were not unfounded. Months later, Maggie applied for a full-time job at another preschool. She was told she had the job and the director introduced her to other employees as "our new baby room teacher" who would be "a great part of our team." "Welcome aboard," she was told. But before Maggie's first day, the job offer was suddenly withdrawn because of negative comments from Maggie's former boss, the director of Angie's preschool. The director of the new center told Maggie she withdrew the offer because she was reluctant to hire someone who might be "controversial."

After my conversation with Maggie, I called Ms. Williams to find out what was going on. She told me she had visited the school and had interviewed the teachers and director. She told me how impressed she had been with the director, because she was so "upset and concerned about this whole thing and promised to do everything she could to cooperate." "That certainly will be in the school's favor," she added.

I told Ms. Williams about my conversation with Maggie and how the director had made her turn in her questionnaire to her. Ms. Williams said the reason the director had done that was because DHR had asked her to collect the forms for them. I asked her if the questionnaires were at least sealed for confidentiality. They were not.

Two weeks later, I saw Maggie again when I picked up Angie from her Girl Scout meeting. I asked her if she had ever talked with Ms. Williams and she said she had not—she was still afraid the director would find out. She also said the teachers were still unable to find out about the investigation. They had held two staff meetings since DHR's visit to the school and the investigation was never mentioned. Maggie said it was as if nothing had ever happened.

Once more, my frustration got the best of me and I called Ms. Williams. She wasn't in, so I asked to speak to her supervisor, as Ms. Williams had told me to do anytime I couldn't reach her. I told the supervisor that I was just checking on the status of DHR's investigation and that I was especially concerned about the teachers' situation at the school. The supervisor told me that "quite frankly," how DHR conducted its investigation was none of my business. I wasn't prepared for anything that callous, and I burst into tears. Apparently my tears unnerved the supervisor, because she softened a little and acknowledged that we had obviously been through a lot. Then she abruptly transferred my call to another investigator who was working with Ms. Williams on Angie's case.

I stopped crying long enough to tell that investigator about my conversations with Maggie, and I asked if she could call Maggie at home, since Maggie was so intimidated by her boss, the director, that she was afraid to call them. Then the investigator lashed out at me. She said she couldn't "buy" the intimidation story. The teachers were given a chance to talk with DHR, and if any of them had anything else to say, it was up to them to come forward, instead of "running around stirring up trouble." I tried to explain how my conversations with Maggie had come about, and that no one was running around stirring up trouble, but by that time I was crying so hard I couldn't talk. I blubbered a feeble "thank you" and hung up.

A few days later I wrote Ms. Williams a letter to tell her about my telephone call to her office. I told her I wanted to make it clear that I was not trying to tell DHR staff members how to conduct their investigation, but that the information Maggie had given me seemed significant enough that I thought DHR would want to know about it. I wrote, "Mr. Morgan had always encouraged us to call him with any thoughts, information, or questions, and I guess I assumed the parameters were the same with DHR's investigation."

I also explained how my conversations with Maggie had taken place. I told her Maggie had not even known that Angie was one of the victims. I assured her that Maggie "did not seek me out, nor did I seek her out. Neither of us was trying to 'stir up trouble.' You have to understand that the school community is a very small one. I constantly run into teachers, former teachers, board members, parents of current and past students, and people who know people at that school."

I ended my letter by promising that I would not bother her again and asked only that she let us know as soon as possible when the investigation was complete.

I managed to keep my promise not to bother DHR for over two months; then my curiosity got the best of me, so I called Ms. Williams to see where they were with their investigation. It was the same story. She still wasn't sure what DHR would be able to do, but she thought they would have everything wrapped up within a few weeks. I asked if she would let me know when that happened, and she agreed to notify me when some decision had been made.

Another month passed before I called Ms. Williams again. She told me DHR's investigation was in a "holding pattern." She acknowledged that this case was taking a long time, but she said she just had too many other new cases to work on. She said she hoped to have her report ready to turn in to her supervisor in two to three weeks. I asked what the procedure would be once she turned in her report. She didn't know. She said it was possible that her supervisor would make some kind of recommendation, or it might get passed on to a higher level.

I asked Ms. Williams if she would make a recommendation, since she was the one who had conducted the investigation. She wasn't sure. I asked what her recommendation would be if she could make one. She wouldn't say.

Ms. Williams went into the same old story about how she just didn't know what DHR could do. And then she floored me with a new twist. She said, "One thing working in favor of the school is the amount of time that has elapsed." She agreed that this certainly wasn't any fault of ours, because we had cooperated. It was DHR's responsibility, she admitted. "It's unfortunate, but that's just the way it is."

I asked Ms. Williams if DHR felt any responsibility at all to the parents of abuse victims. I asked if parents are typically notified of actions DHR takes against institutions where children are abused. The answer was no. Ms. Williams went on to say that DHR's investigations are confidential, and details are not disclosed to the family. Since we had repeatedly asked for information about Angie's case, however, she would be sure to let us know when their investigation was complete and what action, if any, DHR would take against the school. I hung up the telephone and cried one more time.

The next time I talked with Ms. Williams was two months later. By this time, 11 months had passed since Angie's disclosure. There was nothing new to report. Angie's case was still on hold; Ms. Williams still didn't know what DHR could do; and she still thought something would be decided within "two to three weeks." Once again, I asked if she would let me know when DHR decided to take action of some sort. Once again, she promised me she would. By that time, DHR had me on my knees. I felt completely defeated. I knew in my heart that DHR's investigation had been over before it had even begun.

I wrote in my journal, "What they've done to us is incredibly cruel . . . What hurts so much is that they've made it clear their investigation is none of our business . . . And now they're saying they can't do anything about the school because 'so much time has elapsed,' when they're the ones who let this thing drag out interminably. It is just beyond my comprehension that they're not going to take any action at all against the school. I never expected them to shut the place down. But if that school doesn't deserve at least a token fine, who does? How can DHR totally absolve the institution where this was allowed to happen—especially with all the other things that went on there?"

My journal continued: "What a wonderful philosophy of justice DHR has. Let time elapse and eventually everyone connected with the crime will leave. Maybe we should apply DHR's ideas to our entire justice system. It would be a great way to clear out the prisons. After all, if we wait long enough, every criminal will die a natural death. As far as I'm concerned, DHR's action, or lack or action, condones the crime committed against my child."

I was hurting pretty badly by that time, and to give myself time to heal, I forced myself into a state of self-decreed indifference and vowed I would not care whether the system worked or not. It was obvious that DHR was not going to do anything, so I kept telling myself it didn't matter. I tried not to think about it because I knew I could never accept the way things were turning out.

Over the weeks and months that followed, my anger cooled and I really did stop—for a while—caring about what I saw as DHR's travesty of justice. The problem was that I still needed some kind of closure. I still found myself wondering if DHR would ever officially close their case. Finally, three months after my last conversation with Ms. Williams, and 15 months after Angie's disclosure, I called Ms. Williams one last time.

Ms. Williams sounded surprised to hear from me. I asked about the status of DHR's investigation, and she replied, "Oh, we closed that case in July."

"In July!" I gasped. "But I talked to you in July and you promised you would call me when your investigation was complete!"

Ms. Williams stammered a little and replied that she had "just gotten sidetracked, I guess." She wouldn't volunteer any information, so I had to pull it out bit by bit. She finally told me that they had sent a letter to the school three months earlier, citing them for "harsh and unapproved disciplinary procedures" because several teachers had admitted that they sometimes yelled at children.

"What about the sexual abuse?" I asked. Ms. Williams replied that DHR had been "unable to find evidence to substantiate those charges." I was so shocked I could hardly speak. By this time, I had expected DHR to close the case without taking any action, because Ms. Williams had repeatedly said she didn't know what they could do. I had never dreamed they would conclude that the abuse never occurred!

"Are you saying you don't believe my child was molested?" I whispered. "I'm saying there is insufficient evidence to substantiate those charges," she answered. My old anger began to return. "But all along, you said you believed the girls were molested at the school. You just didn't know what DHR could do about it. What happened to change your mind?" I asked.

Ms. Williams began to hem and haw and said that her opinion didn't really matter. I asked whose opinion did matter, and she said she could not respond to that.

I asked her if the opinions of professionals such as the prosecuting attorney and Angie's therapist had mattered. Ms. Williams answered weakly, "Well, we were unable to come up with any witnesses or confessions." I asked if eyewitnesses and confessions were required before DHR considered abuse charges to be substantiated. Again, Ms. Williams stammered and said she thought there might be other evidence that would be acceptable, but she could not tell me what that evidence might be.

And then Ms. Williams stopped talking. I was so angry that I fired question after question at her, but the only answer I got in return was, "I can't really comment on that." Worn out and frustrated, I asked if I could have access to DHR's report. The report was confidential, she replied. She went on to say, however, that if I wanted a copy of the letter they sent the school, I could file a written request. She wasn't sure what they could send me, but she would refer my request to her supervisor.

Once more I was dumbfounded. It was as though all those earlier conversations and the promises she had made to keep me informed had never happened. I exploded. "I've taken the time to provide you with over a dozen pages of reports, which you requested, and now you're telling me I have to write yet one more letter, just to get information you promised me months ago?" That was the procedure, she replied.

I hung up the phone and I cried again. A few days later I mailed my letter to Ms. Williams requesting a copy of DHR's investigative report "regarding the sexual molestation of our daughter at [school] during the school year 1986–87." Several days later I received a brief note from Ms. Williams saying, "As requested, enclosed is a copy of the letter dated July 26, 1988, concerning findings related to the allegations received in August 1987. Thank you for your cooperation." Period.

The letter Ms. Williams enclosed cited the school for "unapproved disciplinary practices . . . revealed during the investigation: Staff in the past ('86–'87), have yelled at the children and made inappropriate or harsh comments to the children. Current staff have reported that yelling or loud voices are sometimes used by staff members. Your center is hereby cited for being in violation of 290-2-2-07(8) of Rules and Regulations for Day Care Centers . . ."

The charges of sexual abuse weren't even mentioned in the letter. I wondered if there was any rule or regulation against sexually molesting children at licensed child care facilities. Something was obviously terribly wrong with the system, and I promised myself I would do whatever I could to fix it. I didn't know what one mother could do, but I knew I had to try. I also knew I would have to wait until I calmed down to do anything. I was very angry, and I was afraid to lash out in anger. Whatever I did had to be well thought out if I was to be effective.

I decided to take it one day at a time. And so I waited. And I held mental debates with myself. And I prayed. Whatever I ended up doing, I wanted my motives to be right. I wanted to make sure my actions would help other families who, I believed, deserved more from DHR than we had gotten. I wanted to make the system do what it is supposed to do to protect our children. Also, I was already well into the manuscript of this book, and I didn't want to let myself be distracted from my writing unless I really thought I could make a difference.

Fighting City Hall

Two and a half months later, I wrote a letter to the office of the commissioner of DHR. In my letter I said that "DHR's investigation has left me agonizing over four unresolved questions which I hope you will address . . ."

My first question was how DHR could have come to the conclusion there was no evidence to substantiate that my daughter was sexually molested at the school. I pointed out that District Attorney Robert Wilson and Special Prosecutor J. Tom Morgan had told a roomful of parents at the school that their investigation left no doubt in their minds that kindergarten girls had been sexually abused at the school. The reason they would not prosecute the case was because confusion over which teacher had done what to which victim made convictions doubtful. I pointed out that Nancy McGarrah had filed a report with DHR, which, she told me, should have left no doubt in anyone's mind that my child was sexually molested and that the abuse took place at that preschool.

I asked if DHR's conclusion was based on the fact that no criminal indictments were sought against the individuals. If so, why didn't they close their investigation at the time when that decision was made? Or was it because, as Ms. Williams had implied, there were no eyewitnesses or confessions? "If so, DHR will substantiate few, if any, charges of child sexual abuse in the schools and centers they supposedly regulate," I wrote.

My second question concerned the accountability of an institution in which children are abused. I believed that DHR's refusal to address the issue of sexual abuse at the school set a dangerous precedent because it condoned the institution's shrugging off of responsibility for the actions of its employees.

At one point, Ms. Williams had defended the school by saying, "Abuse could, after all, happen anywhere." I asked if that absolved the school from responsibility, especially when there were so many factors that indicated irresponsibility on the part of the school's administration. I pointed out three examples.

The first was the lack of cooperation on the part of the director during the year my daughter was being abused. The second was the board's determination to keep the investigation secret, and the third was the school administration's continued refusal to acknowledge that the abuse charges were legitimate, after the charges became known, and its refusal to take steps to decrease the probability that such incidents would occur again.

For example, there had been one board meeting when Diane, my friend who sat on the school's board, suggested providing some sort of training to make staff members more aware of the nature of child abuse. The director immediately declared that the training was unnecessary because, she insisted, she and the teachers were fully aware of the symptoms of child sexual abuse. In fact, she added, it had already been discussed at their staff meetings. (Her claim was later refuted by teachers who said that child sexual abuse was never mentioned at their staff meetings.)

After the school's parents met with the officials from the district attorney's office, concerned parents asked for information and training about child sexual abuse for the school's parents and the staff. Their requests were refused by the school's administration. The parents finally initiated a program themselves and worked directly with the Georgia Council on Child Abuse to establish a protocol for the school.

My third question involved the manner in which DHR conducted its investigation. I talked about how long DHR had left the case on hold, only to end up using the passage of time as an excuse to do nothing. I told how we had been treated as outsiders, and even as adversaries. I disputed the contention that DHR's investigation was none of my business. I wrote, "As the mother of a child who is in her nineteenth month of therapy as a result of the abuse inflicted on her at that school, I take serious exception to DHR's position that its investigation is none of my business."

My fourth question was a very sensitive one, and I agonized a long time over whether to include it in my letter. Someone within the school's administration was married to a fairly high-ranking state employee. I didn't know if that could be significant or not. First of all, I didn't know how much influence that person really had. Second, I didn't want to believe that DHR's investigation of charges as serious as the sexual abuse of children could have been affected by inside influence. Nevertheless, the surprising end to DHR's investigation and the fact that the school's administration had never shown serious concern over the investigation left nagging questions in the back of my mind. I asked for "some assurance from you that [state employee] was not allowed to provide inappropriate input into DHR's investigation that might have contributed to the case being closed the way it was."

I ended my letter by saying, "The sexual molestation of a child is devastating in and of itself. The short-term effects on the child are heartrending. The long-term effects are terrifying. Adding the trauma of trying to understand why the system did not work has heaped agony on top of our anguish. As the mother of a child who was sexually assaulted at a regulated day care center, I believe I have a right to ask the questions I have asked.

"I also believe I have a right as a taxpayer in the state of Georgia. Child sexual abuse is a crime that is occurring at an alarming rate. Society seems reluctant to acknowledge, let alone understand, this problem, making child abuse one of the most tragically kept secrets of our time. Ironically, the public's failure to accept the sad realities of child abuse helps to perpetuate the crime. While society's indifference is hard to accept, indifference on the part of DHR is incomprehensible. What kind of faith can the public have in the regulatory powers of an agency that turns its back on a sexual abuse case such as this? The taxpayers of Georgia deserve something better.

". . . Child molestation is a horror no child should have to live through. My daughter deserved more from DHR than 'we just don't know what we can do,' 'abuse can, after all, happen anywhere,' and 'it's unfortunate, but that's just the way things are.' "

Everything I wrote in my letter could be confirmed by third parties. For example, District Attorney Wilson and Special Prosecutor Morgan could confirm the conclusions of the criminal investigation. Dr. McGarrah could confirm the effects Angie's abuse had had on her. Diane could confirm the cover-up that had taken place in the school's board meetings. In fact, I urged DHR to contact those individuals if they wanted to confirm statements made in my letter.

I sent the letter off in the first week of January, 1989, 17 months after Angie's disclosure. Then I settled down to wait once again.

About a week later, I received a reply from the commissioner's office saying my letter had raised numerous issues of "grave concern." An internal investigation was being initiated, and as part of that investigation, I might be contacted in the next few weeks. I was contacted. Two weeks later, I met with officials from the Office of Regulatory Services.

I had no idea what to expect when I walked into the office where the meeting was to be held. I didn't even know who would be there. I ended up meeting with two supervisors from Child Care Licensing. The senior person had a fat folder in front of her. On top lay my letter to the commissioner's office, well-marked with highlighter pen. She explained that they wanted to talk with me about their investigation of the preschool. She said it had been a frustrating investigation for them, and she outlined all the problems they had encountered, including never having received any information from the district attorney's office.

This claim floored me, and I said I would ask Mr. Morgan about that the next time I talked with him. She looked surprised, then quickly added that even if they had gotten the report, it didn't necessarily mean they would have reached a different conclusion.

The supervisor went on to say that they had never received parental statements for the other victim(s) and that they had had trouble tracking down the teacher who no longer lived in Atlanta. Besides, she said, the Department of Children and Family Services (DFCS) was legally responsible for the investigation. DHR's responsibility was limited to questions involving the license of the school. DFCS and DHR had an agreement that they would investigate cases like this together, but when DFCS decided not to investigate the school, DHR was left on its own. She also mentioned that the "time frame" of the investigation was a factor. In the end, she said, all they had to go on was "one child's allegations and a report from one psychologist." It was not enough to substantiate a charge as serious as sexual abuse.

Our case was not unusual, she continued. DHR receives many charges of abuse that can't be substantiated for lack of medical evidence, witnesses, or confessions. I was appalled when I heard this.

The supervisor said they were frustrated too, but their hands were tied, because abuse cases, without physical evidence, are "almost impossible to prove." She noted that DHR sometimes took action in the absence of physical evidence if they thought conditions at a facility might have been conducive to an offense being committed. I didn't ask her to elaborate on that point, though I probably should have.

Afterward, as I reflected on the meeting, I thought about the conditions that existed at Angie's school. Why didn't DHR consider them significant? I thought about events that had occurred during Angie's kindergarten year that were, in my opinion, examples of negligence.

There was the unauthorized field trip one teacher took the class on, which I have described earlier. There was another field trip when Angie was accidentally left behind. Angie went to the bathroom before the class left on a field trip, and when she came out, the teachers had gone without her. She ran down the hall to the office, but no one was there. The doors to all the other classrooms were shut. She ran to the door and saw the last of the children rounding the bend in the road. (It was a walking field trip to a nearby park.) So Angie ran out of the school, across the parking lot, down the road, and caught up with the class. The teachers had not even missed her until she appeared.

Another mother told me of an occasion when she came into the classroom during naptime and found the teacher asleep so soundly that she couldn't be awakened. The mother had reported it to the director but no action was taken.

Then there were the unexplained marks on Angie's arm. I had given Ms. Williams a picture of the injury, but it was never mentioned again. I had told Ms. Williams about all these incidents in the course of our telephone conversations. I also told her in writing about an incident when one of Angie's teachers had come into the bathroom when several girls were in there and stripped down to her underwear in front of the children. It had made me think about Mr.

Morgan's comments about the bathroom policies at the school. I wondered what more DHR wanted.

I also knew that Diane had filed two reports with DHR. The first she wrote as a mother, and in it she documented questionable conditions she had observed in the kindergarten room the year Angie was molested there. She wrote the second letter as a member of the school board, and documented the board's attempted cover-up after the members found out about the district attorney's investigation. I wondered why DHR had discounted those reports completely. They weren't even mentioned during my meeting with the DHR officials.

That meeting ended with the supervisor saying that she didn't know what else to do except to turn the case records over to their legal staff to see if the attorneys thought DHR had conducted their investigation properly.

A week after that meeting I talked with Mr. Morgan, and I asked him about DHR's claim that he had never filed a report with them. Mr. Morgan shook his head in disbelief, and said he had made it clear from the beginning that the district attorney's office would not write a report for DHR or send them his records. He said that he had talked with the DHR investigator many times by telephone. He had given her a lot of information in those conversations, and also told her she could come to the district attorney's office at any time to review his case file. In addition, he had told her she could interview anyone she wanted to in the district attorney's office to obtain verbal reports. The investigator did neither.

Shortly thereafter, I received a "documentation" letter from the commissioner's office that summarized my meeting with the child care licensing people. Everything in the letter was accurate except for a comment that I had "agreed to assist by obtaining a copy of the investigation report from the DeKalb County District Attorney's office, which was never received during the course of the investigation." That alarmed me, because I had made no such promise, and I felt it was unfair for DHR to shift that responsibility to me. I called the supervisor with whom I had met and repeated what Mr. Morgan had told me about his report. She sounded completely surprised, as though they had never talked with Mr. Morgan at all during their investigation. She asked me if I knew what information he had that they could look at. I suggested that she call him herself, because I didn't want to get caught between the two offices.

According to Mr. Morgan, no one from DHR ever called him after that conversation, and several weeks later, I received a letter from DHR saying that their internal review was complete. Their conclusion: "It does not appear that there is any more the department could have done in this case." None of my four questions was addressed specifically.

This time I didn't cry. I wasn't even disappointed, because it was the answer I had expected. I supposed DHR would continue to hide behind "confidentiality" to keep from providing me with the information I had requested about their investigation. I can't understand who was being protected by "confidentiality," though, since I was the mother of the victim. And I still don't know why DHR concluded that there was no evidence to substantiate the abuse charges, but if their only standard for the substantiation of child abuse allegations requires physical evidence, eyewitnesses, or confessions, their investigation conformed to their internal guidelines. The best I can hope for is that the questions I raised will form some sort of base on which future reforms can be built.

To other parents, there isn't much I can say. By the time DHR's investigation got started, I was asking questions I should have asked. I just couldn't get any answers. I can't think of anything else I could have done to lessen our frustration. Sometimes I am tempted to wonder if the parents of the other victims did the smartest thing by refusing to talk with DHR at all, but I really can't let myself believe that. I believe all parents have an obligation to cooperate with the system, at least initially. They should file a report with the proper authorities and at least give the system a chance to work.

The DHR supervisor told me in our meeting that their investigations are often hindered by parents who will not cooperate. Many parents choose not to file parental statements because they would rather "just forget the whole thing." If that is true, then they are all part of the problem. Cooperating with the authorities may not guarantee that the system will work, but failure to do so guarantees that it will not. Parents of sexual abuse victims should not be afraid to go on record. Once they do, however, they should not torment themselves by expecting too much. My family's experience shows that they may very well end up with nothing at all.

CHAPTER 14

The Civil Arena:
To Sue or Not to Sue

The idea of filing a civil suit against the individuals who hurt our child, and the institution at which they worked, was not the first thing my husband and I thought about. It didn't take long for the idea to present itself to us, however. Ironically, the first person to mention that option was Ms. Williams, the DHR investigator. She brought the subject up at the very first meeting we had with her, and she reminded me in subsequent conversations that taking civil action against the school was an option we could consider.

There were others who whispered "sue the bastards" in our ears as news of Angie's abuse became known to the people around us. We live in a litigious society, and most of us assume it is easy to leap into a lawsuit and collect damages from people who cause us injury and pain. The injury and pain inflicted on my child were obvious, and no one ever disputed that we had valid grounds for a civil suit.

We were encouraged when an attorney told us that civil cases are easier to try than criminal cases because the standard of proof is different. In a civil suit, one has only to "tip the scales of justice enough to convince a jury that the preponderance of evidence is on your side," whereas in a criminal case one has to convince a jury "beyond a reasonable doubt." It gave us a small degree of comfort to know that a civil suit was an option, but it was a long time before we seriously considered taking action.

We never thought of the civil suit as a way to collect monetary damages. For us it was a means of justice, a way of compelling the people who had hurt our daughter so badly to accept responsibility for their actions. If these individuals had been tried in criminal court, we would never have given a civil suit serious thought. It wasn't until the criminal case fell apart that we consulted an attorney to explore the feasibility of suing the individuals and the school.

Legal Advice

That first meeting was brief. The attorney told us a successful civil suit would have to show that Angie had suffered injury. That part would not be difficult. In addition, we would have to prove that the defendants had contributed to her injury either directly or through negligence. The fact that criminal charges were never pressed against Angie's teachers was a drawback, because many of the same problems the prosecutor had faced would have to be overcome in a civil suit. It didn't invalidate the civil suit, however, because the fact that there had been no indictments could not be introduced as evidence in the civil suit. Also, the burden of proof would be less rigorous. (In fact, I have since read and heard reports of civil cases involving sexual abuse that were won after defendants were acquitted in criminal trials.) Proving negligence on the part of the school would be more difficult, but not impossible. The fact that Angie had not been the only victim would be significant evidence in our favor.

The biggest problem with filing a civil case, however, came down to the issue of "deep pockets." The object of a civil suit is to win a cash settlement. Winning wouldn't accomplish anything if the defendants couldn't pay the awarded damages. In our case, none of the individuals were wealthy, and the school traditionally operated on a shoestring. Further, child care facilities are not required to carry liability insurance in Georgia. We could not know for certain if the school was insured until after the suit was filed, and then it would be too late to turn back.

My husband and I were more concerned with principles than money, but there was no way we could afford attorneys' fees out of pocket. Therefore, we had to find an attorney who was willing to take Angie's case on a contingency basis. The attorney we consulted was not willing to invest the time and effort this case would take unless there was someone with deep pockets who could pay the damages if the suit should be successful. In other words, the potential reward was not worth the risk. The attorney recommended that we not pursue a civil suit.

It seemed incredibly unfair, but at the same time, I was relieved. The idea of dragging Angie through a lengthy lawsuit bothered me. It had taken me a long time to get used to the idea of a criminal trial, but finally I decided it was something that had to be done. Mr. Morgan was a pro and I had a lot of confidence in him. The attorney we consulted later had never tried a case like Angie's. In addition, Angie would have had the county's victim advocate to help her through the criminal trial, whereas we would be on our own in a civil suit. Finally, a criminal case could have gone to trial within months, but civil cases typically take years to come to trial. It looked like a no-win situation.

As DHR's investigation of the school dragged on, the idea of filing the civil suit worked its way to the front of our minds again. The irresponsibility of the school's administration after news of the abuse became known strengthened our belief that something had to be done, even if we had to do it ourselves. The only thing we had control over was a civil suit. It was a need that arose from our frustration over the failure of the system to work the way it should have on its own. It represented a way of taking matters into our own hands.

And so, ten months after Angie's disclosure, we consulted another attorney. This time, we found someone with expertise in child abuse cases. We couldn't find anyone who had handled a case exactly like Angie's, but the attorney we chose had experience with custody cases that had involved child sexual abuse.

The attorney asked us to bring to our first meeting a picture of Angie and any documentation we had involving the case. When I went through my pictures of Angie to find one to take to the attorney, I was startled by how clearly they reflected the effects Angie's ordeal had had on her. I found a picture taken right before she entered kindergarten. She was an angelic five-year-old with an exuberant smile and shining eyes. Then I found the picture that was taken at school just months later, in her kindergarten year. She had a smile on her face, but it was the forced kind of smile that comes from saying "cheese." There was no smile at all in her eyes, and her hair hung dull and limp around her tired little face. It was obvious my angel had turned into a rag doll in just a matter of months.

The latest picture I had of Angie was one taken just three and a half months after her disclosure. Her natural, spontaneous smile was back, but the circles under her tired eyes reflected her struggle to cope with the terror and pain she was experiencing at that time. The story those three pictures told was so dramatic that I took all three to show the attorney.

The attorney listened as we outlined the events of the previous eighteen months, and then she tried to discourage us from pursuing the civil case. She started out by saying that child sexual abuse cases are almost impossible to prove in court unless there is physical evidence. Angie would have no credibility before a jury, the attorney continued, simply because she was a child and it would be her word against the word of adults. The defendants could "get up in court and lie between their teeth," the attorney said, and the jury would still believe them, because people just naturally believe that adults are more truthful than children. The fact that Angie was so bright would also work against her, the attorney continued.

I could hardly believe my ears. She explained that the defense would turn Angie's intelligence into precocity and make the jury believe her story of abuse had been born in an overactive imagination. "But," I protested, "if she were less intelligent or less verbal, they would say she wasn't smart enough to know the difference between telling the truth and telling a lie!" "That's right," the attorney agreed, and I was exasperated at this catch-22.

The attorney went on to say that the trial would be messy because the abuse had occurred at a school, and the defense would bring in all the other children who had been in Angie's class, as well as their parents, to testify in support of the teachers and school. We, however would have a hard time convincing people to come forward in our behalf. I found that hard to believe, but the attorney insisted that people who were supportive now would "disappear" when it came time to go to court.

And then we got down to the deep pockets question again. Because there were no obvious deep pockets, the attorney explained, we would have to sue "everyone we could get our hands on." That would include everyone who had served on the preschool's board during the year the abused occurred and every year thereafter. That way we could collect damages from a lot of different people. The problem, though, was that having so many defendants would make the case very messy, lengthy, and expensive. A number of defense attorneys would be involved, and that would be especially hard on Angie.

There is still a lot of room for improvement when it comes to protecting children during criminal trials in Georgia, but when it comes to civil cases, children have virtually no protection at all. The defense attorney in a criminal case cannot question a child victim until he or she cross-examines the child in court; but in a civil case, the child may be subjected to lengthy, brutal depositions. Depositions are statements made under oath in advance of the trial, and they may be presented in court as evidence.

Cross-examination of a child victim in court is conducted in front of a jury, so the defense attorney has to be careful not to turn the sympathy of the jury toward the child. No jury is present, however, during a deposition, and this gives the defense attorney much more leeway as he or she tries to tear apart the victim's story. The defense will try to wear the victim down—and time is on their side, because there is no limit on how long a deposition can last. I heard of one four-year-old who was grilled during a deposition for over eight hours. In addition, defendants have the right to be present during a deposition, so children may come face to face with offenders without the comfort of knowing that police officers are there to protect them.

According to the attorney we consulted, Angie would have been subjected to depositions from a number of defense attorneys. Theoretically, the purpose of a deposition is to obtain information, and all of the attorneys could have questioned Angie at the same time. Realistically, however, each of them would have deposed Angie at a different time in an effort to wear her out and to get us to drop the case. As the attorney told us, they would "put her through absolute hell" because as defense attorneys that would be the smart thing for them to do. "I know that's what I'd do if it were me," she added.

For the first time, I began to realize that our American legal system is not necessarily designed to ferret out truth and justice. Rather, it is designed to reward the strength and persistence of ad-

versaries. The person with the greatest personal and financial resources is the one who wins the contest—or even gets to compete
in the first place.

The attorney said that if we really wanted her to, she would
discuss our case with her partners to see if the law firm was willing
to take it on. She also wanted to talk with Mr. Morgan about his
criminal investigation, and she suggested we talk with Dr. McGarrah
about the effects a trial would have on Angie. We said that we wanted
her to proceed, and we agreed to meet again after she reviewed all
the information. Then the attorney concluded by asking us to consider dropping the idea of filing a civil suit. We would be better off
just forgetting what had happened and getting on with the rest of
our lives, she said. As for Angie, it was unfortunate but she "just
had to learn a little earlier than most kids that life isn't always fair."

That last remark, delivered with no feeling whatsoever, stunned
me, and I walked back to my car in a daze. I think that deep inside
I knew I did not want to proceed with the civil suit, but I had a hard
time accepting that end to our last hope of ever seeing some kind
of justice done. Not being able to file a civil suit was strike three,
and it really hurt to have to walk away, knowing that the people
who had sexually assaulted my child were going to get off free and
clear. I wondered how many other little girls were going to be hurt
by them because the system didn't work.

We went back for that second meeting with the attorney, but I
had cold feet about the civil case long before we got there. The low
probability of winning a large cash settlement didn't bother me. It
would have been nice to have Angie's extensive medical and counseling bills paid, but I knew there was no way I could ever profit
from the settlement personally—it would be too much like blood
money. All I wanted was to see Angie's offenders answer, in court,
under oath, for what they did to her and to stop them from doing
it to others.

One of the things that bothered me was having to sue so many
other people. Diane had been on the school's board. Would she have
been included in the suit? I never asked that question, but I assume
the attorney would have said yes, because she told us it would have
to be "all or nothing." We couldn't pick and choose, she had said
at the first meeting. In no way could I consider dragging Diane into
a lawsuit when she had fought the rest of the board so hard to get
them to take a stand against child abuse at the school. And as much

as Carla had hurt me, I didn't want to include her in the suit either. Her husband was a hardworking, self-employed businessman, and a lawsuit could have wiped out the family. I was angry with the school. I believed the school's administration had acted irresponsibly, but when it came down to thinking about the individuals, I knew I couldn't live with myself if we tried to assuage our own pain by destroying others in the process.

Even greater than my concern for these others was my fear of what a civil case would do to Angie. I did talk to Dr. McGarrah about the effect a trial might have on Angie. Dr. McGarrah sketched personality profiles of several types of children and how each typically reacts to the courtroom situation. She went on to say that some children benefit therapeutically from a court experience. Children who are very bright, verbal, and do well with role-play situations can be helped. We both agreed that Angie fit that profile. We also agreed that Angie was still having trouble finding closure, and that a trial might help with that.

Dr. McGarrah said the situation was comparable to that of a child who waits anxiously for months for the birth of a sibling, until Mom goes to the hospital, the baby is stillborn, and she comes home empty-handed. A child in that situation will often have trouble coming to terms with what has happened. It helps if the family has a funeral or a memorial service for the baby, because it gives the older child an ending of sorts. A court case can do something similar for children who have been molested. Whether the civil suit is won or lost doesn't seem to matter to the child. In either case, going to court marks the "end" for them and it helps them put their ordeal behind them. Although a trial would not be easy on Angie, it could be therapeutic for her, Dr. McGarrah said.

Despite this conversation, though, the attorney's description of how the defense attorneys would try to tear my child apart to discredit her story haunted me. I could not bear to think of Angie being dragged through deposition after deposition, month after month, and I knew I couldn't file the civil suit.

Nevertheless, my husband and I did go back for the second meeting with the attorney. I guess we just needed her death-blow to make it final in our minds. The attorney started out by saying that she had talked with the prosecutor about our case and she and her partners had spent a lot of time trying to decide what to do. She said she wanted to make it very clear that no one doubted that our daughter had been sexually molested and that she deserved damages, but the firm had decided to decline the case because the potential payoff just didn't justify the amount of resources they would have to commit to the case. It would be a hard case to win, and if they did win they would have nothing to show for it. She said, "I thank you for bringing this opportunity to us, but we have to decline," and then she handed us the file of information we had given her. Case dismissed.

Civil Remedies in General

So what does that mean for other parents of molestation victims? I struggled with that question, because our experience with those two attorneys left me with a lot of unanswered questions. Some of what they told us made sense; some of it I just couldn't buy.

To get those questions answered, I decided to seek a third opinion. I interviewed Mr. Thomas G. Sampson, an Atlanta trial lawyer, about civil cases involving child sexual abuse. Mr. Sampson had successfully litigated a highly publicized case on behalf of two girls who were sexually assaulted on a school bus en route to a state school for the handicapped. My conversation with Mr. Sampson centered on two issues—what factors contribute to the probability of a civil suit being successful and what effect such a trial would have on the victim.

In Mr. Sampson's opinion, psychological evidence presented by credible expert witnesses is critical in a child sexual abuse case. Physical evidence would make the case stronger, but its absence would not be fatal to the case. The fact is that physical evidence is lacking in most sexual molestation cases, while psychological evidence has gained credibility in courtrooms in recent years. Sexually abused children exhibit a distinct psychological profile. The abuse syndrome, presented by credible expert witnesses, can outweigh the absence of physical evidence.

If physical evidence does exist, timing is critical. A child who experiences physical trauma should be examined as soon as possible after the assault. Some physical evidence, such as a discharge specimen, has to be obtained within 48 hours. It would also be important to a civil case to have expert witnesses backed up by testimony from other credible adult witnesses. Civil suits are based on the questions of damage and accountability. The psychological evidence is critical in establishing the fact that the abuse (damage) has occurred. Then, testimony by additional adults indicating who committed the assault is needed to link the defendants to that damage (accountability). The testimony of a verifying adult, along with the psychological evidence, can effect the successful prosecution of a civil case, even when physical evidence does not exist.

As in criminal prosecution, hearsay evidence is admissible in civil court in Georgia. Any information about the abuse that the child has disclosed to an adult can be presented in court. The outcome of the criminal investigation, however, is not admissible, so that the absence of an indictment and/or conviction has no direct bearing on the outcome of the civil case. Neither would the results of any regulatory investigation bear directly on the civil case.

One factor that will affect a civil case is the length of time between the occurrence and the reporting of the abuse. The sooner the crime is reported, the stronger the evidence will be. Evidence of multiple incidents of abuse and/or other victims would also strengthen the case.

I asked Mr. Sampson if it is standard procedure to "sue everyone in sight." He explained that the typical strategy in civil cases is to "sue everyone who initially appears to have some reasonable nexus" to the case. This strategy protects the case from falling prey to the statute of limitations. Also, it is easier to release individuals from the suit during the discovery process than it is to try to bring additional defendants into the suit after the fact. The existence of evidence that will support a successful civil case is only part of the equation parents must consider when deciding whether to file a lawsuit. Parents also have to consider what effects a civil suit might have on their child. Mr. Sampson agreed with Dr. McGarrah that the courtroom experience can provide therapeutic benefit for victims in some cases. Those benefits do not come without considerable risk, however.

Except for the hearsay statute in child abuse cases, the state of Georgia provides no special consideration for child witnesses in civil court. The victims are afforded no protection whatsoever, so it is up to the child's attorney to present the case in a way that will protect the child as much as possible from additional emotional trauma.

If the child will not be a witness in the case, the attorney can file a motion to keep the defense from subjecting the victim to a deposition. If the child is going to testify, however, there is no way he or she can be protected from being deposed. The defense is entitled to the deposition, and any defendant in the case may be present during the deposition. There are no limitations on the time or the conditions under which it takes place, so all the child's attorney can do is file motions seeking protections for the victim. For example, if a number of defense attorneys try to depose the child at different times, the child's attorney can request that all the attorneys question the child at the same time, arguing that repetitive questioning would result in unnecessary emotional trauma for the child. How the court rules on those motions for protection will depend entirely on the judge.

As in the case of criminal prosecution, parents of molestation victims should ask their attorneys what kinds of examinations, if any, the child will be subjected to in a civil case. In Georgia, victims are not protected from multiple examinations in the civil arena, as they are in criminal court. Defense attorneys can request that independent medical and/or psychological examinations be conducted by their own expert witnesses. It will be up to the victim's attorney to protect the child by filing motions of his or her own to block the defense's request. Whether the child is in fact protected will depend upon whether the judge understands the trauma that multiple examinations inflict on the victim.

Parents of molestation victims have no say about the people who will conduct criminal and regulatory investigations of their child's case. In civil court, however, the choice of the attorney who represents their child rests squarely on the parents' shoulders. Parents should take that decision very seriously, because an attorney who is sensitive to the welfare of the victim is the only thing standing between that child and additional emotional trauma. The attorney must be willing to fight for the child and protect him or her to the greatest extent possible, especially in states like Georgia, where the child victim can be legally thrown to the wolves in civil court.

In searching for an attorney to represent their child, parents have to find someone with trial experience, experience in litigating sexual abuse cases, and sensitivity to the special needs of the sexually abused client. How do parents find such an attorney? Primarily by word of mouth. Referrals from local bar associations can point the parent toward experienced trial lawyers, but they probably won't help find an attorney with expertise in sexual abuse cases. There is a big difference between litigating auto accident claims and litigating cases of child molestation! A better source of referrals would be the network of professionals who deal with child sexual abuse—the child's therapist, social agencies, child advocacy groups, or special prosecutors.

Once parents find an attorney with whom they and their child feel comfortable, they should ask the same kinds of questions they would ask the prosecuting attorney in a criminal case. They should listen carefully to the advice of the attorney and the child's therapist and keep in mind that each case is unique. As in the criminal prosecution of abuse cases, generalizations are hard to come by. In the end, parents have to weigh the benefits and risks of a civil suit and go with their gut feelings about what will be in the best interests of their child in the long run.

PART IV

What to Expect from Yourself

Give us grace and strength to forbear and to persevere. Give us courage and gaiety and the quiet mind, spare to us our friends, soften to us our enemies.

—Prayer from the memorial to Robert Louis Stevenson
in St. Giles Cathedral, Edinburgh, Scotland

INTRODUCTION

L ife is harder on some of us than on others, but no one escapes without some hurt and tragedy. A near-fatal accident in my infancy, followed by the breakup of my parents' marriage, ensured that my life would be no exception. Looking back on the sad events of my life, I can honestly say that none of them—accidents, family hostilities, a home destroyed by fire, serious illnesses, and even the deaths of people I loved very much—were as hard to cope with as the sexual abuse of my child.

Since Angie's disclosure, I have worked through phases of mourning much like those people experience around the death of a loved one. My initial reaction was disbelief. Then came periods of guilt, anger, depression, and finally, after a long, hard struggle, acceptance. The difference between coping with death and coping with the sexual assault of a child is that we, as a society, are better prepared to deal with death—a corpse and a funeral help bring home the awful reality that death has taken place. Also, family, friends, and acquaintances offer immediate support. This is not true when child molestation strikes a family.

It is very difficult for the parents of child sexual abuse victims to work through the phases of mourning and reach that final stage of acceptance. I can look back now and see how I wavered back and forth between the different stages without being able to find any real resolution of my turmoil. It was difficult to work through my grief and find a feeling of closure. For months, the only consistency in my life was a persistent feeling of pain. Sometimes it was a muted ache, sometimes the sharpest agony, but the hurt was always there.

Support systems for the families of molestation victims are sorely lacking. I guess it's because so few people understand the crime that most can't comprehend the effects it has on the victim and her or his family. And so I was, for the most part, on my own.

Considering the effects Angie's abuse had on her, the reactions of others, and our frustrating encounter with the system, it should not be hard to understand the disruption I felt in every corner of my life. It affected my relationships with friends, coworkers, and others. It affected my relationships with my daughter and my husband. And it affected my relationship with myself, as it ripped me apart emotionally, physically, and spiritually.

During the months following Angie's disclosure, I poured so much energy into attending to her needs that I never took time to consider my own. Even now, I feel self-conscious talking about my own pain, fears, and anger because it was Angie who was the victim. Her pain, fears, and anger were overwhelming. She was the victim, and it was natural to focus on her.

Yet we parents of molestation victims need to acknowledge that we are victims too. When someone hurts our child, we hurt. And we have a right to feel anger, bitterness, helplessness, and all the other emotions that come with that hurt. We need to acknowledge our own feelings, accept them, and work them through, because that is the only way we can sustain the level of strength we have to muster to help our child put a childhood back together.

CHAPTER 15

MOODS OF MOURNING

As I went through my own phases of mourning, my emotions were often mirror images of Angie's. As I watched the emotional turmoil raging inside my daughter, I struggled with my own fear, anger, guilt, and depression. My emotions often seemed to merge with Angie's until I felt as though our grief was one. I could understand and accept Angie's feelings, but I continually fought my own. I thought that giving my full attention to Angie would speed her recovery. Now I see that denying my own feelings did not help either one of us and only prolonged my own mourning.

By the time Angie disclosed her abuse, I had spent almost a year trying to solve the mystery of her sudden change in personality. One would think that my pent-up frustration would have burst into instantaneous anger when Angie's sudden disclosure answered the questions I had been asking for so long. It didn't. My immediate reaction, instead, was calm, analytical disbelief.

When we are injured physically or psychologically, our first response is shock. Shock is a reflex defense mechanism that numbs us and temporarily shields us from the pain. A friend once told me about her husband's injury during the Vietnam war. He was wounded when the shrapnel from an exploding grenade tore into his neck. The first thing he remembers about his injury is how puzzled he felt when he realized that his arm, which had been in the process of lifting a cigarette to his mouth, was suddenly dangling at his side. An instant later he felt blood spurting from the wound and realized he had been hit. Calmly, he held the severed vein together with his hand and kept himself from bleeding to death until he was rescued.

We protect ourselves from psychological trauma in much the same way. We go into shock. We feel numb and our minds seem to go blank. Yet years later we can remember minute details about that moment of shock. And so I can remember how I reacted to the news that my daughter had been molested.

First Came Denial—

I was out of town attending a seminar when Angie disclosed during therapy that she had been sexually abused by her kindergarten teacher. (The involvement of the second teacher was revealed later.) My husband told me of Angie's disclosure that evening when I called home. I can still remember every detail of that conversation. I remember my physiological response—the tightening in my chest and how heavy the telephone felt in my hand. I remember the sound of my husband's voice and how quiet everything suddenly became, as though I had just entered a great vacuum. The sounds from the conference center's kitchen and dining room dimmed into the distant background, and I was conscious of each breath I took.

I didn't cry. The tears did not come until much later. Instead, I calmly walked into the dining room and joined my colleagues for dinner. My cabin-mates at the conference were two of my best friends from work. As the three of us walked back to the cabin after dinner, I repeated the conversation I'd had with my husband. I quickly added that I was sure there must be some misunderstanding. I wondered if Angie was overreacting to an accidentally misplaced touch by the teacher.

I knew the teacher was very physical with the children. She was always hugging them, kissing them, and holding them on her lap. She would scoop them up in her arms and tell them, "Come on, give me a big body hug." A body hug meant that the children wrapped their legs around her waist and their arms around her neck and hugged her as tightly as they could with the whole body. It seemed harmless enough at the time.

My friends reacted as calmly as I did. They assured me that it couldn't be anything serious. And that was the end of it. We spent the rest of the week concentrating on the class we were attending. It was a very intense week of learning and all of our time was spent either in class or studying. With my friends' help, I managed to put Angie's disclosure out of my mind. Looking back now, I am amazed that I was able to concentrate on financial analysis for the next three days. But I did—except at night when I finally crawled into bed, turned out the lights, and tried to go to sleep.

That's when the tears came. I couldn't put into words the thought behind my tears. It was just a deep feeling of foreboding. At night when I was alone, I knew that what had happened to Angie was very serious. I hardly slept for the rest of that week.

After a five-hour exam at the end of the seminar, I ate lunch, climbed into my car, and headed toward Atlanta. I can hardly remember the trip home. The car must have been on automatic pilot, because my mind was swirling with thoughts of Angie. I wanted desperately to have her there to hold. I wanted to tell her I loved her and would make everything all right for her. I felt sorry for my husband because he had been there alone when all this came up. How were they doing? What was waiting for me in Atlanta? What would happen next? It was the longest 90-minute drive of my life.

My husband and I spent that weekend going over and over what had happened so far. There wasn't much to talk about. All we knew was that Dr. McGarrah was taking what Angie told her "very seriously." Neither of us fully understood what that meant. Everything else we talked about was speculation. We knew that we were to be contacted by the DHR, the DFCS, and the police. We didn't know what that meant either. We were careful to keep our discussions out of the way of Angie's ears. I hoped she would not sense my anxiety.

I met with Dr. McGarrah after the weekend. I was groping for answers, but I didn't know what questions to ask. The main thing I remember was telling Dr. McGarrah that I believed Angie when she said her teacher had touched her in "places she shouldn't," but I wondered if it was some sort of misunderstanding on Angie's part. I told Dr. McGarrah how the teacher was always hugging and kissing the children. Maybe she had inadvertently picked Angie up the wrong way or something. Dr. McGarrah's response was quick and decisive. "Don't you believe that for a moment," she said. Angie had already described to Dr. McGarrah three specific incidents when she had been molested by the teacher, so Dr. McGarrah knew details I didn't.

I'm not sure why I tended to defend Angie's abuser at the beginning. Maybe it was my way of denying that this could have happened to my child. Also, I think I was afraid to fly off the handle and unjustly accuse anyone of something so serious. I immediately recalled a news program that had been on TV several years earlier about a college-age baby-sitter who had (supposedly) been falsely accused of molesting a child in her care. The program was so one-sided that I couldn't help feeling sympathy for the young woman and disdain for the child's parents. They were criticized for reporting the suspected abuse to the authorities instead of confronting the baby-sitter first and giving her a chance to defend herself. I didn't want to identify with those parents.

Another reason I had a hard time believing that Angie's teacher was a bona fide child molester was my complete ignorance about child molestation. I would never in a million years have suspected sexual abuse. The teacher Angie named as her primary offender did not fit the stereotype of a child molester at all. She was female. She was young. She was always sweet and smiling and very affectionate with the children. I remember her laughing and telling me, "I'm the one the children love because [other teacher] is the one who disciplines them. I'm easy on them."

The all-or-nothing myth also kept me from accepting Angie's disclosure immediately. That is, I was confused by the inconsistencies in Angie's behavior during her kindergarten year.

She had said that she hated her teachers. But there were also times when she seemed to adore them, and I couldn't help but remember the good days, in between the bad, when she had enjoyed school. I remembered the page in Angie's yearbook where the children had been asked what they had liked most about kindergarten. Angie was quoted as saying, "I love my teachers." (Months later she explained, "I had to say that, Mom. I hated them, but I *had* to say that.")

My period of denial was fairly short-lived. The truth began to penetrate my defenses within days of my conversation with Dr. McGarrah. As Angie disclosed more and more details of the abuse, it became indisputably clear that this was no misinterpretation of a misplaced touch. My daughter had been sexually molested on at least three occasions. The abuse had been deliberate and mean. I began to realize there had been another side to her teacher's personality, and it was not the sweet, smiling side I had seen the year before.

I wondered how I could have been so blind. Why couldn't I have seen what was going on? I shuddered when I realized that I would never have known Angie was a victim of sexual abuse if she had not come forward on her own and talked about it. I shed my armor of denial and plunged headlong into guilt.

Then, Guilt

I have the kind of conscience that would make Jiminy Cricket look like an amateur, so guilt came easily for me. Since Angie was molested in a preschool, my first wave of guilt stemmed from being a working mother. If I had been at home with her "where I belonged," I reasoned, this would never have happened. The abuse occurred during Angie's kindergarten year, so I tried to defend myself by thinking that it could just as well have happened in any other kindergarten. It was a feeble defense, because the primary reason I had left her in that particular school for kindergarten was its day care. If I had not been working, she would have been in another school.

Working motherhood can be a guilt trip in the best of circumstances, although I had not indulged much in the feeling during Angie's early years. I had been able to juggle home and work fairly well and I never felt that my working had detrimental effects on Angie. All that changed, though, when things began to unravel during Angie's kindergarten year. During one of our conferences that year, the school's director suggested that Angie's stress was a reflection of my own work-related stress. I knew that wasn't true, but it still made me stop and contemplate the possibility. Maybe the previous five years had not gone as smoothly as I thought. Maybe my working during Angie's early years was catching up with us and she was beginning to pay the price. The director and teachers had deliberately directed my search for answers to Angie's unhappiness away from school and toward home. I took the bait, and by the time Angie disclosed her abuse months later, I already had a foundation of guilt on which to build.

I agonized over whether I could have done more to help Angie during the year she was abused. It was hard to defend myself against Angie's anger because I had the same questions she did. Why had I not been able to protect her? I was her mother and it was my job to keep her safe. Somehow, I had failed her. I also struggled with doubts about the quality of my relationship with Angie. We had always been very close. We always communicated openly and clearly with each other. Now I wondered why she had not told me what was happening. Was there something wrong with our relationship? As Angie struggled with her feeling of guilt, I reassured her that what happened to her was not her fault. I was unable to convince myself that the same held true for me.

With a little help from my friends, I found a lot of other reasons to feel guilty during the months following Angie's disclosure. Even people who meant well were unintentionally accusatory as they tried to understand how this could have happened to my daughter. After a moment of shock, one man blurted out, "Well, I guess that's the price you pay for having such a beautiful daughter." (That must have been a corollary to the old "Women who dress provocatively deserve to be raped" theory.) Another person (a teacher) quizzed me on whether I had done anything to antagonize Angie's offenders. Her hypothesis was that they had abused Angie to get back at me for something I did.

My greatest source of guilt was my friends, who constantly pressured me to "just forget it." I was criticized for wanting to see Angie's offenders prosecuted for their crime. I was advised to "drop the charges" and get the district attorney's office to stop its investigation. The pressure was even greater when we considered filing a civil suit. I was reprimanded for making too much of Angie's experience. One friend pointed out that "a lot worse things happen to children" and I should "just be grateful she doesn't have leukemia or something." I was also advised to stop thinking about it so much because I was making it harder for Angie to forget. I was supposed to "move on with life" and pretend nothing had happened.

Most people don't understand that parents of molestation victims have a need and a right to work through our grief. We can't be expected to steel our minds into forgetting it happened. To do so would be unhealthy for ourselves and our children. Further, to do so would be virtually impossible considering the many reminders we face as we "move on with life."

For one thing, TV and newspapers constantly supply reminders, as they increasingly tune in to child sexual abuse. Each time I see a news report about child molestation, I identify with the victims and their families and relive our own experience. I never know when such reminders will invade my life.

For example, I was having lunch with a customer and another representative from my company when the conversation unexpectedly turned to child sexual abuse. The topic was on everyone's mind at that time because a highly publicized molestation case was making the headlines every day. So there I was, trying to conduct "business as usual" in the midst of a debate over whether the sentence the alleged offender received was unduly harsh!

Even recreational TV brings back memories. One evening, nine months after her disclosure, Angie turned on one of her favorite sitcoms to find that it was about a child encountering a child molester at camp. I debated whether to let her watch the show. Angie said she wanted to see it and I decided I couldn't protect her forever from reminders of her own experience. We watched the program together. Angie was very quiet during the show. Afterwards she became agitated and had a hard time settling down to sleep. I could understand her reaction, but the intensity of my own response surprised me. The show was very low-key—it was, after all, a prime-time family sitcom. Nevertheless, I struggled to control the tears that welled up in my eyes throughout the half-hour show. I felt extremely anxious, and like Angie, I had a hard time sleeping that night.

Reminders were not always that innocuous. Three months before Angie and I watched that TV program, an envelope addressed to both of us came in the mail. I casually slit it open and saw an invitation to a baby shower—a baby shower for one of Angie's kindergarten teachers! I freaked out. My whole body started to shake. I shoved the invitation into my pocket and ran for the bedroom. I sat there for a long time and just stared at the invitation. I felt as though I were floating through some surrealistic, off-Broadway experimental play. Real life just couldn't be this bizarre!

Other reminders are much more subtle. I may be going through Christmas ornaments when I find a decoration Angie made in kindergarten. Anything at all that reminds me of her kindergarten reminds me of the abuse she suffered there. Like Angie, I have encountered strangers who resembled her offenders and felt an immediate aversion to them. And I still see people who were or are associated with the school. I never know when a cue will bring memories to mind and tears to my eyes.

Then, Fear

Like Angie, I also lived with fear after her disclosure. And my fears, like Angie's, revealed themselves in nightmares. My nightmares were usually variations of the same theme—Angie was drowning and I was unable to help her. In my dreams I would watch her fall into water of some kind—a pool, a well, a muddy pond—and find myself unable to save her for one reason or another. I couldn't swim, or I was too far away to get to her in time, or there was some other restraint. Other times I would dive in after her and be unable to find her because the water was too murky. In one of my dreams, Angie was floating peacefully on a rubber raft on a clear, calm lake. Her raft drifted behind a wooden diving platform and out of my sight. I waited for her to come around the other side, but she never reappeared. I swam to the platform and found to my horror that she had disappeared completely.

One of my most terrifying dreams began with Angie and me walking through a beautiful woods together. We were having a wonderful time. She was laughing and happy. And then we came to a tumbling, rocky stream. It wasn't wide, but the water was fast. I stepped onto the rocks that led to the other side of the stream. As I turned around to take Angie's hand, she slipped and fell into a pit I had not even noticed. I could hear her screams as she plummeted into the hidden cavern. I heard a crack from far below, and then there was silence.

I can't describe the sense of panic I felt when I awoke from some of those dreams. I could never go back to sleep afterwards. I would get up and go to Angie's room to make sure she was there and safe. I would kiss her on the forehead, tuck her in, and say a prayer of protection for her. Sometimes I sat on the floor next to her bed and watched her sleep. Other times I spent the rest of the night reading, writing, cooking, smocking dresses for Angie, or doing whatever it took to distract myself.

I didn't experience the same kind of terror Angie suffered, but I still worried about her. Angie was terrified that her former teachers would come back to get her. I knew that was not a serious threat, but I wondered if they might try to get to Angie and intimidate her into silence. I was worried about one teacher in particular. Would she be foolish enough to try to talk to Angie? I wasn't sure. That fear was heightened after the teachers and the school's board found out about the investigation.

The day after Mr. Morgan interviewed the first teacher, we received the first of a string of hang-up telephone calls. Was it a coincidence? We had no way of knowing. My husband and I sat long into the night discussing how to protect Angie. We decided not to let her answer the telephone for a while, and we considered getting an unlisted number. (I learned later that the parents of the other confirmed victim did change their telephone number after one of the teachers called several times.) We also decided to talk with the principal of Angie's current school to make sure she would not be allowed to leave school with anyone who had not been properly authorized by us. And we asked to be notified immediately if anyone not associated with the school tried to approach Angie on the playground or in the halls.

Did we overreact? Maybe so, but we were scared.

My husband and I had other fears as well. One was the fear that the school or individuals connected with the school could somehow come back and sue us if Angie's teachers were not ultimately convicted. It seemed far-fetched, but the hostility of the school's administration was extreme. (I heard through the grapevine months later that someone at the school had threatened to "sue anyone and everyone who talked about the investigation" after finding out that the district attorney's office had decided not to prosecute.)

Dr. McGarrah told me about one case in which the parents of a molestation victim were successfully sued for not reporting the abuse. The suit was brought by parents of a second child who was subsequently molested by the same offender. So parents can be "damned if they do or damned if they don't."

Closely related to our concerns about legal aspects was the fear of publicity. One part of me wanted to see the story of Angie's abuse made public so that her offenders would know they had not gotten away with their crime entirely. It would also be a way to get the message out that child sexual abuse can and does happen to anyone. Those thoughts were overruled by my concern over the effects the publicity would have on Angie. It was ironic that the need to protect my child also provided protection for the people responsible for hurting her.

Parents of molestation victims have a lot to worry about. Some of my fears were short-lived; others haunt me even now. Many of them were fears of the unknown—about the long-term effects Angie's abuse might have on her. Angie's emotional health was so fragile following her abuse that I worried about her ability to cope with any additional traumas life might throw at her. Will she be more likely to engage in early sexual activity or drugs? Will she be able to form normal, healthy relationships later in life? Could she become a child molester herself? Her six-year-old talk about wanting to "just go ahead and die" haunted me, and I wondered if she would be more likely to become a teenage suicide statistic as a result of her abuse. I worried about how others would respond to her if they found out about her victimization. Would she be stigmatized? Would it affect her academic and social development?

The more I read and learned about child sexual abuse, however, the more I realized that many of my fears were legitimate. Victims of child molestation are not automatically condemned to a life of crime or deviancy, but their abuse does place them at greater risk than their nonabused contemporaries. One fear that continues to haunt me is that Angie might become a victim of sexual assault again. The probability of rape or additional incidences of child molestation is greater for victims of child sexual abuse than for the general public.*

It is important to recognize that this threat of revictimization does not mean that the victim does anything to invite assault. In some cases, subsequent abuse occurs because the perpetrator knows the victim has already been assaulted. Victims may be perceived as easy marks; offenders see them as "damaged goods," already "experienced," or less likely to defend themselves or to be believed if they report subsequent assaults.

Another element that puts molestation victims at risk for later assault is the "victim syndrome." Sexual abuse shatters a child's self-esteem, and a person who projects an image of low self-worth is more likely to be targeted for assault than one who is self-assured and confident. In my opinion, this is the primary reason that long-term therapy is critical for victims of child molestation.

My fear of stigmatization was also a legitimate one. Angie still has trouble accepting herself because she feels different from her friends. Recently she explained, "It's like all the other children are in the sunshine and I'm always stuck in the shade." Would Angie's

---

*   Researcher Diana Russell reports that 65% of incest victims and 61% of extra-familial abuse victims were sexually assaulted later in life, compared to 35% of women who were not sexually abused in childhood [*The Secret Trauma: Incest in the Lives of Girls and Women*, New York: Basic Books, Inc., 1986].

belief that she is different from other children be reinforced by her friends and their families if they knew? I have read and heard accounts of parents who did not want their children to play with child molestation victims.

That people think there is something wrong with child abuse victims was made clear in a recent local news article. It was a story of one community's fight to keep a group home for abused children out of their neighborhood. The home would have provided shelter for six children, ages five to 11, who were victims of physical and/ or sexual abuse. One resident explained the neighborhood's concern this way: "People are scared they [the children] will steal things and break into houses. It would hurt this street . . . It would go down." [*Atlanta Journal*, Monday, May 8, 1989, C-2].

She went on to say that she felt sorry for the children, but believed they should be put out in the country somewhere, presumably because they would be less likely to get into trouble if they were kept a safe distance from other people. It was a chilling example of how insensitive people can be toward victims of child abuse.

Then, Anger

Dr. McGarrah told me once that some people burst into anger when they first learn their child has been sexually abused. Most people, however, experience disbelief first. The anger comes later. For me, anger came much later.

It takes a lot to get me angry, and I seldom make it beyond a nasty case of irritability. I fought my anger over Angie's abuse a long time because I remembered Dr. McGarrah's warning: The school's defense would be that I was a vindictive mother who had made up the charges of abuse to get back at them for something. I was afraid to be angry because I didn't want to validate their accusation. For weeks I worked hard at maintaining an air of calm, controlled objectivity.

Once my anger broke through, however, I was furious with everyone and everything. Obviously, the first targets of my anger were Angie's kindergarten teachers. I was angry that people I had trusted could have hurt my child so badly, and I was livid when I remembered how they had set up and then covered up their crime. It was bad enough that they abused her, but the way they protected themselves by trying to make me believe Angie was a lying, spoiled little problem-child was cruel beyond words. I was even angrier when I thought about how they had bad-mouthed Angie to other people.

I particularly remembered an incident following one of our teacher-director conferences. During her kindergarten year, Angie often said that her teachers hated her and that she was "the stupidest kid in the world." She believed it because their response to her work was always lukewarm, while they praised other children's work profusely. She pointed out that they never displayed her work, and I mentioned this during one of our conferences. One teacher immediately replied that they only hung up work that was perfect; if Angie's work wasn't hanging up, it was because it was not perfect. The other teacher, however, agreed to be more sensitive, and she did begin to hang up all the children's work, including Angie's.

Shortly after that, Diane walked into the room when the "sensitive" teacher was in the process of hanging up a picture of Angie's. Diane commented on the picture because she thought it was particularly well done. Angie had drawn a picture of the galaxy. Instead of stars, she had drawn tiny hearts scattered among the planets. On the picture she wrote, "My love covers the whole world." It was a great picture. The teacher's reply to Diane's comment, however, was very sarcastic.

She explained that she *had* to hang it up because "someone, we won't mention who, but you can guess what little girl it was, had her poor little feelings hurt and her mother complained." It was an incredibly cruel thing to say, considering all the times we had sat in those conferences and puzzled over the sudden drop in Angie's sense of self-worth. The teachers had always acted so surprised and concerned. Now their duplicity made me furious.

My anger also flared every time Angie disclosed more details of the way she was abused. I remember feeling that I was going to choke when she told me how one of the teachers had slapped her on the leg and held her down when she tried to resist. I was angry with myself, too, for having been so gullible. Why had I not been able to see the vicious side of that woman?

My first wave of anger was toward Angie's abusers. The second volley was aimed at their supervisor. My frustration turned to fury when I remembered how defensive and unresponsive the school's director had been during the year Angie was being molested. I was enraged when she continued to support the teachers and to insist that the child molestation charges were frivolous, even after the prosecutor told her he believed the charges were legitimate.

I was especially upset when someone told me that, after the meeting between the district attorney and the school's parents, the director called a staff meeting and told the teachers they were all in this together. She said something like the following: "You have to realize that this could just as easily have happened to any one of you. What you have to think about is how you would feel if some unhappy child decided to get back at *you* by making up a story that you molested her. How would you like to have *your* life and career ruined like that?"

As the school administration's cover-up policy unfolded following Angie's disclosure, my anger spread from the teachers and director to the school's board. Each time I heard something new about the board's position, it was as though someone twisted a knife in my back. It was painful beyond words. I was living every day with my daughter's nightmares. Every day I looked into her sad, hollow eyes and remembered how sparkling and full of life she had been only months before. And still the people who ran the school where she was sexually abused were calling my baby a liar. It hurt—it still does—and you'd better believe I was angry with those people!

I was also mad at the school's parents who refused to believe children had been molested there. I was even angrier at those who believed it but thought it was "a lot of commotion over nothing." After the parents' meeting with the people from the district attorney's office, a petition was circulated asking the parents to pull together and show their support for the school's administration. Many of the parents were more concerned about the school as an institution than as a guardian of the children entrusted to its care. My daughter had her childhood stripped away from her at that school and only a handful of the other parents cared at all.

Once I got used to my uncharacteristic outbursts of anger, I really let it roll. I was angry at the parents of the other victims for the position they eventually took regarding Mr. Morgan's attempts to prosecute the case. I was also disappointed in them because I thought we could have helped and supported each other. Instead, they withdrew into themselves. As much as I respected Mr. Morgan, there were times I was angry at him when his investigation kept stalling out. I couldn't understand why he couldn't do *something*. I was even angry with Dr. McGarrah at times because she didn't have a miracle cure for my child.

A lot of my anger was unfocused. I was just "mad at the world." I was mad because I had no family nearby to lean on when I needed them so badly. I was mad at my friends because they were happy and I wasn't. Some of them were sympathetic, but they never fully understood or empathized with how bad a time I was living through, and I resented it. And I was mad at God for allowing this awful thing to happen in the first place.

People in mourning often pass through a phase of "bargaining," when they think they can somehow negotiate away the reality of their situation. When I could no longer deny the fact that Angie had been sexually abused, and I was exhausted by my fears and anger, I had no place to go but to the bargaining table with God. If we could have struck a deal, I would have lived the rest of my life in letter-perfect adherence to the Ten Commandments. I was even willing to throw in a few extra rules as sweeteners. Apparently there was no demand for new saints, because I never awakened one morning to find this was all a bad dream. Angie never miraculously "got over" her abuse. And when I realized God wasn't willing to negotiate, I was furious with Him.

Then, Depression

Anger is exhausting, and when I was emotionally, physically, and spiritually spent, I collapsed into feelings of frustration, helplessness, and depression. I was frustrated over the criminal and regulatory investigations. I was frustrated by the overwhelming lack of concern I saw for the victims of child sexual abuse—not only from individuals I knew, but from society at large. And I felt helpless because there was nothing I could do to change any of it.

I wanted to see Angie's offenders prosecuted for more than sheer vengeance. Of course I wanted them held responsible for the hurt they caused my child, but it was just as important to me to know they would not go free to abuse other children. Child molesters keep abusing children until they are stopped. I know that as long as I live I will never stop wondering how many other little girls have been hurt by Angie's offenders. Knowing those women are out there destroying other childhoods still leaves me with a terrible feeling of helplessness.

My frustration over the school's response to the abuse that took place there was overwhelming at times. Eight months after Angie's disclosure, those feelings expressed themselves in a nightmare that left me weak and weeping.

I dreamed Angie and I were back at the school. It was "now," not "then." I don't know why Angie was going to that school again, but for some reason we were both trapped there. I brought Angie to school late and we were met at the door by the director. She was standing there with a smirk on her face, and she told me that she was going to levy a fine because Angie was late. I knew this was not typical, and I got angry. I said, "You're just trying to punish me. You're trying to get back at us for telling about the abuse."

Other parents, including the president of the board and Carla, gathered around and started laughing. They said there was nothing I could do about it—I had to pay. I began to scream. "What about the children? Don't you care about what happened here?" The director looked at me very calmly, very coldly, very unemotionally, and said simply, "It didn't happen."

I was on my knees, crying. Everyone else stood there and looked amused. "It did happen. You hurt my baby," I sobbed. The director just looked right through me and kept saying in a cold, level voice, "It didn't happen." And then I woke up. I felt as though I would suffocate, and like many times before, I got up and read because I knew I would not sleep again that night.

The emotion I felt myself fighting most often was depression. There were times I was so engulfed in despair that I had to concentrate on whatever task I was engaged in at the time to make it through the day. The past was too painful and the future seemed too hopeless to think about. It was hard to see a light at the end of the tunnel.

When we experience trauma in our lives, the anguish can knock us flat. When that happens, we regain emotional strength slowly. We creep, we draw ourselves to our knees and crawl for a while. We pull our feet under us and stumble along, and eventually we walk again. When Angie was sexually abused, I felt as though I were watching my child die over and over again. Every time I thought the worst was over, I was knocked flat on my face again.

I have written about the emotions I experienced as though I progressed through distinct phases. I did not. I was caught in a vicious circle, and my emotions often seemed to feed on themselves. Even though I accepted early on the fact that Angie had been sexually molested, I sometimes found myself trying to deny the seriousness of that abuse. Each time Angie entered a new phase of disclosure and turmoil, it brought new doubts and fears, or resurrected old ones. And then I would get angry again, feel guilty over feeling angry, feel helpless because I couldn't do anything about it, get depressed because I felt helpless, and then get angry again at the people who were responsible for it all in the first place—or at the people who weren't doing anything about it.

The emotional and behavioral cycles that victims of abuse go through make it hard for their parents to find closure. The hurt just goes on and on. A lack of understanding about what is going on with the child or what to expect next makes it even harder. My own emotional recovery was also impeded by the way the criminal and regulatory investigations dragged on and then never really ended. The way the school's administration dealt with the situation knocked me down over and over again and prolonged the agony. Just as Angie's emotional turmoil resulted in behavioral havoc, my own behavior reflected my emotions and affected my relationships with the people around me.

CHAPTER 16

REDEFINED RELATIONSHIPS

Sometimes I felt like I was careening through an emotional time warp, and I had to work hard to maintain some sort of status quo in my relationships with the people around me. I've already explained how relationships with people associated with the preschool where Angie was sexually molested were affected. Although it was less obvious, my emotional state affected how I interacted with other people as well.

I had a hard time accepting my own emotional volatility during those months, and the only way I could control those feelings was to erect a glass wall between myself and the rest of the world. I learned to slip in and out of a mask—a calm, sometimes smiling mask—that enabled me to interact with others on a superficial level even though my guts were churning.

Like Angie, I often felt different from my friends. I was the only one I knew who was struggling with the daily dilemma of trying to parent a victim of child sexual abuse. The holiday season was especially hard for me. My friends were wondering what to wear to their Christmas parties. I was wondering if my child would ever smile again. Emotionally, I withdrew from the people around me— it was the best defense I had at the time.

We have visited with relatives several times since Angie's disclosure. Each time, I had to rely heavily on my glass wall, because my husband and I had agreed not to tell Angie's grandparents about her abuse. It was particularly hard when my mother, stepfather, and grandmother came to visit us shortly after the situation blew up at Angie's former preschool. During the day-by-day developments at the school, there were also highly publicized reports on TV about a Catholic priest who had allegedly molested a number of boys at a nearby church. I spent that week babbling on with neutral conversation, while my mind was racing off in other directions. It made me feel very defensive around people with whom I normally felt relaxed.

The changes in my relationship with Angie following her abuse were hard for me to accept. Even at an early age, Angie's extraordinary ability to communicate had contributed to our very close relationship. We were friends as well as mother and daughter. Normally, when I disciplined Angie, I would wait a bit and then ask her if she wanted to talk about it. She always did—and we would sit in her room and talk and make up afterwards. She would tell me why she thought I had been unfair, I would explain why she had been disciplined, and we would both say how much we loved each other in spite of it all. We always ended with a hug and a promise to do better next time.

After Angie was molested, our old channels of communication were often closed. She refused to talk with me, and she had attacks of hostility that lasted for days. There were times when she would get out of bed in the morning, look me straight in the eyes, and calmly announce, "I hate you." It was a devastating way to start the day. Sometimes, when I drove her to school, she would turn her back to me and scrunch down in the corner of the car, as far away from me as she could get. If I tried to communicate silently by reaching out and patting her on the head or shoulder, she would cringe from my touch. I can't begin to describe how much it hurt to suddenly be afraid to touch a child who had freely given and accepted hugs and kisses before. I understood her hostility and anger, but that didn't make it any less painful for me.

Angie's relationship with her father was even more volatile than her relationship with me. My husband is the strong, silent type, but he couldn't mask the bitterness he felt over the hostility Angie directed at him, and it scared me. I wondered if their relationship could possibly survive. Angie had a difficult time believing that I loved her after she was abused. I had to work hard to help her understand that what had happened to her was not her fault, that there was nothing wrong with her, that she had a right to be angry, that I understood her feelings, and that I still loved her no matter how angry she felt toward me or anyone else. She didn't receive that kind of support from her father, and I think that's why her anger toward him was more intense.

From the beginning, my husband had a harder time than I did accepting that Angie had been abused. I talked with Dr. McGarrah about it and she told me that my husband's reaction was not atypical. She said it was normal for parents to go through a period of denial and disbelief. It was also typical for one parent, usually the mother, to work through that denial faster than the other parent. Fathers often have a harder time accepting their child's having been abused, she said. If that was true, our family certainly fit the norm.

Once the reality of Angie's abuse hit me, I was very frustrated when my husband continued to deny the facts that were unfolding before us. He thought I was overreacting, and kept saying that we had to "maintain an attitude of healthy skepticism." That was the beginning of the tension that invaded our home in the months that followed.

Eventually my husband realized that his daughter had been sexually assaulted, but even after that first step toward acceptance, he was unable to understand the impact it had on her. He was sympathetic when she suffered nightmares, fears, and guilt, but he couldn't handle her anger and behavioral problems. He knew she had been sexually molested, but he didn't think the abuse was any "excuse" for her outrageous behavior—especially when it was directed at him. He often returned her anger with anger of his own. Naturally, that response only escalated their conflicts.

Conflict like this was new to our family, and I often felt helpless and frightened as I watched our family fabric unraveling before my eyes. I usually tried to intervene and defuse their hostility before one of them blew up. Sometimes it worked and sometimes it didn't. Angie went through a particularly bad time right before the Halloween following her disclosure. When I saw the tensions mounting between Angie and her father, I took Angie aside and talked with her until she calmed down. That also gave my husband time to collect himself. Then Angie and I returned to the kitchen to decorate a Halloween cake. By the time we had the cake frosted, Angie decided she wanted her daddy to help her decorate it. They had a good time turning the cake into a pumpkin face, and the evening ended on a pleasant note.

Less than a week later, my family hit rock bottom and all three of us fell apart at once. No one incident precipitated the blowup that evening. Angie just kept testing her father. I could see his frustration and anger mounting. I tried to separate them, but Angie kept going after him. He finally lost his temper and spanked her. She started screaming and hitting him back. I held her back and physically stood between them, but they continued to yell at each other. Then I broke down and ran out of the room crying. Angie ran after me, crying hysterically. And my husband came running after both of us, still angry and shouting. We finally all calmed down a little and sat there without saying anything. We just sat and sobbed. We were all numb.

Angie and I eventually went to her room. She was still hostile. She didn't want to talk, but she didn't want me to leave, either. We sat there in silence for a long time before she finally said I could talk if I wanted to. I said that we should all be working together to get over the hurt her teachers had caused instead of fighting with each other. Angie was still very angry with her father, but she agreed to go outside to look at the moon with me. That's one of my favorite things to do when I need quiet time, and Angie enjoys it, too. That night the moon was the biggest, most beautiful moon I had seen in a long time, delicately framed by a few wispy clouds. Angie and I sat there and enjoyed it in silence for a long time. Finally I asked, "Well, what do we do now?" Angie perked up a little and said, "A meeting. We have to have a meeting. You and Daddy and me."

We went back inside and had a family meeting in Angie's "clubhouse." Angie began by saying that she thought we should all tell what we were so upset about and what we thought we should do to fix it. Her sensitivity and perception were amazing! I said that I was upset because Angie and her daddy were not getting along and I was frustrated because I couldn't do anything to help. I thought we all needed to help each other instead of fighting among ourselves. My husband said that he was upset because Angie was always saying, "I hate you," and he really believed she didn't love him anymore. Angie replied that she didn't think her daddy loved her anymore, and then she added that we should all try to love each other again.

By bedtime, we were all emotionally exhausted, but a lot calmer. That incident was one of the worst the three of us experienced, and it shows how the tension of trying to cope with child sexual abuse can disrupt a normal family and threaten to tear it apart.

Several weeks later, my husband was out of town on business when Angie startled me by asking, "Mom, you know ... about [preschool] ... do you believe me ... about, you know ... about what happened to me there?" I assured her that I believed her with all my heart. She thought a little and then added bitterly, "Well, Daddy doesn't believe me!" I told her that he did believe her. He was just having a hard time understanding how much it had hurt her. I promised her that Daddy and I would talk about it when he returned from his trip, and she seemed relieved.

Angie's relationship with her father did improve over time. Setting aside one-on-one time for them helped a lot. My husband took a day off from work to go to her field day at the new school the following spring. Angie was delighted to have her daddy there to cheer her on. Sometimes my husband took Angie to see the Atlanta Ballet, and those were also special times for them.

Even though my husband's relationship with Angie gradually improved, my relationship with him continued to suffer. We had been married 18 years when Angie was sexually molested in kindergarten. During those 18 years, we had supported each other through a number of tough times. We had pulled each other through college and graduate school. We had leaned on each other when serious illnesses, deaths, and divorces struck our families. But for some reason we couldn't help each other cope when our daughter was sexually assaulted.

Sometimes our relationship dissolved into open hostility, primarily because we couldn't agree on how to discipline our "new" Angie. My husband was more likely than I was to resort to physical punishment, and he got angry at me when I tried to intervene. I think he felt I was taking sides with Angie against him. He also resented the fact that Angie was taking up 100% of our attention and we no longer had time for each other. Further, he was having a hard time keeping the pressures at home from affecting his work, and I think he resented that intrusion into his professional life.

As for me, I felt as though my husband had deserted me. He often withdrew into himself, and that left me carrying the full load of parenthood alone. Besides having to deal with Angie, I had to struggle with what was happening to him and to us. I resented having to bear that extra burden at the time I could least afford it. I just didn't have enough emotional energy to go around.

Most of the time, though, my husband and I didn't fight each other. We had occasional arguments, but the biggest problem was that we just went our own ways, trying to nurse our own wounds instead of helping each other. Instead of pulling together, we were like two toddlers engaged in parallel play. Our relationship didn't go from plus to minus—it just slipped out of gear and got stuck in neutral.

The stress and tension of dealing with Angie's abuse severely strained all of the relationships within our family. And we had been a strong family unit before all that happened. It makes me wonder how families manage to cope with child sexual abuse if they are not on solid ground in the first place. What if there are already family tensions, such as financial difficulties, religious differences, or career conflicts? What if other family tragedies strike, such as serious illness or death in the family, the loss of a job, or an unwanted transfer? Any weak links in the family chain will be vulnerable under the strain of child sexual abuse.

How do families survive? I have not seen statistics on divorce rates for the parents of extrafamilial molestation victims, but it would not surprise me if the incidence is statistically greater than that for nonvictim families. Child sexual abuse is hell on the family!

CHAPTER 17

DESTRUCTIVE VERSUS CONSTRUCTIVE COPING

To *cope*, according to the dictionary, is to contend with difficulties and to seek to overcome them. Contending with difficulties is a normal part of everyday life. We all do it. The trick, however, is to do it in a healthy, constructive way. Parents of sexual molestation victims have specific feelings to resolve, but how effectively we cope with them can either help or hinder our progress. Further, how we handle our own stress sets an unspoken example for our children, so it can help or hinder their recovery as well.

Coping with the sexual assault of a child is an exhausting process for two reasons. First, it overpowers every aspect of our lives at once. No matter where we turn—work, home, family, friends— our lives are suddenly out of equilibrium. Second, there is little help available for families of molestation victims. Finding the support we need can be exhausting in and of itself.

Coping with Your Child

When any aspect of our lives is thrown out of equilibrium, we experience stress and discomfort. To cope with those unpleasant feelings, we seek to gain or regain control of the situation. The sense of control is an important part of coping with everyday life.

Control is especially critical when it comes to parenting a child who has been sexually assaulted. The victim needs help in reestablishing equilibrium in his or her disrupted childhood. But just when the child needs parental support the most, parents have to contend with emotional turmoil of their own. As parents struggle to regain the control they need to put their family's life back in order, it is easy to overreact or underreact. Parents may flip-flop from one extreme to the other, trying to find the balance that will allow their family to get on with life.

I frequently found myself overreacting to everyday situations after Angie was abused. When I realized what I was doing, my efforts to compensate made me bend too far in the other direction. I struggled to find the proper balance in many aspects of my family's life, from discipline to structure in bed-, bath-, and meal-times. Parenting situations that had been routine suddenly became hard work.

When I first learned that Angie had been sexually abused, I felt so sorry for her that I wanted to do anything I could to make her life easier. It is very tempting to spoil a child who has experienced severe trauma!

Shortly after Angie's disclosure, I went shopping to buy a few last-minute things for school. I suddenly realized I was walking around the children's department with my arms loaded down with clothes. Angie could never have worn half of what I had selected for her, but there I was, pulling things off the racks with no regard for whether she needed them or how much they cost. I came to my senses and put most of it back that day, but since then, my shopping habits have remained fairly impulsive where Angie is concerned. There have been times when Angie could have asked me for the moon and I would not have hesitated to charge it to MasterCard®. And there have been times when I refused her tiniest request, simply because I had to convince myself that I wasn't the overindulgent parent I had, in fact, become.

When it came to diet and exercise, my husband and I had been fairly health conscious. We rarely had soft drinks, chips, or sweets in our house, and Angie's favorite "fast food" was a peanut butter and apple sandwich from a local health food restaurant. In the months following her disclosure, though, I became uncharacteristically lenient with her diet. I didn't flinch when she asked for colas or candy bars. And then, when I realized how much junk she was eating, I did an about-face to get back to normal. The result was a very inconsistent diet for all of us. One week we ate hamburgers and fries and the next week it was sprouts and yogurt.

While I was struggling to maintain normalcy in our daily family routine, I also had to avoid extremes in reacting to the abuse itself. When was I being cautious and when was I being overprotective, as I tried to shelter Angie from new risks? Did I overreact to her behavioral problems? When was her behavior related to the abuse and when was it simply a normal phase for her age? Did it even matter?

When it came to discipline, I think it did matter. I was much more effective in dealing with Angie's behavioral problems when I focused on the emotions driving her behavior. That focus also helped my own attitude. I was less likely to take Angie's "I hate you" personally when I understood the source of her hostility.

I probably spent too much energy, though, trying to analyze whether individual behaviors were directly related to her abuse. After living with a child abuse victim for several years, I have come to the conclusion that each day's behavior can't be defined directly in terms of the abuse trauma. That doesn't mean the effects aren't there, however. When I am having a particularly difficult time with Angie, other parents sometimes will point out that they are having similar problems with their children. So, is this just a "normal phase" all children her age go through?

The answer, in my opinion, is yes and no. On the one hand, a particular behavior may be characteristic of all children her age. On the other hand, Angie's behaviors are often intensified because of her past trauma. She doesn't bounce back as easily as other children seem to. If she has a fight with a friend, for example, the other child can usually forgive and forget within minutes or hours. Angie will retreat into feelings of worthlessness. She may be depressed or hostile for days. One relatively minor incident may set off a chain reaction that Angie will take days or weeks to pull out of.

To cope constructively with a sexually abused child, parents have to be knowledgeable about the nature and effects of sexual molestation. Most parents, like the rest of society, know very little about child sexual abuse and its effects on the victim. Parents who are burdened with the standard myths and stereotypes around child sexual abuse will have a harder time dealing effectively with their child. For example, knowledge about child molesters—who they are, why they molest, how they select their victims and set up opportunities for the crime—will help parents understand and *believe* that their child was not responsible for the abuse. Only then will they be prepared to help the child deal with his or her guilty feelings.

Parents must understand the behavioral dynamics of child sexual abuse, and accept their child's emotions, before they can help the child accept her or his own feelings. Those feelings are as much a part of the child's being as her heart and lungs. The child needs to learn to distinguish between feelings and behavior. Parents who focus only on behavior will be of little help to a child who is trying to come to terms with the emotional turmoil raging inside.

The more knowledgeable parents are, the less likely they are to fall back on knee-jerk reactions to the child's experience. No one is born knowing about child molestation, and parents who look for information about it may have a hard time.

I remember how frustrated I was when I set out to search for information. One afternoon I called one social agency after another asking for help. Everyone I talked with was sensitive, sympathetic, and kind, but no one could help me. The people who knew something about child sexual abuse worked primarily with incest victims, and they all referred me somewhere else for information about third-party abuse. After each frustrating call, I hung up the phone, cried a little, and then dialed another number.

Finally, one person recommended several books she thought might be helpful. When I tried to find them, I discovered that most libraries and bookstores carried very little on the subject of child molestation. I did find a feminist bookstore that covered the subject extensively, and I wondered why sexual assault on children was of interest only to feminists. Even there, most of the material dealt with incest and/or was written for professionals.

Public awareness of child molestation has improved somewhat in the past several years. This book has a resource list so that other parents will not experience the difficulty I did in getting information.

I recommend that parents begin their search for information with the first professional they come in contact with—the child's therapist, social agency workers, or the special prosecutor. These people may have suggestions on where to look. Parents who follow whatever leads these people provide will find that eventually the pieces of information start falling into place. Local affiliates of the National Committee for Prevention of Child Abuse are also good sources of information and referrals. Persistence is important. Parents should not give up if information is not readily available.

I think it is also helpful for parents of victims to learn more about normal child development and constructive disciplinary approaches. Child molestation victims are, after all, children, with the same needs and developmental characteristics as other children. The impact of abuse trauma is superimposed on their basic emotional and behavioral profiles. I think it helps parents to have that developmental background as a base on which to build. The knowledge can also strengthen parental confidence at a time when it is easy to feel like the worst parent in the world.

Coping with Others

The general lack of enlightened attitudes toward child sexual abuse is a reality parents have to face. The best line of defense against overwhelming frustration is knowledge. Knowing the facts about child sexual abuse can lessen parental vulnerability to the insensitivity of others. Parents who feel secure about the job they are doing in guiding their child through his or her posttrauma childhood will be better equipped emotionally to withstand the pressures and frustrations of the outside world.

I stumbled along from day to day, and the lack of support and understanding I met along the way often hit me hard emotionally. I could not understand why no one else seemed to care about the damage done to my child's life. Society's attitude toward child sexual abuse is abominable, but if we take it personally, we and our children are the ones we hurt most. It helps to keep in mind that most of the people who hurt us behave out of ignorance rather than malice. Unfortunately, human frailties sometimes show up when we are least able to cope with them.

Most people mean well, but they just don't know what to say when someone is in pain. People don't say dumb things—like "Just be grateful she doesn't have leukemia or something"—only to parents of molestation victims. They also try to comfort parents who lose a child by telling them they can have another baby, as though children can be replaced like broken appliances. Or they tell someone whose loved one has died unexpectedly to be grateful he or she didn't suffer a long, painful death, as though that will lessen the survivor's sense of loss. People don't realize that what victims of any trauma need most is a gentle hug and an understanding presence.

Coping with the antagonism of people who do act out of malice is another matter. The negative way people at Angie's preschool reacted to news of the abuse charges hurt a lot; it was salt in the wounds my family was struggling to heal. It is hard to know when to engage in open confrontation and when to walk away. The only thing parents can do is keep their priorities straight, and the number one priority should be to take whatever action will be in the best interests of the victim and other children who might be harmed.

Parents will encounter many situations when they must decide what to do. Should they back off and seek support from more enlightened sources? Or should they hang in there and try to educate others about child sexual abuse? In my opinion, one place where it is imperative for parents to dig in and educate/advocate in behalf of their child is at the child's school.

Teachers have a significant impact on a child's life, and yet many of them are uninformed about child sexual abuse. Teachers may be trained to recognize symptoms of physical abuse so that they can report suspected cases. Few, however, understand the emotional or behavioral impact that physical abuse and sexual abuse have on children. One of my dearest friends is a special education teacher in a public school system in the midwest. It is her job to work with children who have special educational needs—and yet she admits that she knows nothing about child sexual abuse. It seems incredible, in light of the statistical incidence of child sexual abuse in this country and the impact that abuse can have on victims' behavior and performance in the classroom, that the subject is not a required part of the teacher-education curriculums. According to my teacher friends, it is not.

When Angie started first grade, almost immediately after her disclosure, I knew it was important to talk with her teacher about the trauma and its effects. I also realized I might have to have the same conversation with her second grade teacher the following year. I also remember thinking that by the time Angie reached third grade, a conference with her teacher would not be necessary, because by that time she would surely "be over it."

Little did I know, when all of this started, that advocating for my child would become a permanent part of my parenting responsibilities. And little did I know that it would become more difficult with time. When my husband and I met with Angie's first grade teacher, we were still reeling from Angie's recent disclosure. It was easy for all of us to understand the turmoil Angie was experiencing. The further we move away from the time Angie was abused, however, the harder it is for people to understand the effect it continues to have on her.

The parent's initial conference with the teacher is important. It is equally important to keep the lines of communication open throughout the school year. A teacher has a roomful of other children to contend with every day. That, plus the fact that his or her emotional investment in the child is nowhere near that of the parents, makes it easy for the teacher to burn out before the school year is over. Even a teacher who begins the school year with an enthusiastic pledge of support for the child may become less tolerant of the victim's problem behavior after a few weeks or months.

During one conference, Angie's teacher mentioned that she sometimes noticed Angie staring into space as if she were in a trance. What the teacher had witnessed were "flashback" episodes when someone or something triggered a painful memory for Angie. When that happens, she will suddenly get a dazed, blank look on her face as her mind disengages itself from the present and returns to the past. As Angie describes it, "It feels like I'm asleep, but I know I'm really awake." It is as though she were daydreaming a nightmare.

I was pleased with the teacher's perceptiveness when she acknowledged that Angie was probably "having a bad memory." It would have been easy for her to assume Angie was just not paying attention in class and discipline her. Unfortunately, the teacher went on to say that she thought it was time for Angie to forget about her experience and get on with the rest of her life.

When something like that happens, I have to fight an impulse to jump in and vehemently defend my child. Instead, I try to retreat to more neutral ground and talk about child abuse victims in general— about why the abuse is so traumatic for the victims and about the process of recovery all victims face. Even kind, sensitive, dedicated teachers have to be educated about child sexual abuse if they are going to provide the nurturing support a molestation victim needs.

It is easy for parents to assume that teachers will be responsive to a child's special needs once they understand the trauma she or he has experienced. Unfortunately, that may not be true. Teachers walk into their classrooms with the same range of biases and misconceptions about child abuse as the general public. They also are products of their own past experiences, and parents may find themselves dealing with a teacher who is a survivor of child sexual abuse. That is not an improbability, considering the number of women (and men) who have been sexually assaulted in childhood!

I asked Nancy McGarrah whether that probability is serious enough to concern parents. She acknowledged that it is. Most of the time, parents will never know why teachers react to their child the way they do. Dr. McGarrah was aware of several situations, however, where classroom teachers were known to be survivors of abuse. She pointed out that dealing with a child victim may resurrect old memories for an adult survivor. Also, adult survivors may feel uncomfortable or may disapprove if the child's coping mechanisms differ from their own.

Dr. McGarrah went on to say that teachers who are adult survivors may treat child victims in several ways. They may be overly protective of the child, treating her or him more like an adopted child than a student. Or they may demand perfection from the child, so that nothing the child does is right in the eyes of the teacher. The teacher may be unusually harsh and punitive with the young victim of abuse. The same teacher may exhibit both extremes of behavior as he or she tries to deal with a victim of child molestation in the classroom.

Parents may experience difficult situations as they advocate for their child. All they can do is accept the reality that they can't control other people's reactions. They have to try to gain the support their child needs to recover from the abuse trauma, but they also have to be prepared for the likelihood that support may not be forthcoming.

The child's parents and therapist also should work with the victim so that he or she will eventually be strong enough to accept negative reactions from others without internalizing guilt or shame. Sexually abused children must come to believe that what happened to them was not their fault, and that they did nothing to deserve the assault. It could just as easily have happened to any of their classmates. If other people react negatively to a child because of the abuse, the child must learn that it is the other person who has a problem, not he or she.

Coping with the System

To cope with the system, parents have to recognize how it works and what its weaknesses are. They should not expect too much, because even in the best of situations, much is unfair when it comes to children in general and child sexual abuse in particular. Sometimes it seems as though society is more concerned about the rights of animals than it is about the welfare of our children.

Although parents also have to realize that most of what happens within the system is out of their control, there are two scenarios, I think, in which parents may find themselves working to confront or change the system. First, parents may have no choice but to challenge the system directly if it fails to protect children who are threatened with additional abuse. It may be a situation where a child is returned to the custody of an abusive parent (or a parent living with an offender). Or it may involve an institution where repeated allegations of abuse go unheeded by the authorities. As long as children are in danger of future abuse, parents should take every avenue open to them to protect the victims.

If all else fails, parents may want to seek help from the media. I have heard of situations where media attention generated support for victims who had fallen through the cracks of the system. Before taking such a drastic step, however, parents should know how the media work. Many reporters are moved by social issues, but they are reporters first and foremost. Their job is to report stories that are newsworthy and of interest to society at large. They cannot champion every cause they encounter. Also, the media have to be cautious because of the threat of lawsuits. They generally will not print stories they cannot substantiate or that are not public information. (When legal action of any kind is taken in an abuse case, that situation enters the public domain.)

Parents also have to consider how publicity will affect their child. I believe most members of the media act responsibly and will agree to protect the child's identity. After all, they are interested in the story, not in traumatizing a child. Parents with a story that interests the media possess some degree of power, and they should be able to insist that their child's privacy be protected as much as possible.

The other scenario involves parents who do not need to confront the system to protect their child. Rather, their own frustrations with the system may create a desire to do what they can to improve the system. They can undertake a number of actions. One may be as private as offering financial support to organizations providing services for child abuse victims. For more active involvement they can work with those organizations as volunteers. Parents who are really tough may get involved in letter-writing campaigns or lobbying for child advocacy legislation.

Parents should do what is right for them, waiting to do it until they can be effective. The first impulse may be to charge off and start slaying dragons. Before they sharpen their swords, however, they should understand that they won't meet with as much sympathy or support as they might expect. They may be viewed as bitter parents who are simply out to vent their venom, rather than as people who are really interested in bringing about changes within the system.

Parents should not rush into active advocacy for several reasons. First, they have to learn their way around the child advocacy network. Second, they need time to deal with the more immediate crises they face at home. The early months of their child's recovery will demand an incredible amount of energy. Parents may not have the physical or emotional strength left over to devote to child abuse issues outside their immediate situation. Third, parents will need enough emotional stamina to withstand the many disappointments they will encounter, and to be able to avoid taking setbacks personally. I have found that people—even professionals within child advocacy networks—are often uncomfortable with parents who choose to speak out.

I decided to work as a volunteer with a local child advocacy organization. I chose the speakers bureau because I believe that education about child abuse is the first step to take before we can deal effectively with the crimes being committed against our children. People have to get their heads out of the sand and start talking about what's happening to children, because child abuse is one widespread problem where what you don't know *can* hurt you—or someone you love. People have to learn what's going on before they can care enough to look for solutions to the problem. Working with this particular organization gives me an opportunity to educate people about child abuse in general. I am not comfortable talking publicly about my family's personal experience, however. I thought I was, until I had an opportunity to do so—and then I really blew it.

A year and a half after Angie's disclosure, I was invited to speak before a state House Judiciary subcommittee that was considering several pieces of legislation concerning the testimony of children in abuse cases. I jumped at the chance. Legislative lobbying seemed like the quickest, most powerful way to get things done, but my enthusiasm didn't last long because the experience turned out to be devastating.

The problem was that I walked in blind—I had no idea of what to expect or what was expected of me. As soon as I started talking, I knew everything I was saying was wrong. It was obvious the legislators didn't want to hear some little mother's sad story about the effects of sexual abuse on her child's life. They wanted to talk about the nuts and bolts of the proposed legislation, something I knew nothing about. In a panic, my mouth went on automatic pilot while my mind tried to figure out how to salvage the situation. I ended up digging in deeper and saying some things that were inappropriate. That embarrassment, plus the emotional intensity of speaking publicly about Angie's abuse for the first time, wiped me out. I left the State Capitol, walked back to my office, headed straight for the bathroom, and threw up.

Talking to a bunch of strangers about what had happened to Angie was harder than I had ever imagined it would be. The worst part was that after putting myself through that ordeal, I didn't have anything to show for it. It was apparent from the legislators' questions and comments that nothing I said had made a bit of difference to anyone on that subcommittee. After that experience, I vowed to stick with finding ways to educate laypeople about child sexual abuse and leaving the political activities to individuals with stronger stomachs, at least for the time being. It will be a long time before I go back to the State Capitol, unless it's to see the stuffed birds in the museum! To repeat, parents should do what they're most comfortable with. And they should also be tough enough to cope with disappointment.

Coping with Yourself

Parents who can cope with their own emotions will be better able to deal with the uncertainties and frustrations they encounter both within their families and with the world outside the family. Feelings of denial, guilt, fear, anger, and depression are normal for parents of sexual abuse victims. Extreme and/or prolonged periods of emotional upheaval, however, can be counterproductive to the healing process. And a delayed recovery for the victim's parents can impede the victim's recovery.

I have talked throughout this chapter about the importance of knowing the facts on child sexual abuse. Being knowledgeable can help parents cope with their child, the system, and people outside the home, and it can help them cope with their own attacks of denial as well. It is important to realize that denial doesn't refer only to that initial period of shock when we tell ourselves over and over, "This just couldn't have happened to my child." Denial recurs throughout recovery.

I accepted, within a fairly short period of time, the fact that Angie had been sexually molested. I think that was because I had seen the dramatic changes in her personality during kindergarten and had spent almost a year before her disclosure trying to figure out what had caused them. I had a harder time understanding and accepting the impact the abuse had on Angie's behavior. I could understand her initial guilt, fear, and hostility. It has been much harder to accept the longer-term, more subtle effects on her personality that I continue to see every day. The problem is that what happened to Angie is a permanent part of our lives that I can never seem to get away from. And so there have been times I just wanted to shut down and pretend it never happened—or to acknowledge it happened, but pretend it was over.

I went through a whopper of a denial phase almost a year after Angie's disclosure. It was when Angie was still struggling to get over the unfortunate end to her first grade school year. I was still hearing stories about the upheaval at Angie's former preschool. The DHR representative was still whining, "I just don't know what we can do." And, I had just walked out of the trial lawyer's office after she declined the case. That was the straw that broke my back.

It wasn't the attorney's legal opinion as much as the cold, insensitive way she delivered it. Not only did she shrug off Angie's abuse as an early introduction to the world's unfairness, but she also laid a heavy guilt trip on my husband and me. She implied that we were lousy parents to have even considered filing a civil suit. How could we think about subjecting our daughter to the trauma of a court battle? If we really cared about our daughter, she advised, we would just forget what had happened, help Angie forget, and get on with our lives.

I walked out of her office thinking, "OK—everyone keeps telling me to forget it—then that's what I'm going to do!" And I launched my personal campaign to "forget about it." I took every reminder of Angie out of my office at work so her pictures and the millions of paperweights she had made over the years wouldn't distract me. And then I dug into my job with a vengeance. I filled every waking moment with activity. When I wasn't working, I read or watched TV. I gave up smocking because that kept my hands busy but not my mind. When I was in my car, I kept the radio blasting away and I sang along with it. I stayed up late at night and got up early in the morning to make sure I would be tired enough to sleep through the night. And I asked my husband to take Angie to her appointments with Dr. McGarrah.

That routine lasted for several weeks and ended August 11, 1988, at 5 A.M. That's when I sat down and began writing this book. Denial can't last forever.

Guilt, Depression, and Other Pitfalls

I had an especially hard time handling the guilt I felt after I found out Angie had been molested. I really beat up on myself. I cross-examined myself more brutally than any defense attorney could ever have done. First of all, there were questions in my mind about whether I might have been responsible in some way for Angie's abuse. I went beyond wondering why I had not pulled her out of that school sooner than I did. After I learned that children of sexual abuse survivors are more likely to become victims than children from families with no history of abuse, I began to examine my own childhood. I was the product of a broken home. I had not gotten along with my stepfather. Were there memories I was repressing? I examined every corner of my own childhood to make sure I had not been a victim of sexual abuse myself.

Also, the sudden chaos in my family's life shook my self-confidence as a mother and wife. My home and family had always been the most important things in the world to me, but now I threw myself into homemaking with unsurpassed passion. I made sure the cookie jar was full of homemade ginger snaps, and it got to the point when my house was so spotless I started to crave dust.

I became very defensive about my child. I bristled if anyone criticized her, or even if I suspected someone disapproved of something she did or said. When the people at Angie's former preschool accused her of being a spoiled brat who had made up the abuse charges, I held mental debates to prove she was not spoiled. Sure, she had a lot of pretty clothes, but that was because smocking was my hobby, not because I bought her expensive things. She had a collection of dolls, but that was because she saved her allowance to buy them herself. These dialogues with myself were serious enough at the time, though they sound silly now.

My reactions weren't quite as extreme when it came to coping with my own fears. I knew it would be easy to overreact, and I frequently found myself stepping back to do a reality check. That doesn't mean the tendency to be overly protective of Angie wasn't there, though. Even now, I have to cope with fears of the future. I worry about how to protect her from the attitudes of others. It is a fear made even more acute by the publication of this book. Even though I am not using Angie's real name, people who know me will know who she is. Also, there are a number of people at our church, at Angie's school, and at her after-school and summer camps who were associated with the school at the time the abuse charges became known. They know she was one of the "alleged" victims. I can't control their reactions.

All I can control is how I respond to their reactions. And I will do everything I can to prepare Angie for the negative reactions she may encounter. She has no reason to be ashamed. She was the victim of a crime that affects thousands of children every year. If people can't understand that, it is their problem, not Angie's. I hope she will be strong enough to believe that some day.

Rationality helped me control my fears. It didn't help when it came to coping with my anger, however. Let's face it, the only cure we want for anger is vengeance; and the criminal, regulatory, and civil systems denied us their "cures."

I have enjoyed some feelings of what I call "constructive vengeance." For example, seven months after Angie's disclosure, I had a conference with her first grade teacher to go over her achievement test scores. The scores were outstanding, and the teacher recommended that Angie participate in a program for gifted children. I couldn't help but remember back to less than a year earlier, when Dr. McGarrah had given Angie a battery of tests that showed a large discrepancy between her aptitude and her achievement. In only months, Angie had closed that gap significantly.

I walked out of the school elated. I remember thinking how nice it would be to tell Angie's offenders, "See, you tried to destroy my child, but you didn't succeed. She's fighting her way back. She'll be

OK. She is OK, in spite of everything you did to her!" It was the sweetest kind of revenge any mother could ever hope for.

I suffered pangs of guilt and flashes of anger, but the hurt, ranging from sadness to despondency, was the most overwhelming emotion of all. I knew those feelings were unhealthy if I nursed them too long, so I fought to keep them from getting the best of me. When I started getting really down, I looked for activities to keep me busy. I tried to turn my thoughts outward instead of dwelling on myself. For example, Angie and I worked more actively with a shelter for the homeless that we had supported in previous years. I also agreed to head up a fund-raising event at Angie's new school. On a more frivolous note, I took a microwave cooking class I had wanted to take for years, but had never found time for. The trick is to keep your perspective. There is a fine line between denial and healthy distraction! I stepped over that line more than once.

I really overdid it when I threw myself into preparations for Angie's seventh birthday party. It turned out to be a production that would have made Disney proud. We used a Snow White theme and decorated the entire house accordingly. The children played a coin toss game in Snow White's wishing well. They bobbed for poison apples in the wicked queen's dungeon. They played Musical Dwarfs' House in a cottage constructed out of plywood and poster board, and they hunted for treasure in the dwarfs' Heigh Ho Mine.

The hit of the day was the Magic Mirror on the Wall. We took the heavy, ornate mirror off an old dresser and propped it up on the tool bench. We covered the front of the workbench with poster board and decorated it like an old dresser. We cut partial openings in each of the "drawer pulls." Then I made a furry paw out of fake fur and prerecorded a bunch of corny two-line responses to the question, "Mirror, mirror on the wall, who's the fairest one of all?" When the children stepped up to the mirror and asked the magic question, the mirror "spoke" to them. And then a furry paw (worn by my husband who was hiding behind the poster board) came out of one of the handles and gave each one a prize. The children loved it, but the party left me completely exhausted at a time when I had no energy to spare!

One thing that helped immensely was keeping a journal throughout this period. I have always enjoyed writing, and the journal provided an outlet for my frustrations and pain. Writing my feelings often helped me sort them out. I didn't have to worry about how it sounded because no one else would ever read it. It was probably the most therapeutic thing I did for myself.

The biggest mistake I made was trying to cope with everything on my own. I did talk with Dr. McGarrah occasionally, but we talked about matters directly related to Angie's therapy and progress. I should have had someone to talk with just about me.

My need to talk about Angie's abuse went from one extreme to the other. There were times it was almost a compulsion and I had to fight the urge to talk to anyone who would listen. Other times, I cringed from every thought and didn't want it mentioned at all. Talking with a professional would have given me the outlet I needed, and probably would have tempered the extreme reactions I experienced.

It would also have helped for my husband and me to talk with someone together. This would have lessened the tension in our home. In retrospect, I recommend that parents of molestation victims seek professional help for themselves as well as their child, even if it is only for one or a few sessions. There is no reason why parents should stumble blindly through the maze by themselves. As with the child's therapist, parents should search for someone with pertinent expertise.

I thought about getting professional help a number of times, but never did. I had lots of excuses. For one thing, there is a stigma in our society against seeking psychological help. I wanted to believe I was strong enough to cope on my own. Also, Angie's weekly therapy was already expensive in terms of time and money. How could we afford to have the whole family in therapy at once? Finally, I was well aware that the people at Angie's preschool thought I was some crazy, vindictive mother. If they ever found out I sought psychological help after Angie's abuse, they would have used that information to support their claim. I don't think that was idle paranoia on my part. One of the first questions Carla asked me when she called after the parents' meeting at the preschool was whether I had been in therapy myself.

I did try to find a parents' support group immediately after Angie's disclosure. The few groups that existed, however, were full because the demand for groups was so great. It took two years for my name to make it to the top of one waiting list! Nevertheless, I recommend that parents search for a support group. I hope it won't take them two years to find one. It would have been a tremendous help for me to have other parents of victims to talk with and listen to. I wouldn't have felt so alone.

Bad Times and Good

I did participate in "group therapy" of sorts. I found it was a great help to get away occasionally with my friends for "girls' night out," when we met for dinner, a movie, or shopping. I really needed the company of other mothers. I mentioned earlier how important it is for parents of victims to be knowledgeable about child development in general. Meeting with my friends and listening to the frustrations they were experiencing as they tried to cope with working motherhood contributed to my knowledge.

I could put Angie's behavior in perspective when I heard about the rough times Angie's friends were giving their parents. I remember one time when I didn't think I could bear another day of Angie's hostility. I was so tired of hearing her call me names and say how much she hated me. Then a friend told me how exasperated she was with her daughter, who was going through a rebellious phase that included an outbreak of name-calling. "If she calls me 'Pig-Face' one more time...," she said, and I broke out laughing. That was more therapeutic than a month of counseling could ever have been!

Parents should take care of their spiritual and physical health as well as their emotional health. They should not hesitate to seek support from within their religious communities. Parents need all the help they can get because living with the tragedy of child sexual abuse day after day can push one's spiritual strength to its limits. When confronted with other stressful situations, parents may develop a "Job complex," and like the biblical character, begin feeling that nothing will ever go right again. The complex hit me especially hard when Angie had a serious accident less than a year after she was sexually abused. Only instead of reacting with Job's patience, I exploded in anger.

I was at work when I received the telephone call saying that Angie had been hit in the head with a brick at after-school camp. Twenty minutes later I walked into the room where the doctor was working on Angie, and almost passed out. In one glance, I saw her battered face with a large gaping hole above her left eye. She was covered with blood from head to toe. The doctor showed me Angie's wounds. The worst was a long, deep gash which started at the left eyebrow and angled up toward the hairline. It took ten stitches to close. She also had a smaller, three-cornered cut next to the large one, which took two stitches to close. There was a large scrape running outward from the outer corner of her eye and a fourth gash that ran the length of her nose, near the inner corner of the eye. He closed that cut with butterflies. Angie was extremely fortunate that her eye was not damaged.

By the time I got her home, Angie's face was swollen and bruised. I spent the evening pampering her and trying to make her comfortable. By 7:30, she was asleep. And by 7:35, I collapsed in a heap of tears. The anger roared from every corner of my body and soul, and I aimed it straight at heaven.

"Why Angie?" I screamed silently. "Why her? Hasn't she been through enough? Please, please, please . . . just leave her alone!"

It was just too much to handle at one time. A clergyman told me later not to fight my anger. "Remember," he told me, "anger can itself be a prayer." It sounded strange to me at the time, but the more I thought about what he said, the more it made sense. Anger might be a desperate plea for help!

With all the emotional and spiritual turmoil that goes on, it shouldn't be hard to understand how the sexual abuse of a child can take a toll on the parents' physical health. A major problem I had was that I was unable to talk with anyone about Angie's abuse immediately after I found out about it. Mr. Morgan was in the initial phase of his investigation, and I could not say anything about the investigation until he interviewed the parents of the other girls in Angie's class. I kept everything bottled up inside for over a month, and after a few weeks I was experiencing full-blown anxiety attacks, complete with chest pains, shortness of breath, and numbness in my left arm.

Health and fitness are important to me, but I no longer had the time or energy to think about my own health. I stopped exercising. I began to eat junk I wouldn't have considered before—fast food, no food, candy bars in the afternoon. With Angie's nightmares screaming at me night after night, I began to go two and three nights in a row without sleeping. I lost weight I couldn't afford to lose.

I didn't turn myself around physically until I took my leave of absence from work, during the spring after Angie's disclosure. I knew I was in bad shape, so I put myself on a strict health regimen. I began running and working out on Nautilus at the YMCA. I started eating sensibly again. And for an extra pickup, I treated myself to a makeup lesson at a local salon. I called it my New Thighs, New Eyes Program!

Parents of molestation victims have to maintain their physical, spiritual, and emotional strength, because burnout is a real danger. They can do a number of things to help themselves, but some things they can do could be detrimental. Coping with it all is such a constant struggle that parents may feel an overwhelming need to get away. As with everything else I have talked about, extremes can be counterproductive. Distractions are beneficial, but a healthy balance is necessary. It is important to take time for yourself and spend time with friends, and husbands and wives should definitely get away by themselves and work hard on maintaining their relationship, but the urge to get away may be so strong that it turns into a flight from reality. A retreat into alcohol, drugs, extramarital affairs, or other false cures might be tempting, but it would definitely undermine the healing process.

Literal flight to a new location might also be tempting. It seems like an easy way to "get away from it all and forget this ever happened." I wished many times that we could have picked up and moved far away. It would have been easier to cope with the outside world. I wouldn't have had the constant reminders every time I drove by the school where Angie was molested or bumped into people associated with the school. It would have helped Angie with her fears to know that her offenders wouldn't be able to find her. But no matter where parents go, they should realize that they can't get away from the reality of their child's abuse. The family's fears, anger, guilt, and hurt will go along with them. There are just no easy cures.

It sounds simplistic, but a positive attitude is one beneficial coping mechanism. Dealing with child sexual assault can engulf the entire life of a family. I found myself thinking about life in an entirely new time frame. B.C. and A.D. became Before the Crime and After the Disclosure. I didn't think I'd ever smile again. But if parents can step back now and then and appreciate the little joys in life, the pain won't seem quite so overpowering.

There is an entry in my journal that shows how emotionally beneficial an event that might ordinarily seem insignificant can be to the parent of an abused child. On October 30, 1987 (two months after her disclosure), I wrote, "Well, this afternoon, I went to Angie's Halloween party at school . . . [It] was the best part of my whole week. It was that little bit of happiness I was looking for. I was surprised to find myself smiling and laughing for the first time in ages. It was just so much fun to see the children dressed up. They paraded across the stage to model their costumes. Then they played a game. Finally, they decorated cupcakes and ate them with some juice. Angie made it a point to get a cupcake I had baked. She was especially happy because after the party, she went home to play with a new friend. For 45 minutes, Angie and I were just another mother and daughter having fun at an elementary school Halloween party!"

It helped especially to sit back and look at the little things that showed how much progress Angie was making in her recovery. One day, nine months after her disclosure, Angie and I were on the way to school. We saw a little chipmunk cross the street, and Angie said, "I like chipmunks . . . and I like squirrels . . . and I like you and Daddy . . . and I like Mrs. Davis (her teacher) . . . and I like myself." "Do you really like yourself?" I asked. "Yes, I do," she answered. I had thought I would never hear her say that again. It had been so long! I went to work that day with the best feeling I'd had in a long time.

I also made sure that when Angie was able to laugh again, I wasn't so bogged down with my own problems that I couldn't laugh with her. I remember one night when she was feeling very affectionate. She put her arms around me and told me, "All mommies are different, but you're the greatest mom in the world. You're sweet, gorgeous, intelligent, and str . . ." She paused and put her hand on my arm. "Let's see your muscles, Mom." I bent my arm and flexed my muscles. "No really, Mom, show me your muscles." "I am," I answered. Angie grimaced and finished her list of accolades: ". . . and you've got muscles like chopped liver!"

Laughter can be healing, and parents will find that there are some good days sprinkled in with the bad. The good times will increase in frequency. Parents should soak up those moments of happiness when they can. They will give them strength for the hard times still ahead.

CHAPTER 18

SPECIAL ISSUES

A Word about Incest

When I began my search for information about child sexual abuse, most of what I found dealt with intrafamilial (incest) situations. As the parent of a child who was sexually molested by third-party offenders, I had a hard time mentally making the connection between my family's experience and incest. But actually, much of what I have written about in this book—the impact child molestation has on the victim, the family, the community, and society—is true whether the offender is related to the victim or not.

The dynamics of the crime are basically the same, but the sexual abuse of a child by a relative adds other dimensions to the crime. My daughter was hurled into a hell no child should ever have to endure, and it was hard for me to imagine that the pain my family experienced could have been worse. But I think it would have been even harder to cope with if someone in our own family had been responsible for the damage inflicted on Angie. I believe that Angie's fight to recover would have been more difficult if she had been incestuously abused.

She still can't understand why her teachers hurt her. They were authority figures she had been taught to trust and respect. Even now, years after her abuse ended, Angie will ask me, "Why, Mom? Why did they do it? Tell me why they did that to me. What did I do to deserve it? Why me?" It would be even harder for her to understand if the injury had been inflicted by a relative she loved. I think her guilt, her anger, and her sadness would have been more intense if she'd had to struggle with that kind of betrayal.

I also believe that the support others provide incest victims and their families might be weaker than that offered in extrafamilial situations. A greater stigma is attached to incest than to third-party abuse. Further, when the abuse is perpetrated by a relative, support from the victim's immediate and extended family would be even more tenuous than in third-party cases. The family would be torn by conflicting loyalties. Not only would family members be more likely to deny that the abuse occurred, they would also be more likely to pressure the child and nonabusing parent to "forget it." Parents who report the abuse to the authorities may incur the wrath of family members who think the information should be kept within the family. The conflicting pressures exerted by others on the victim and his or her parents could be overwhelming.

Parents of incest victims would not have to deal with reactions from ancillary organizations. Neither would the question of filing a civil suit be an issue in most incest situations. The system, however, often presents hurdles for nonabusing parents of incest victims trying to protect their children from continued abuse that parents of extrafamilial abuse victims don't have to face.

I doubt that anyone would challenge my right to remove my daughter from the school where she was molested. I doubt that anyone would condemn me for doing everything within my power to keep her from ever again having to see the people who abused her. Nonabusing parents of incestuously abused children, however, may face the added horror of seeing their children forced by the court system back into contact with the offender, often a spouse or former spouse.

I remember how terrified Angie was that her teachers would come to get her and hurt her again. Even after all these years, that fear still raises its head occasionally. I can't imagine anything more devastating for a parent than to have the right to protect one's child taken away. How can children ever learn to trust again when they are subjected to continued abuse after confiding in adults they expect to protect them?

It is a nightmare I can't even comprehend after knowing the pain my own child has endured. Yet, that is the nightmare many victims and their nonabusing parents face every day, when the child molester is a parent or stepparent. The right of an offender to exercise his or her parental rights often conflicts with the child's right to protection. Nonabusing parents who try to protect their children are accused of dirty tricks in custody battles. It is appallingly common for judges to grant custody or unsupervised visiting privileges to abusive parents (or to parents living with abusers), even when there is strong psychological and/or physical evidence to support the abuse charges. In those situations, nonabusing parents have no choice but to go head-to-head with the system to try to protect the victim. It is a fight they lose far too often.

With the added dimensions incest heaps on the trauma of child sexual abuse, I can understand how much harder it must be for those parents to cope. The denial, the guilt, the anger, and the depression must be even more intense than what I experienced.

In talking with the mother of two incestuously abused children recently, I was struck by how often she used the word *shame* in describing her feelings. Shame was one feeling I don't remember having to cope with, but this woman seemed overwhelmed by the shame she felt because she had been unable to protect her children in her own home. Incest introduces even more horrifying parameters to the crime of child sexual abuse than those my family had to face. And we faced more than any family should ever confront.

When There Are Siblings

Angie is an only child, so I didn't have to worry about the effects her experience might have on other children in the family. The difficulties a family encounters when a child is sexually molested will be more complex if there are siblings. Further, if more than one child within the family is victimized, the problems will increase exponentially. Disclosure by one victim might put that child in conflict with siblings who are not emotionally prepared to talk about their own experience with abuse. Conflicting reports, retractions, and antagonism among siblings could result. All relationships within that family would most certainly feel the impact.

Just as child sexual abuse victims develop social problems outside the home, they also meet trouble in their relationships with siblings. The victim's anger is often directed at the person nearest, so a sibling, especially a younger sibling, is a likely target. Nonvictimized siblings would have to cope with the erratic behavior of the molested sibling. They might resent the sudden demand the victim makes on their parents' attention. Depending on the age of the siblings, they might also have to cope with the reactions of their peers, if news of the sexual abuse became public information. Although the parents' first wave of concern will naturally be for the welfare of the victim, they must cope with the stress their nonvictimized children will experience as well.

Siblings should be part of the "recovery team," but their own needs must not be overlooked. They will struggle to understand what happened to their abused brother or sister. They may experience their own feelings of denial, guilt, fear, anger, and depression. Parents have to help them understand what happened on a level appropriate for their age. They will need one-on-one time with the parents more than ever. Perhaps several sessions with a therapist would be beneficial for brothers and sisters of the victim. Nonabused siblings should not be allowed to get lost in the turmoil that engulfs a family when one of its members is sexually molested.

Daddies Are Parents, Too

This book has been written from my perspective as the mother of a sexual abuse victim. Most of what I have said should be relevant to both parents, but I think fathers deserve special attention. When I first searched for a support group, I wanted to find one for parents because I felt that both my husband and I needed the support of other parents. There were no parent support groups then, only groups for mothers of abuse victims.

Public awareness of child molestation has evolved slowly over the years. The sexual abuse of children has been going on for centuries, but no one talked about it until recently. Even now, when the subject is discussed, the focus is on incest. Over and over, the organizations and agencies from which I sought help told me that their efforts were concentrated on incest victims. Publications about child molestation were written primarily about incest; child sexual abuse seemed almost synonymous with incest.

The emphasis on incest may have been the result of several factors. For one thing, the need for intervention from outside the family to protect the child from further victimization may well be greater in incest situations than in cases of third-party abuse. That, plus the complexity of family dynamics in incest cases, may have necessitated the concentration of limited resources on intrafamilial abuse situations. I also believe, however, that the public preferred to equate child sexual abuse with incest because then it was easy to think it would never affect them personally. Incest was something that happened to other families in another part of town.

Contrary to that popular belief, Diana Russell's survey indicated that only 29% of perpetrators were relatives, versus 60% who were known, but unrelated, to their victims. Nevertheless, it wasn't until the highly publicized McMartin day care case in California a few years ago that people began to realize that children could be abused outside the home as well. With increased media coverage of third-party abuse perpetrated by day care workers, teachers, scout leaders, and clergymen, the public's attention is finally beginning to focus on the extrafamilial sexual abuse of our children.

What does all that have to do with fathers of sexual abuse victims? Simply this: as long as the public equated sexual abuse with incest, the father of a molestation victim was often equated with the offender. Actually, according to Russell's research, incestuously abused children are more likely to be victimized by uncles, stepfathers, and cousins than by their biological fathers. But as long as *father* was synonymous with *offender*, help for nonoffending parents focused on the victims' mothers.

The increasing awareness of third-party abuse may begin to focus attention on the needs of fathers as well. I am aware of two support groups now meeting in Atlanta that include fathers of victims. One group is for nonabusing parents of either incest or third-party victims. The other is only for parents of third-party molestation victims. I hope more resources will be channeled into programs that help both parents of child sexual abuse victims. And I hope that fathers will reach out and accept the help that becomes available to them.

Fathers are often less likely than mothers to turn outward for help in coping with trauma in their lives. Men in our society are socialized from birth into being "strong and silent." Expressing feelings is too often seen as a sign of weakness. Men are conditioned not to cry. I can't imagine how any parent of a sexually assaulted child can help but cry. Daddies need hugs, too!

The Dollars and Cents of Child Sexual Abuse

I have read a number of articles and books on the subject of child sexual abuse in the last two years. I have seen and heard reports about the crime on TV and radio. I have attended workshops on the subject. I have yet to come across anyone who has focused on the economic impact the crime has on individual families and on society as a whole.

In the first two years after my daughter was molested, the cost of the crime totaled over $16,500. Of that amount, my husband and I paid over $7,000 out of our own pockets. Those are only the hard dollar costs directly related to the abuse—Angie's medical bills during the period we searched for physiological answers to her somatic symptoms, the cost of therapy, and the income I lost while on leave from my job. That does not include indirect costs such as my own medical bills, transportation costs, or lost productivity and lost salary increases at work.

My husband and I are fortunate because a portion of Angie's medical and therapy bills has been covered by group health insurance. We also have two incomes to cushion the amount we have had to pay. Nevertheless, the expenses have placed tremendous stress on us at times. For one thing, we have had to build a permanent "float" factor into our family budget to cover the period between the time we pay for the services and the time we are reimbursed by the insurance company. Even more significantly, we don't know how long those benefits will continue. We never know if or when the insurance company will dispute the legitimacy of keeping a child in therapy for the length of time Angie will need it.

Our policy has both annual and lifetime limits on coverage for psychological care. Our expenses have exceeded the annual limit, and the lifetime limit probably will be reached before Angie reaches adulthood. Further, we never know if we might lose our insurance benefits because of a loss or change of employment. If that happens, will Angie be insurable under a new policy with her history of claims? Will she be able to get coverage on her own as an adult?

Finally, we are depleting insurance benefits that might be needed at a later date if Angie ever suffers a catastrophic illness. The financial uncertainty presented by Angie's future need for therapy is frightening. Other parents are saving for their children's college educations. We are saving so that Angie will be able to have the therapy she may need in the future. I don't know how parents who are already financially stressed cope with the additional burden.

We are in a relatively secure situation, with two incomes and group health insurance, and we still feel very vulnerable. The problem is that there are no guarantees when it comes to health insurance coverage, especially now that companies are cutting back on health care benefits and shifting more and more of the cost to employees.

I know of a child who was denied therapy for months, even though one of her parents was employed and the family had health coverage. The problem was that the family was insured by an HMO that required its members to use a therapist from their approved list of contract specialists. None of the therapists on the list was experienced in working with molestation victims, and the parents couldn't afford to pay the full cost of therapy if they used an "unapproved" therapist. As a result, the child lost valuable therapy time, while her parents worked through months of formal protests and red tape, until she could be seen by a child psychologist who specialized in abuse cases. And then the HMO limited coverage to 20 therapy hours per year.

Many families fall through the health care cracks completely. A lot of people earn too much to be eligible for public assistance, but too little to manage the cost of long-term therapy for a child who needs it. Even those children who qualify for public assistance may not receive the help they need. In Georgia, for example, Medicaid will pay for a maximum of nine hours of therapy (including evaluation) per year for children who have been abused. When a group of mental health professionals lobbied to have those benefits increased, legislators asked for proof that longer-term psychological intervention was needed. Unfortunately, no such proof existed, because little research has been done on this aspect of sexual or physical abuse. It is a vicious circle. The public sector is afraid to commit funds to a problem they know little about, but the necessary research is not going to get done without proper funding.

Child abuse—and I am talking now about physical, emotional, and sexual abuse—is already costing the public sector dearly. And we, as taxpayers, are the ones who ultimately pay that bill. For fiscal year 1991, for example, Georgia's Department of Human Resources requested $55 million for the direct costs of programs that protect children, many of whom are at risk because of abuse. The funds were earmarked for services for abused and neglected children, for emotionally disturbed children and juvenile offenders, and for teens at risk for early pregnancy and substance abuse.

Indirect costs are also associated with child abuse. Local governments across the nation are struggling with the problem of overcrowded prisons. According to the Georgia Council on Child Abuse, Inc., 90% of the people confined to those prisons were abused as children. Abuse victims are more likely than nonabused individuals to turn to lives of crime, drugs, and alcohol abuse. Further, child abuse is a self-perpetuating crime. Abuse victims who do not receive the treatment they need may grow up to be abusive adults. The cost of abuse increases exponentially if intervention programs aimed at stopping the cycle of abuse are not available.

Angie's abuse has already cost my company thousands of dollars in health insurance benefits, sick days, and lost productivity. And considering the high incidence of child abuse, I know I am not the only employee of this company whose child has been a victim of the crime. If my company could put a dollar sign on the cost of abuse, I have no doubt our management would be shocked at the impact on our bottom line.

What I don't understand, either as a mother or as a business-woman, is why no one has figured that out yet. I think the problem is the same in both the public and the private sectors. Those who hold the pursestrings put their money where their mouths are—and no one is talking about child abuse. Conversely, they put their mouths where their money is—and no one has bothered to calculate how much child abuse costs.

Many companies acknowledge how much alcoholism, drug abuse, and employee stress affect their bottom lines. Consequently, they invest in programs to encourage healthy life styles or in assistance programs for employees needing help with substance abuse. But these same companies—these corporate community leaders—don't even want to think about child abuse.

I know of two major southeastern corporations that shied away from presentations on child abuse at their employees' "lunch-and-learn" series. Lunch-and-learn presentations are informal noontime talks about health and public interest issues, such as how to handle stress. At one company, employees who were concerned about increasing media reports of child abuse suggested a session on the topic. I talked with the person in charge of programs for that organization.

She told me that child abuse would not be an appropriate topic for the series because the company's management wanted to steer away from controversial topics. "Controversial?" I asked. "Well, maybe not controversial . . . but, you know . . . sensitive." "Why would child abuse be considered a sensitive subject?" I asked. She answered, "Well . . . people who attend the session might be stigmatized by their fellow employees. I mean, people might think that anyone going to it must be a child abuser."

This is a sad and frustrating state of affairs. What can be done to change it? I believe that families of victims and professionals in the field must become more vocal. Government and business leaders have to be educated until they care enough to commit resources to combating child abuse. Too many politicians pay only lip service to protecting our children. Publicly they say all the right things, but when it comes down to funding programs, they'd rather see limited public dollars go into steel and concrete. And business leaders aren't saying anything at all because the plight of abused children has not yet hit their social or fiscal consciences. The cycle of abuse is going to be broken only if business and government leaders are willing to join forces to tackle the problem.

I was amused recently by the cover of a local business magazine, which featured a miniature yuppie on its cover. It was a picture of a small boy dressed up in pinstriped suit, button-down shirt, and power tie. The magazine featured a series of articles about the role businesses are playing in local educational systems. Business leaders are concerned that a declining quality of education will threaten their future pool of qualified employees. As a result, local companies are participating in innovative programs to improve the local educational systems.

The problem of child abuse needs that same level of concern and innovation. The Georgia Center for Children is one example of what can be done when public and private interests join forces. The Georgia Center is a nonprofit organization offering services to victims of sexual abuse. Since it began operation less than a year ago, the center has provided treatment for 63 abuse victims ranging in age from 17 months to 18 years. Although some government grants contribute to its support, the center is funded largely by contributions from individuals and businesses.

The Georgia Center is a private organization that was founded largely by the efforts of individuals within the DeKalb County District Attorney's office. Former District Attorney Robert Wilson serves as chairman of the center's board and District Attorney J. Tom Morgan and former Prosecutor Steve Roberts sit on the board, along with individuals from the business and professional communities. The center is working closely with government agencies, local police departments, and the judicial system to break the cycle of abuse. The center is a wonderful example of what can be done, but it is not enough.

Businesses do contribute to child advocacy organizations. That commitment is nominal, however, compared with their support for other types of nonprofit organizations. Programs that protect children from abuse should receive more priority than they currently do. Few individual citizens, public officials, or business people would dispute the idea that children represent the future of our country. Those same people must come to understand the far-reaching effects that child abuse has on all of us. They should begin working together to break the cycle of child abuse. Until that happens, the lives of our children, and the future they represent, will be in jeopardy.

EPILOGUE

Five Years after Disclosure

I began writing this book one year after Angie's initial disclosure of having been abused. The changes I had witnessed during that first year were so dramatic that at that time I believed her pain, for the most part, was over.

The early months after her disclosure, the short-term period of her recovery, were dominated by daily terrors. By the time I began writing, it was easy to assume the recovery was over, because I remembered how much worse things had been only months before. Now, as I reflect on the four years since I began writing, I realize that Angie's recovery wasn't as complete as I initially thought. In fact, the end of that first year had marked, not an endpoint, but a milestone in her recovery. It was the beginning of my daughter's long-term recovery, a process that I now know will continue indefinitely.

Even now, five years after Angie's initial disclosure, we continue to ride our roller coaster of discovery and recovery. Should I rewrite what I wrote back then to reflect my current perspective, or leave it as it was originally written? I have decided to take the latter approach. I think it will be more honest, and, I hope, more useful, for others to see the evolution of Angie's recovery through the eyes of a mother whose own moods and perspective were constantly changing. So I will simply update what I wrote those many months ago.

Angie: The Long View

I never know what to expect next from Angie, and that has made it hard to write about the long-term effects of her having been abused. Sometimes I feel pessimistic when Angie is experiencing a new round of difficulty. But sooner or later she recovers, and I feel optimistic because I can see the progress she is making. She really is okay! And yet I can't be too positive, because I know there is a lot of pain still to come in her life. I guess it would be most accurate to say that Angie is coping as well as any child who has experienced the trauma of sexual assault can be expected to.

Five years have passed since Angie began talking about the abuse she suffered in kindergarten. She is nearing her twelfth birthday. Eighty percent of the time she looks and acts like any other fifth-grader. She's an affectionate, creative, bright little girl who has outgrown dolls but still loves ballet. She enjoys having girlfriends sleep overnight at her house and she thinks boys are the greatest nuisances on earth.

What makes Angie different from her friends is the current of sadness that is never far below the surface of her smile. And when that sadness erupts into anguish, it makes the other 20% of her life hell. I never know when that's going to happen, but by now the sequence of events is predictable.

It will begin when something happens to stir up painful memories for Angie. The cue that sparks the upheaval may be a direct reminder of the abuse Angie suffered in kindergarten; I may see an immediate, dramatic breakdown in her behavior. Other times, a less concrete, less obvious cue will bring on a more subtle deterioration in her behavior. Angie will become increasingly anxious, with no apparent cause. Sometimes she will complain of feeling "afraid," but she can't verbalize the source of her fears. She will begin to have trouble sleeping at night, and within days her sleeplessness will leave us both exhausted and craving one good night's sleep. Sometimes Angie will lapse back into her old pattern of refusing to flush the toilet. She will become more and more agitated, and then all hell will break loose.

Angie may or may not experience a flashback, but the behavioral effects are the same. What I see next is the old "push-pull" syndrome. On the one hand, she will show regressive behavior while she clings to me for protection from her torment. On the other hand, she pushes everyone away with her aggression and/or hostility, which may be passive or active. The first thing to crumble will be Angie's self-esteem, and her self-hate will translate into behavioral problems at home and social problems with her peers.

The severity of Angie's setbacks vary in intensity, but eventually she will bottom out and then slowly begin to recover. It may take days or weeks before that happens, but her behavior typically stabilizes after one and a half to two weeks. When Angie experiences a setback, it demands an incredible amount of patience and support on my part. Children who have been abused require a lot of what I call "nurturing discipline." They need support and understanding. They also need constancy in family routine and discipline. When Angie is going through a rough period, I try extra hard to keep disruptions in our routine at a minimum so we can maintain some sort of equilibrium. Angie's flashback/setback periods are exhausting for both of us.

No matter how many episodes we go through, I am never prepared for the next one. It never gets any easier. And when things are going smoothly, I can never relax completely because I never know when something will happen to throw Angie out of equilibrium again.

Shortly after Angie started third grade I took her to lunch at her favorite Southern-style restaurant to celebrate the beginning of a new school year. As we waited for our food to be served, Angie sat across from me in the booth, bubbling over with tales of her first week of school. She liked her new teacher. She was excited about having history for the first time. She had gotten a perfect score on her first math quiz. The move into third grade brought a big jump in expectations in conduct and academics at her school and Angie was feeling like a big girl. She was proud of her new status as a third-grader, and she told me excitedly about the book reports and the geography project she would work on during the year. And then Angie froze.

I followed her stare across the room and saw a father who had just entered the restaurant with his small son. The child was wearing a T-shirt from the preschool where Angie had been molested. In an instant, the beaming smile on Angie's face was replaced by the now-familiar look of despair. I reached across the table and took Angie's hand in mine. We sat in silence for a while. Angie looked dazed.

"Angie," I asked softly, "are you OK?" Without a word, she got up and crawled onto the seat next to me. She drew her legs up under her and curled up as small as she could. I put my arm around her and she pressed against me for protection. When she began to talk, she had reverted to disjointed baby-talk sentences. In a matter of seconds, a $6 T-shirt had reduced my big-girl third-grader to a whimpering, frightened preschooler.

As she has so many times before, Angie asked me why "that" had happened to her, and she wanted to know why I had put her in that preschool. I tried to remind her of the good times she'd had there before kindergarten, but Angie stared at me blankly. She seemed to have no recollection of her earlier years at the preschool. I wondered if she was beginning to block out the good parts of her childhood along with the bad. And now I wonder how much of her childhood Angie will lose because of those nine months when her childhood went wrong for her.

I wish those people who criticize Angie and/or me because we haven't "forgotten" her abuse by now could have been in that restaurant that day. I wish they could have seen her smile turn to pain. I wish they could have felt my own happiness sink and disappear.

Not long ago someone wondered out loud if Angie wasn't "deliberately hanging on to those memories so she can get attention." The memories of the crime committed against my child will be with her forever, but it is not through any choice she has made. It is absurd and cruel for people to believe Angie wants it that way.

New Disclosures

Early in chapter 3, I talked about the cycle of disclosure, upheaval, assimilation, equilibrium, and disclosure that Angie experienced during the first year of her recovery. While the effects of Angie's abuse have been constant reminders of what happened to her, Angie eventually stopped talking about the specific incidents of abuse after the first year of her recovery. It was not until the summer after second grade, two years after the abuse stopped, that Angie unexpectedly disclosed new information.

One day at summer day camp, Angie found herself alone with a counselor in the kitchen. Nothing happened, but the situation—being alone in a room with a "teacher"—triggered the first of a series of flashbacks. The following three weeks were terrible for her, and as we talked our way through her latest round of anguish, she began to disclose details she had not mentioned before. Gaps in the information disclosed by Angie and the other confirmed victim had left unanswered questions regarding the exact involvement of one of the kindergarten teachers. The new details that Angie disclosed answered most of those questions, and the early inconsistencies in the victims' stories finally made sense. They also explained why Angie was so much more terrified of one of her offenders than the other. To my dismay, I learned that Angie had been molested many more times than we had previously believed.

This unexpected volley of information took me completely by surprise, so I consulted Dr. McGarrah about it. She said that it is not unusual for abuse victims to disclose new information years after the actual incidents. It may be that deeply repressed details surface as a result of therapy and/or external cues. It also may be a function of the child's changing perspective on past events as she or he grows older.

I was surprised by how calm Angie was as she revealed these new details of her abuse. She was clearly upset, but the hysterics of earlier disclosures were gone. Old fears were resurrected, but the terror didn't overwhelm her as in the past.

Angie's bad times are fewer and farther between, but they still exist. She continues to experience feelings of guilt, fear, anger, and depression. She still has bad dreams occasionally. They don't overwhelm every day of her life as they did at first, but they are still there to haunt her.

Angie once described the fear she continues to feel toward her offenders in extremely graphic terms. "I can't stop seeing their faces," she said. "No matter how hard I try, I see those faces coming at me. There aren't any arms or legs or bodies—it's just their faces, coming at me and coming at me and coming at me, and I can't stop them." And then Angie ran into a closet and scrunched down in the corner, making herself as small as possible. She curled up on her knees, her back hunched over, and covered her head with her arms as if to protect herself from falling debris. "Even if I do this," she continued, "I still see their mean faces coming at me."

Angie remained in weekly therapy with Dr. McGarrah for three and a half years. We dropped her back to every-other-week appointments while she was in fourth grade. That schedule lasted for one year, until the trauma of her parents' divorce necessitated a return to the weekly sessions. Several years ago, Angie wrote this about Dr. McGarrah:

Nancy is my psychologist and a good friend of mine. For at least a year I have been going to her with all my problems. I talk to her about friends or if I get in a fight with

*my mom. She has been very nice to me. She told me that
I was not the only one that got hurt. It makes me feel good
inside to know that my mom, dad, and Nancy all care.*

As hard as it has been to see Angie struggle with understanding
what happened to her, I know it would have been much harder if
she had not had her friend, Nancy McGarrah, to help her. Sometimes
the benefits from therapy are hard to see, but there have been times
when I could see them very clearly.

Once, when Angie was nine years old, my husband was caught
outside in a sudden summer cloudburst. Angie called to him from
inside, "For heaven's sake, Daddy, come in out of the rain. You are
so stupid!" She hesitated and then explained, "I'm sorry, Daddy. I
didn't mean to call you stupid. I know you're not stupid, but standing
out in the rain isn't a good thing to do, because you might get sick."
I smiled to myself to think that Angie was finally beginning to
distinguish between one's self and one's behavior.

I continue to seek opportunities that will build on Angie's im-
proving self-confidence. She played T-ball and baseball for several
summers. Learning to play a team sport was very good for her. She
was fortunate to have wonderful coaches who were more interested
in reinforcing basic skills and having fun than they were in competition. Having pets around the house has also been good for Angie's
growing sense of self-worth. There is nothing like the unconditional
love of a puppy to let a child know she is loved!

I have found that giving Angie responsibilities around the house
helps her feel she is an important part of the family team. Chores
don't have to be a source of conflict. Handled positively, Angie's
chores have helped her feel more self-confident. She is very proud
of herself when she helps me clean or when she learns to cook
something new.

School Life

Looking back over the past five years, it seems to me that Angie's
first grade school year, the first year following her disclosure, was
characterized primarily by her lack of confidence in her academic
skills. Despite Angie's intelligence, she was convinced she was the
dumbest kid in her class. She tried hard, but she was never pleased
with her work. With the encouragement of her first grade teacher,
she slowly began to believe in herself.

Her second grade teacher also helped Angie recognize her academic strengths. Angie's second grade school year was characterized primarily by social problems. She complained that no one liked her because she was "different." Angie felt different because she thought she was the only one who had been "hurt like that." When she felt bad about herself, she set up situations that would validate that self-concept. It became a vicious circle. Angie felt different, so she did things to push the other children away from her. Then when they called her "weird" or didn't want to play with her, Angie accepted that as proof that she was right all along about being different.

Then came third grade, a year that started off with promise. I remember how Angie came home beaming with pride when she was placed in the advanced reading group, and when she got another perfect score on a math test. "I had no idea I was that smart," she said in amazement.

It still amazes me that this child, who is incredibly bright, is surprised at her own academic achievements. She talks about her successes as though they are freak accidents! Her academic self-confidence came a long way in third grade—until January, when her classmates discovered her "secret" and everything fell apart.

A new school offered a fresh start. I did not tell Angie's fourth grade teacher about her history of abuse. The need wasn't there as it had been in the previous three years. Angie was given her chance to prove she was not "a bad kid in school," and she passed the test with flying colors. Her academic performance has improved dramatically, and she is no longer the friendless "kid from outer space." During the summer between third and fourth grades, Angie participated in group therapy with other preteen female victims of sexual abuse. It was a pilot program led by Dr. Marianne Celano and supported by the Georgia Council on Child Abuse. While the children met with two therapists in their group, the parents met with Dr. Celano in a support group.

Both Angie and I benefited immeasurably from this program. Even though three years had passed since Angie's disclosure, I wept as I realized that all the questions, fears, and feelings I have discussed in this book had been experienced by the other parents. I wasn't alone. And Angie learned that she wasn't alone either. Being in a group with other children who looked and acted "normal" reinforced what Dr. McGarrah and I had been telling her for years—that there wasn't anything wrong with her. Sexual abuse does happen to other children. She really wasn't from outer space after all!

Friends and Others

Angie and Jessica are still friends, as are Diane and I. Carla and I, however, have only recently begun to speak to each other again, mainly because she seems to be reaching out to me. For months, Carla had acted as though nothing ever happened at Angie's preschool, and she chatted brightly whenever we met at church or school. Then she began to avoid me. I don't know whether something happened or she simply sensed my discomfort. When a meeting was unavoidable, we spoke as little as possible and then went our own ways.

Some other parents from Angie's old school have also become a bit more cordial recently. I think they have forgotten the entire situation. And why shouldn't they? To them, it's as though nothing ever happened.

The preschool where Angie was abused has not only survived, but is stronger and more prosperous than ever. The board's defensive policy worked quite well. There was some disruption initially, but as that group of parents moved on, everything returned to normal. The school had a strong reputation before the abuse, and it was able to skip over that brief period and continue building its reputation as a premier Atlanta preschool. I suspect that most parents who have their children enrolled there now don't even know children were sexually abused at the school.

To Tell or Not to Tell

I continue to struggle with the question of whether or not to tell people about Angie's trauma. As Angie has grown older, an interesting twist to the dilemma has developed. Other than the authorities, Angie had talked about her abuse only to Dr. McGarrah, her father, and me. She didn't want anyone else to know about it. Now that she's a little older, however, she's beginning to feel a need to confide in other people. I try to encourage her to do that if she's comfortable with it, but this means Angie is having to learn how to balance the pros and cons of telling certain persons, just as I have had to do.

Many people believe child sexual abuse should be kept a deep, dark secret. It's an idea that is reinforced by offenders to keep their victims from telling. Unfortunately, it also gives victims the message that they have done something terrible—that there is something dirty or bad about them—something so awful that no one will like them if people find out.

The hardest part of Angie's recovery has been helping her believe that she didn't do anything to deserve being abused. When Angie wants to talk about what happened to her, I try very hard not to overreact. I listen to what she has to say and then I try to respond calmly. I tell her that I wish I could wave a magic wand and erase what happened to her, but I can't. The fact is that it did happen and we can't change that. What we can do is make sure it doesn't ruin the rest of her life. And the first step to take is to understand that she didn't do anything to deserve what happened to her. She was just in the wrong place at the wrong time. It could just as easily have happened to any other child. And it does happen to other children—lots of them.

If I suddenly start advising Angie not to tell anyone about her abuse, it would make a lie out of all of that. It would give her the unspoken message, "There must be something bad about me after all, and we don't want anyone to find out about it." Angie has to know, however, that it is not wise to stand on the street corner and shout it out to anyone and everyone. With Dr. McGarrah's help, I am trying to help Angie learn to be selective as she decides in whom to confide. And I am trying to prepare her for a variety of reactions.

Knowing what to expect is the hardest part for both of us. Except for one major flashback episode that threw Angie out of equilibrium for about three weeks, she had a great time the summer following second grade. She especially enjoyed her summer day camp, and became very fond of her camp counselor. While she was struggling with the turmoil following the flashback, Angie said she wanted to confide in her counselor. It was the first time Angie wanted to talk with someone outside the family about her abuse, and I immediately panicked. I didn't want her to do it. I liked Angie's counselor, but she was young and I wasn't sure how she would react.

I swallowed my fears and told Angie I would support her decision, no matter what she decided to do. Angie announced that she was going to talk with the counselor the next day. She was both anxious and excited. It was almost like the night before a ballet performance—full of anticipation mixed with fear.

The next morning, Angie wasn't sure she was going to go through with it, and I assured her that whatever she decided would be okay. When I picked her up that afternoon, she was ecstatic. She had mustered the courage to talk with her counselor, and the counselor had reacted positively. She told Angie she was sorry that had happened to her and said Angie could call her anytime she wanted to talk.

For the next few days, Angie became overly attached to the counselor. She didn't want to leave her side, and became jealous of the attention the counselor gave other children. Then the counselor began to distance herself from Angie, and Angie felt bitter and betrayed. Angie and I talked about the situation and I explained the counselor's position. Angie had to appreciate that the counselor was responsible for the other children, too, and couldn't give all her attention to her.

After a week or so, Angie's unrealistic expectations became more reasonable and her relationship with the counselor settled into a special, yet professional, friendship. That summer is long past, but the counselor is still Angie's friend—and her baby-sitter.

Working that episode through was very difficult for me. When Angie was younger, I was the one who decided whom to tell about her abuse. Now I am having to turn some of that control over to Angie, and it's scary. I want to protect her from being hurt, but as she takes more risks in confiding in others, the chance that she will be hurt by someone increases. Her first experience had a happy ending—her second blew up in her face.

Angie and a classmate had been best friends for two years. One day, when they were in third grade, Angie confided to her friend that she had been abused in kindergarten. The child kept Angie's confidence for months, but eventually she told several other girls at school that Angie had been "child abused." The news spread quickly and Angie was bombarded with questions from children who didn't know what being "child abused" meant.

Many of the comments were innocent. Some were downright mean. Angie heard, "Don't play with Angie—she's creepy," "My mother told me not to play with you," and "Do you have some kind of disease or something?" Within days the curiosity died down, and I believe most of the children forgot about it, mainly because they really didn't understand what it was all about. Angie, however, couldn't forget.

Once more she had been betrayed by someone she trusted. And one of her worst fears was confirmed—children who were once her friends treated her as though she was "from outer space or something" when they found out she was a molestation victim. Immediately after that incident Angie's academic performance and social behavior dropped precipitously. I consulted with her teacher and found little sympathy. The teacher was critical of Angie for telling her friend. She also criticized me for my volunteer work with a local child abuse prevention organization, because she thought my involvement in the speakers bureau made it obvious to everyone that Angie had been abused. And she scolded Angie in front of her classmates, saying, "I don't care what your problems are, I don't want to see you bring them into the classroom."

Angie responded to all of this by walling herself off, and she ended her third grade year feeling friendless, stupid, and generally worthless. It seemed as if Angie's reputation with her classmates and teachers had now been set in cement, and after much soul-searching, we agreed it would be best for her to change schools. She needed a fresh start. As Angie put it, "I need to prove I'm not a bad kid in school, Mom."

As expected, the decision to change schools was criticized by people who thought I was teaching Angie to "run away from her problems." It is a criticism I have never taken lightly. After a lot of thought, however, I don't believe Angie is running away from her problems. In fact, Angie has shown remarkable strength these past five years. She has dealt with the problem of sexual assault as well as any child—or adult, for that matter—could do. I just think she should not be expected to face other people's problems at the same time!

The System

Dollars and Cents Revisited

My life at work finally took a new turn. I was on a probation of sorts for 18 months after I returned from my second leave of absence. I worked hard and had two very good performance reviews. Finally, my boss reassigned territories again, and I now handle some "high-profile" accounts. It's a good feeling to know that my boss and colleagues have confidence in me again, but I also know I've lost three years from my career that will never be recovered. The financial consequences of that hiatus will continue to compound indefinitely.

In chapter 18, I talked about the Medicaid limitations on therapy for abuse victims. That limit increased from nine to 41 hours of therapy per year (including evaluation) in 1990. To fund that increase, however, the Georgia legislature eliminated all coverage provisions for adults. This elimination is especially significant for victims who are incestuously abused because the victim will be the only family member eligible for benefits.

As far as my own family goes, comments I made in chapter 18 proved to be painfully prophetic. The direct costs resulting from Angela's molestation five and a half years ago now total over $30,000. That cost used to be cushioned by group health insurance and two incomes. Those cushions no longer exist; once again, I am afraid for my child and her future.

When my marriage began to crumble, I decided to add Angie to my group health insurance plan. It was "insurance insurance"—with her covered on both parents' policies, I thought she would surely be protected. Angie's coverage under my policy was declined, however—she was uninsurable because of her history of therapy.

I appealed the underwriter's decision to an employee benefits board within my company. My appeal included three arguments. In my underwriting argument, I pointed out that, with the exception of her therapy, medical claims had been fairly routine. I could understand their excluding therapy as a preexisting condition, but couldn't they at least request a physical exam to determine her medical insurability?

My second argument was based on employee relations issues. My company, like many in this country, is worried about the effect rising medical costs are having on the bottom line. In an effort to control those costs for the company, it is excluding as many employees as possible from the group plan. Employees who are covered are bearing more of the costs through higher premiums, larger deductibles, and larger coinsurance payments. As a businesswoman, I understand the dilemma American businesses faced. But, I asked the board, is it really in the best interests of companies, in the long run, to place ever increasing numbers of their employees in a position where they face potential financial disaster?

My final argument was a social one. I talked about the revictimization of child abuse victims and their families. This was one more example of revictimization. Declaring my daughter uninsurable now could deny her both health and life insurance coverage for the rest of her life, because applications for insurance always ask if previous requests for coverage have ever been denied. Once more, my daughter's future was in jeopardy because, at the age of six, she was the victim of a crime.

On the basis of my appeal, the benefits board overturned the underwriter's decision and Angie was added to my group policy. Her need for therapy was ruled a preexisting condition and would be excluded from coverage for one year. I was relieved—but not for long.

Several months later, my company announced that it was replacing our traditional health insurance plan with a "managed healthcare" plan. Managed healthcare is similar to an extended HMO plan, in which employees choose a primary care physician who is a member of the plan's network. Employees cannot consult a specialist unless one is recommended by the primary care physician. Anyone who is treated by a physician outside the network is penalized by significantly higher deductibles and coinsurance payments.

My immediate concern was the effect this change would have on Angie's therapy with Dr. McGarrah. The insurance company answered that the only way Angie could continue to see Dr. McGarrah without incurring excess costs was for Dr. McGarrah to join their network. Even if Dr. McGarrah agreed to join the network, though, her acceptance into the group was not automatic—it would depend upon the insurance company's need for additional therapists in that area of town. A PruCare representative told me later that they already had two "therapists who specialize in abused children" in our geographic area. The representative suggested that I switch Angie to one of those therapists.

I asked for the names of the two specialists so I could check them out. I found that neither was a psychiatrist or a psychologist. One was a licensed social worker who was "interested in" working with abused children. The other was an R.N. I ran both names through the child abuse network, and no one I consulted was familiar with either one. They may be well qualified in their fields, but as "experts in child sexual abuse," their credentials were nowhere near Dr. McGarrah's.

Even if I had been satisfied with the therapists' credentials, I would have been apprehensive about sending Angie to someone new.

I would be losing the four years of rapport that Dr. McGarrah has established with my daughter and replacing her with an unknown. How would that affect Angie?

I asked Angie how she would feel about seeing another therapist. A look of panic flashed over her face and she cried, "No, Mom. I won't talk about what happened to me with anyone but Nancy. She knows me. She's my friend. I won't talk to anyone else about it. I won't, I won't, I won't. I'd rather die."

Discouraged, I decided the safest route would be to ask Angie's father to continue carrying her on his group policy. Less than a week after reaching that conclusion, I learned that my husband's job was being abolished as part of emergency state budget cuts, along with all other state-funded research positions in mental health.

After months of red tape, the insurance company agreed to cover Angie's therapy with Dr. McGarrah for a limited time. That helped a little, but now I am having to pay the higher, out-of-network costs—costs that are prohibitive on a single mother's budget. Further, coverage for outpatient therapy is limited to 20 visits a year. And for all of this, I am paying a higher premium than I was under my company's old insurance plan!

Sadly, my experience is not unusual. A therapist told me recently that more and more people are falling through the mental health cracks. More and more people who don't qualify for public assistance are finding themselves uninsured. And those who do have health insurance are finding that insurers won't cover the amount or type of therapy they need. Breaking the cycle of abuse is becoming more and more difficult.

The Legal System

The Georgia Legislature has dealt with several children's issues in the last three years, and a number of measures to protect children have been passed. The measure that stirred the most controversy was the amendment of the competency statute: children no longer have to be prequalified before testifying in court.

The afternoon I observed the state house judiciary committee and subcommittee meetings was an eye-opener—something every taxpaying citizen should experience at least once. All the myths and stereotypes of child abuse I have written about throughout this book were right there in living color. I was amazed at the ignorance our legislators displayed when they discussed the issues. Even more appalling was the callousness some of them exhibited. I will never forget the way several men snickered about the courts being jammed with "crazy people complaining they were abused" if "idiots and lunatics" were included in the amendment that freed children from the competency statute.

There are some good people in the Georgia legislature. I saw them in action, too. But they are a minority, and they fight an uphill battle every time child advocacy legislation is proposed. Let's face it, children can't vote. Therefore, only legislators who are sincerely committed to the welfare of those too helpless to protect themselves will engage in that fight.

Many of the legislative gains that have been made in behalf of children have been muted by a lack of subsequent funding. This was especially true in 1991, when Georgia, like many states, experienced a budget crisis. In cutting $415 million from the state's budget, the governor boasted that his goal was to use a "scalpel instead of an ax"; that he wanted to cut out the "fat, not the muscle" in state spending. Unfortunately, the governor's "fat" included significant funding reductions to a number of programs that helped abused and disadvantaged children.

Some of the governor's recommended cuts were canceled or reduced in the budget the legislature finally approved. Nevertheless, the final budget included a $50,000 cut in funding for the Georgia Council on Child Abuse and a $135,000 reduction in funding for the Children's Trust Fund. The Trust Fund had been established by a former governor in 1988 in recognition of the growing threat of child abuse in Georgia. The trust supports community programs to prevent child abuse and neglect, like the Georgia Center for Children, which I discussed in chapter 18.

These cuts were described as "nominal" compared to reductions made in other areas. And part of me—the businesswoman—understands that argument. But the other part of me—the mother—doesn't buy it at all. Considering the magnitude of the child abuse problem, the relatively small amount Georgia spends on child abuse programs, and the struggle of existing programs to meet current demands, I find budget reductions of any size incomprehensible. I just don't think our state political leaders comprehend the magnitude of the child abuse problem and the impact that problem has on all of us. Despite all that has been written and said these past few years, they still don't seem to get it.

What makes this especially difficult for me to accept is the continuous reports I see in the news on political waste and abuse in state government. For example, as over 2,200 state employees were losing their jobs in "emergency" budget cuts, a number of high-paying jobs created for political appointees—mostly former state legislators—continued to enjoy protection. When the governor was questioned by the media about several of those jobs, he defended them by saying that those men "do a good job." I think the child abuse programs that suffered budget cuts do a good job, too. It's all a matter of government leadership and political priorities!

I wrote in chapter 12 that Georgia is a relatively progressive state when it comes to child advocacy matters. The key word is relatively. Georgia still has a long way to go to protect its children. The rest of the country must be in an even worse state of apathy when it comes to the health and welfare of the children who are the future of this country.

Family Life: Ourselves

My family's day-to-day life eventually began to feel like it was stabilizing. Two years after Angie's disclosure, I wrote, "We still get thrown out of equilibrium when Angie has her rough periods, but by now we're pros at taping things back together afterwards. Relationships within our family continue to improve, although we still have a long way to go. We all have scars which will take a long time to heal—some may even be permanent—but we're working hard to put the hurt behind us. Much of the bitterness is gone from my relationship with my husband, and with the help of a counselor, we are learning to communicate about Angie more openly than in the past."

I was optimistic because my husband and I had just begun marriage counseling. Months later, however, I began to suspect that counseling had come too late. In chapter 16, I spoke of the difficulty my husband had in accepting Angie's abuse and how he resented the time and energy I devoted to her recovery. His resentment and ultimate withdrawal from our marriage and family life, coupled with my anger over his emotional desertion, created a schism much deeper than I realized at the time. The extent of the damage became more and more obvious as we proceeded through our nine months of counseling.

I think our relationship could have survived if both of us had been committed to it and to the counseling process. Unfortunately, a new crisis doomed whatever hope I had of saving my marriage.

During the time we were in counseling, my husband fell into the false cure trap, and she was the "difference" that ultimately became "irreconcilable."

Friends have asked me if the trauma of Angie's abuse caused the breakup of my marriage. It is a difficult question to answer. No, it was not the cause. Yes, it was a major contributing factor.

It frightens me to say that, because I don't want Angie to ever interpret that yes to mean that her parents' divorce was her fault. It wasn't. Her father and I were adults—the success of our relationship was our responsibility. Every relationship has weaknesses. Those weaknesses are magnified many times over when a couple faces a major trauma in their lives. Angie's father and I were unable to overcome those weaknesses when we most needed to. They split us apart when we needed to draw together. It was our failure, not hers.

My relationship with Angie has improved immensely over the past several years. I remember how thrilled I was two years ago when she came to me and said, "Mom, can we talk?" Now we have a talk time every night before she goes to bed when we discuss whatever is on her mind. Sometimes we talk about something related to the sexual abuse she experienced. Sometimes she just tells me about her day. And sometimes she'll say something like, "Tell me about life, Mom. I mean, there's so much I don't know. Like, I don't even understand how a check works. How can that little piece of paper be worth money? How will I ever learn everything I need to know about life?" Whether I'm wiping away tears brought on by her painful memories, or explaining how a check clears through the Federal Reserve, those are special moments. It's wonderful to feel that old closeness again!

Angie's relationship with her daddy has continued to be volatile. Over all, though, it has improved a lot, especially since our separation. Her father still has difficulty parenting Angie during her bad times, but a regular visitation schedule is giving her one-on-one time with him that she didn't have before. How Angie feels about her father much of the time is reflected in this poem she wrote.

What Is a Father?

A father is someone who cares for you.
Who holds you in its arms.
And plays with you above all cares,
And keeps you from dangers and harms.

One gentle love, one gentle care,
For he is one strong man.
And if you are in a tight squeeze,
He will lend a helping hand.

If you want to play with him,
He will say, "That is no bother."

And this is how I'll end my little poem
—I have one hell of a father!

Angie, August 23, 1992

The Healing Continues

Although Angie has come a long way in these past five years, she still has a long way to go. Her recently reconstructed self-esteem is still fragile. She still dresses in the bathroom at ballet school. And she still asks why "it" had to happen to her.

Angie is also becoming aware of the larger issues of child abuse. After seeing a recent TV news report about a molestation case, she exploded. "People talk about children getting abused, but what do they care? They don't care. Nobody cares because they don't know what it's like. They don't know what it feels like inside. I know. I know how bad it feels . . ." And then she began to cry, and she asked me one more time, "Why?"

Angie is right. Most people, unless they have lived through the horrors of child abuse themselves, can't possibly know how it feels. As the mother of an abuse victim, however, I think I can come close to knowing how it feels, because Angie's pain has been my pain, too. Watching her struggle these past years has been a gut-wrenching experience.

I can't help but remember Angie's preschool days, when she used to ask me how much I loved her. It was always the beginning of a game we played. I would answer, "I love you more than the biggest number in the whole wide world." "Even more than a million?" she would ask. "More than a billion," was my answer. "What's more than that?" Angie would continue. "A trillion." And from a trillion, I went on to tell her I loved her more than a googol (which, of course, is even bigger than a trillion)—and more than a gaggle—and more than a giggle—and by that time we both would be giggling uncontrollably, and she knew I loved her more than the biggest number she could imagine.

After Angie was molested, she stopped asking how much I loved her, because she was convinced I didn't love her at all anymore. It has taken years for her to trust and accept my love again. But recently she began to ask me why I love her. Now she wants to know, "Do you love me because I'm your daughter or do you just feel sorry for me because of what happened?" So I am having to convince her that I love her because she is Angie.

Yes, I feel sorry for her because of the pain she has endured these past six years. But her victimization has not made me love her more or less. I love her because I love her. I also have a tremendous amount of respect for my daughter. The strength that tiny person has shown during these years of recovery has been awesome. I pray that strength will help her through the rest of her life.

As for me, I have also come a long way in these past years. I can't really say I have "accepted" my child's trauma—I just don't fight it anymore. The old feelings of guilt, anger, fear, frustration, and depression sneak back into my life occasionally, but for the most part I feel calm. I still feel the hurt, and probably always will, but I don't feel bitter anymore, and that is probably the best news. I think bitterness was the feeling that scared me most of all.

There were times after Angie was abused when I prayed to God to make me hard and cold so I could stop feeling the pain. And then when it seemed that I was getting my wish, it scared me—I really didn't want to grow up to be a bitter old woman!

I think I was able to put my bitterness behind me partly because of the support I received from people like Dr. McGarrah, Mr. Morgan, and a few close friends. Their help only took me part of the way, however, because the negative reactions of so many other people often overpowered the positive responses I received. In the end it was my religious faith that gave me the inner strength I needed to survive the past several years without bitterness.

Spiritual strength is an important part of healing for anyone who experiences trauma, and it should not be ignored. I know how important my own faith is to me, and I hope my daughter will have faith of her own to help her continue her healing. It worries me to see her doubt God's love because she can't understand why He let something like this happen to her. She is at an age when most children simply accept that God loves little children, but she feels that she has been rejected by Him and she can't understand why. "God doesn't love children like me," she says sadly.

In the course of researching *The Secret Trauma: Incest in the Lives of Girls and Women* [New York: Basic Books, Inc., 1986], Diana Russell found that 53% of incest victims, versus 32% of nonabused women, rejected the religious faith of their upbringing in adulthood. Catholic victims were twice as likely to reject their faith as their nonabused counterparts. Those figures make me wonder if Angie's faith will survive. And yet there are times when she shows a spiritual depth far beyond her years. She made her First Communion in second grade. First Communion is an important day in the lives of Catholic children, and the instruction she received before the event brought Angie face-to-face with her doubts over God's love for her. But then, a few days before her First Communion day, Angie wrote this poem.

The Oak

> *There stands an oak as tall as the sky;*
> *And hanging from that big great oak hangs a steady swing*
>   *which we sit upon.*
> *Swing, swing we go.*
> *That swing is life.*
>
> *Jesus the Holy Son of God is the great oak.*
> *Taller than all living creatures, he stands there tall and*
>   *steady.*
> *Mary the Holy Mother is the swing.*
> *She rocks us in her arms gently and softly.*
>
> *God the King of all Heaven and earth is the wind that*
>   *pushes us gently through life.*
> *Greediness and cruelty is totally absent from this Great*
>   *Man.*
> *He pushes us through the leaves and bushes.*
>
> *A thorn pricks us.*
> *The thorn hurts.*
> *God puts his hand on our knee and he heals our wound.*

And on and on we go through life.
We get pricked by a thorn.
And on and on God heals it.

Angie, April 30, 1989

I pray that God will continue to heal Angie and all the other victims, and their families, of the hurt inflicted on them by the thorn of child abuse.

RESOURCE LIST

For the Parent

Pamphlets and Booklets

Basic Facts about Sexual Child Abuse. National Committee for Prevention of Child Abuse, 332 S. Michigan Avenue, Suite 1250, Chicago, IL 60604-4357; (312) 663-3520.

Child Sexual Abuse Prevention. Planned Parenthood of Buffalo, Inc., 210 Franklin Street, Buffalo, NY 14202; (716) 853-1771.

Sexual Abuse and Your Child. C.A.R.E. Productions, Box L, #8 12th Street, Blaine, WA 98230; (604) 581-5116.

Tower, Cynthia Crosson, and Susan Russell McCauley. *What Parents Should Know about Child Sexual Abuse.* National Education Association of the United States, P.O. Box 509, West Haven, CT 06516; (203) 934-2669.

Books and Articles

Dziech, Billie Wright, and Schudson, Judge Charles B. *On Trial: America's Courts and Their Treatment of Sexually Abused Children.* Boston: Beacon Press, 1989.

Gilham, Bill. *The Facts about Child Sexual Abuse.* London, England: Cassell Educational Limited, 1991.

Hagans, Kathryn B., and Case, Joyce. *When Your Child Has Been Molested: A Parent's Guide to Healing and Recovery.* Lexington, MA: Lexington Books, 1988.

Hillman, Donald, and Solek-Tefft, Janice. *Spiders and Flies: Help for Parents and Teachers of Sexually Abused Children.* Lexington, MA: Lexington Books, 1988.

McNamara, J.B., and McNamara, B.H., eds. *Adoption and the Sexually Abused Child.* Ossining, New York: Family Resources Adoption Program, 1990.

Pardeck, John T. "Children's Literature and Child Abuse." *CHILD WELFARE* LXIX (January/February 1990), 1: 83–88.

Sanford, Linda Tschirhart. *The Silent Children: A Parent's Guide to the Prevention of Child Sexual Abuse.* New York: McGraw-Hill, 1980.

Tamarack, Lada I. "Fifty Myths and Facts about Sexual Abuse." In *Sexual Abuse of Children in the 1980s,* by Benjamin Schlesinger. Toronto, ON: University of Toronto Press, 1986.

For the Child or Adolescent

Anderson, Deborah, and Finne, Martha. *Margaret's Story.* Minneapolis, MN: Dillon Press, Inc., 1986. (Ages 5–10, Grade 4)

Girard, Linda. *My Body is Private.* Niles, IL: Albert Whitman and Company, 1984. (Ages 5–10, Grade 3)

Morrison, Jan. *A Safe Place: Beyond Sexual Abuse.* Wheaton, IL: Harold Shaw Publishers, 1990. (Adolescents)

Porett, Jane. *When I Was Little Like You.* Washington, DC: Child Welfare League of America, 1993. (Young children)

Sweet, Phyllis E. *Something Happened to Me.* Racine, WI: Mother Courage Press, 1981. (Young children)

For the Adult Survivor

Bass, Ellen and Davis, L. *The Courage to Heal: A Guide for Women Survivors of Child Sexual Abuse.* New York: Harper and Row, 1988.

Bass, Ellen, and Thornton, Louise, eds. *I Never Told Anyone: Writings by Women Survivors of Child Sexual Abuse.* New York: Harper and Row, 1983.

Blume, E. Sue. *Secret Survivors: Uncovering Incest and Its Aftereffects in Women.* New York: John Wiley and Sons, 1990.

Davis, Laura. *The Courage to Heal Workbook: For Men and Women Survivors of Child Sexual Abuse.* New York: Harper and Row, 1990.

Hunter, Mic. *Abused Boys: The Neglected Victims of Sexual Abuse.* Lexington, MA: Lexington Books, 1990.

Lew, Mike. *Victims No Longer: Men Recovering from Incest and Other Child Sexual Abuse.* New York: Nevraumont Publishing Co., 1988.

Russell, Diana E. H. *The Secret Trauma: Incest in the Lives of Girls and Women.* New York: Basic Books, 1986.

Tower, Cynthia Crosson. *Secret Scars: A Guide for Survivors of Child Sexual Abuse.* New York: Viking Penguin Inc., 1988.

For the Child Welfare Professional

Child Welfare League of America (CWLA). *Confronting Child Sexual Abuse: A Video Training Series.* Washington, DC: CWLA and Kingsley Productions, 1993.

Courtois, C. *Healing the Incest Wound: Adult Survivors in Therapy.* New York: W.W. Norton, 1988.

Davis, Nancy. *Therapeutic Stories to Heal Abused Children.* Oxon Hill, MD: Psychological Associates of Oxon Hill, 1990.

Furniss, Tilman. *The Multiprofessional Handbook of Child Sexual Abuse: Integrated Management, Therapy, and Legal Intervention.* New York: Routledge, 1991.

Gil, Eliana. *The Healing Power of Play: Working With Abused Children.* New York: The Guilford Press, 1991.

Gil, Eliana. *Treatment of Adult Survivors of Childhood Abuse.* Walnut Creek, CA: Launch Press, 1988.

McFarlane, Kee, and Waterman, Jill, et al. *Sexual Abuse of Young Children.* New York: The Guilford Press, 1986.

Oster, Gerald D., and Gould, Patricia. *Using Drawings in Assessment and Therapy.* New York: Brunner/Mazell Publishing, 1987.

Sgroi, Suzanne M. *Vulnerable Populations: Evaluation and Treatment of Sexually Abused Children and Adult Survivors,* vols. 1 and 2. Lexington, MA: Lexington Books, 1988.

Wiehe, Vernon. *Sibling Abuse: Hidden Physical, Emotional, and Sexual Trauma.* Lexington, MA: Lexington Books, 1990.

Wilson, Charles; Wilson, Steppe; and Caylor, Susan. *Investigating Sexual Abuse in Day Care.* Washington, DC: Child Welfare League of America, 1986.